Lecture Notes in
Computer Science

Lecture Notes in Computer Science

Lecture Notes in Computer Science

Edited by G. Goos and J. Hartmanis

189

Mark Steven Sherman

Paragon:

A Language Using Type Hierarchies for the Specification,
Implementation and Selection of Abstract Data Types

Springer-Verlag
Berlin Heidelberg New York Tokyo

Author

M. Sherman
Department of Mathematics and Computer Science
Dartmouth College, Bradley Hall
Hanover, NH 03755, USA

CR Subject Classification (1982): D.3.2, D.3.3, D.3.4, E2, I.2.2, D.2.2

ISBN 3-540-15212-1 Springer-Verlag Berlin Heidelberg New York Tokyo
ISBN 0-387-15212-1 Springer-Verlag New York Heidelberg Berlin Tokyo

© by Springer-Verlag Berlin Heidelberg 1985
Printed in Germany

Printing and binding: Beltz Offsetdruck, Hemsbach/Bergstr.
2145/3140-543210

Table of Contents

List of Figures

List of Tables

Acknowledgements

יהי ביתך בית ועד לחכמים
והוי מתאבק בעפר רגליהם
והוי שותה בצמה את דבריהם

פרקי אבות א:ד

Let your house be a meeting place
for scholars,
and sit in the dust of their feet,
and drink in their words with thirst.

Pirkei Avos I:4

One usually acknowledges ones committee, friends and relatives in the acknowledgement section of a thesis. Such a narrow view unfairly reflects the way that research is conducted at CMU. During my tenure here in Pittsburgh, I have spent a great deal of time listening to and learning from other people: fellow students, faculty, official visitors and random hanger-ons. Each contributed to my education and is in some way responsible for my completing my Ph.D. degree. The wealth of opportunities at the Computer Science Department made my studies an exciting and memorable adventure.

Nevertheless, my day-to-day contact with several people helped organize and advance my work on this thesis. Andy Hisgen and Jonathan Rosenberg were always willing to listen to each bizarre new idea and provide helpful suggests and criticisms. Elaine Kant patiently watched my research go through its ups and downs and provided me with technical feedback and encouragement whenever each was needed. Peter Hibbard and John Nestor reminded me that the art of language design is still largely an art. Like all apprentices, I was glad to have these masters around me for advice and help. Cynthia Hibbard read through hundreds of pages of drafts, checking my writing and offering suggestions to improve the writing style. Michael Conner carefully read initial drafts of this thesis and offered helpful technical suggestions.

Nearly everyone who works on a thesis can attest to the frustrating and overwhelming effort it requires. My wife Vera took care to ensure that I never let this thesis oppress me. Without her, this thesis might have never been finished. Last, but not least, I wish to thank her.

Mark Sherman
July 6, 1983

Abstract

This thesis describes a set of language features that supports the specification, implementation and selection of data abstractions. The effectiveness of these features is illustrated through a language, called Paragon, developed for the thesis. Novel features of Paragon include:

- Multiple inheritance of classes (the basic encapsulation mechanism);

- Multiple procedure implementations for a procedure specification;

- Iterators;

- User-provided descriptions of abstract data types;

- User-provided strategies for making representation-selection decisions;

- Compile-time selection of a procedure implementation for each procedure call;

- Compile-time selection of variable representations.

Representative Paragon programs illustrate how this language can be used for defining multiple, simultaneous and interacting implementations of abstract data types. In addition, some refinements of the data abstraction paradigm, such as generalized specifications and shared specifications, are defined in the thesis and illustrated with Paragon programs. I then show how the type-hierarchy facilities in Paragon can be combined with a semi-automated, representation-selection mechanism and some representation-selection strategies using Paragon's notation are provided. To show how Paragon can be implemented, I describe the design of a translator and provide some measurements of a prototype. This prototype demonstrates that the conventional compiler technology can be used for implementing type hierarchies, though it does illustrate possible problems with separate compilation when using multiple, simultaneous implementations of abstract data types. Finally, a critique of the language is provided.

Chapter 1
Introduction

This thesis discusses a new programming language called *Paragon* that supports the specification, implementation and selection of data abstractions. The language uses type hierarchies to specify and implement abstract data types. Further, the Paragon language design integrates the abstract data type facilities with a semi-automatic procedure for making implementation choices for the variables in a program. A prototype for the Paragon design was written and run on several example programs. All of these aspects are considered in detail in this thesis.

In this introductory chapter, the motivation for pursuing this work is presented, followed by a summary of the main results of the thesis. This chapter ends with a discussion of how the rest of the thesis is organized.

1.1. Motivation

Modern software has grown to such size and complexity that programmers can no longer manage all of the details of the programs they write. This lack of management causes the programs being created to be improperly specified (they do not accomplish what the user intended), incorrectly implemented (they do not accomplish what the programmer intended), and inefficient (they produce the wrong answer slowly and at great cost). Programming methods that promote the management of the details of a program can help control the size and complexity of modern software, and in turn, promote the production of correct and efficient systems.

1.1.1. The Use of Abstraction and Refinement

A successful method of controlling complexity in other disciplines is *abstraction*, that is, the suppression of irrelevant details. Various abstraction methods have been introduced into the programming task, notably control abstraction and procedural abstraction.   Control abstraction usually takes the form of *while* loops, *repeat* loops, and *if* statements, each of which suppress the details of specifying nonsequential program flow. Procedural abstraction provides a way for a programmer to specify a black box that can transform some set of values into another set of values while suppressing the details of how the transformation is accomplished.

Although the abstractions initially suppress some details, these details are needed in the final program. The process of introducing details is called *refinement*. Sometimes the refinement is automated, as when a compiler automatically translates a *while* loop into an appropriate sequence of test and jump instructions. Sometimes the refinement is performed by the programmer, as when the programmer writes the code that describes how the specified black box actually works.

Refinement does more than introduce the details suppressed by abstraction. Refinement is also a selection and binding process. There are usually many different models that meet the requirements of an abstraction. For example, a common procedural abstraction is *Sort*. In an abstract sense, a sort procedure accepts a sequence of data and produces a permutation of that sequence that meets a specified ordering relation. There are many different algorithms that meet such a specification, any one of which meets the abstract requirements. The binding of a sort black box in a program to the selected algorithm is a refinement of the program.

Binding details to abstractions reduces the number of choices that a programmer can make for further refinements in the program. For example, if a choice is made to represent an ordered sequence of data as a linked list, a search procedure operating on that sequence can not use a binary search method. The refinement of the abstract sequence to a linked list reduces the number of choices for a searching procedure. As a program is refined further, the program becomes less abstract, more filled with details and more constrained. Therefore refining a program introduces inflexibility.

This inflexibility adversely affects program development and maintenance. As a program is being developed, a programmer may not know which refinement to choose but a programmer has to choose one so that development may continue. Later the programmer might discover that the wrong decision was made, but the inflexibility introduced by previous refinements hinders a better approach from being implemented. This problem is exacerbated for program maintenance since only the fully refined program is available. Because the costs of maintaining a program are far greater than the cost for initial development, inflexibility in a program can exact a high price over the lifetime of a program.

Clearly, an approach is needed that introduces the refinements for constructing a program without eliminating the abstractions. Techniques for introducing details without obscuring control and procedural abstraction are being widely adopted. In control abstraction, the abstraction is provided by the programmer using structured programming techniques and the details are mechanically generated by a compiler. Because of the mechanical nature of the refinement process, a programmer can confidently change an abstraction and rely on the compiler to insert faithfully new details as necessary. In procedural abstraction, the programmer adopts a convention that the interface of a subroutine will remain an invariant abstraction that may be used by the rest of a program. Further, *only* the abstract interface of the procedure may be used by the rest of the program. Because the program using the subprogram relies only on the abstract interface, the refinements inside of the subprogram may be changed without affecting the rest of the program. So for both control and procedural abstraction, there are refinement techniques that retain much of the abstraction, and hence, much of the flexibility.

However, control and procedural abstractions have been used for many years. A newer form of abstraction, data abstraction, is becoming widespread and its refinement techniques are not well developed.

1.1.2. Data Abstraction

Data abstraction is based on the observation that programs conceptually operate on abstract objects that have specific properties unrelated to a computer. For example, a program simulating a traffic intersection operates on objects that represent cars, trucks, streets, and traffic lights. Since the program is ultimately run on a computer and does not manipulate concrete cars, some transformation must be made from the abstract objects to concrete objects that a computer manipulates. The refinements that effect this transformation usually require the addition of a great number of details, and unless carefully done, will cause confusion in the programmer, inflexibility in the program and ultimately, errors in the finished product.

1.1.2.1. The Simple Model of Data Abstraction

There are emerging methods for refining data abstractions that provide a limited way to control the inflexibility and confusion that results from transforming program objects into computer objects. These methods require that each kind of object manipulated by the program have two parts: a *specification* that describes the actions that may be performed on the object, for example, start a car or stop a car; and a *representation* of the object in terms of computer objects, for example, a car is represented by three integers that hold data about the number of people in the car, the serial number of the car and the make of the car. A special piece of a program, called a *module*, provides a set of subprograms that implement[1] the operations that may be performed on a car. Inside of this module, a programmer may refer to the representation of the object in terms of the computer objects. Outside of this module, only the specified operations may be used to manipulate the representation of the object.

Unfortunately, the view that each kind of object be split into two parts is too simple. Although the methodology for building systems recognizes the need for layering for many purposes [Cheatham 79, Parnas 74], the view of providing layers of specifications for abstract objects has not been widely embraced. Yet the single layer of specification is inadequate for many kinds of specifications. Further, multiple representations of an object are not well supported and interactions between representations are not permitted. Each of these problems will be considered in turn.

1.1.2.2. The Limitations Imposed on Abstract Data Type Specifications

The single, isolated specification in a module is too restrictive. Other kinds of specifications that a programmer may wish to write include a specification that is a refinement of another, related specifications that are not refinements of one another and implementation-independent specifications. Each of these three kinds of specifications is illustrated below.

First, one kind of program object may be a refinement of another. For example, a Plymouth

---

[1]The data abstraction literature sometimes uses the word *representation* for the definition of local storage of an object and the word *implementation* for the code that makes up the procedures in a module. It is now becoming accepted that the information in an abstract object may be encoded in either the state of the local storage or in procedures that operate on local storage and so the words *implementation* and *representation* have become interchangeable. They are used interchangeably in this thesis.

object is refinement of an Automobile object. Thus the specification for a Plymouth should be some refinement of the specification for an Automobile. Yet the described method of data abstraction allows only disjoint pairs of specifications and representations, not collections of related specifications and representations. The simple data abstraction method requires different kinds of program objects to be refined independently even when one specification may be a refinement of another's specification.

Second, objects may be related even if one is not a refinement of another. This relationship might be made explicitly by the specification of several objects in a single module or might be made implicitly by the specification of type parameters a module. Neither is permitted in the simple model of data abstraction.

In the simple model of data abstraction, each module may specify exactly one kind of object. However, some specifications are related, such as keyboards and displays. They are clearly separate objects: one might desire many displays to be attached to one keyboard or many keyboards to share a display. Yet they are related: when operating in half-duplex mode, typing a character on a keyboard causes a character to appear on the display. Since the abstract objects, keyboard and display, are related, their specifications should be related and a data abstraction facility should allow both specifications to appear in a single module.

The simple model of data abstraction also provides no facilities for families of specifications. Yet many objects have similar structures. For example, nearly all symbol tables have the same structure: a collection of pairs, where each pair consists of a key and some data. Typically, the keys belong to one type and the data to another type. In the simple approach of data abstraction, every symbol table that uses a different key type must have its own specification and representation. There is no way of defining a class of symbol tables that can be related with another class of objects, namely the different types of keys. Yet the specifications and representations for all symbol tables are nearly identical. It should be possible to factor out the common parts of the specifications and representations into a single specification and representation. Later, a programmer should introduce those details necessary for any particular symbol table as parameters rather than by creating new specifications and representations.

A third way in which specifications in the simple model are too restrictive is their lack of implementation independence. The simple model places strict rules on the relationship between specifications and implementations. In particular, the information available to an implementation is exactly that information provided by the specification, no more and no less. A simple example can illustrate this. The specification of a typical sort procedure requires that the elements to be sorted have a comparison procedure. Any implementation of the sort procedure may use such a comparison procedure, but nothing else. Because the specification is not restrictive, it prohibits bucket sorting, since the bucket sort algorithm requires that the elements to be sorted come from a cross product of ordered sets and that the set of resulting tuples be well founded. Sometimes the opposite problem occurs and the specification is to too restrictive. The specification for sorting might require that the elements to be sorted be tuples in a well found set. This limits the types of elements that may be sorted since many objects may be compared without having a tuple structure. Such a specification effectively prohibits sorting to be done on objects where bucket sort is not feasible. These problems also occur with data abstractions. The specifications for the elements to be stored in a symbol table may require the elements to have a hash procedure defined on them (for example, see the symbol table example on page 164 of the Alphard Book [Shaw 81]). Such specifications limit the possible implementations of symbol tables to those that use hashing functions and those that do not use any element specific functions. In all of these cases, the problem is that information about the refinement process has leaked from the implementation to the specification. A more general facility would include details of refinement where they are appropriate.[2]

1.1.2.3. The Limitations Imposed on Abstract Data Type Implementations

Besides the inadequate support for writing specifications, the simple model of data abstraction does not adequately support multiple implementations of a specification. However, these multiple implementations can be quite useful. For example, an abstract array object allows the assignment and retrieval of data via a list of indices. Two common representations of arrays in linear memory are row-major order and column-major order. Normally it makes little difference which order is used. Sometimes one representation gives a better program performance, for example, because of paging requirements. Sometimes a representation is necessary for properties unrelated to the operations given in the specification. For example, another program may be providing the array in a predetermined format, such as a Fortran subroutine providing an array in column-major order. Therefore it is

---

[2]The restriction imposed by the simple model is not unmotivated. By insisting that all specifications available for the implementation be present in the specification, a compiler may separately check at compile time that the use of a data abstraction is legal, that an implementation that meets the specification, and that both checks are sufficient for guaranteeing that the resulting program can execute.

desirable to associate many different representations with each specification and to select a representation for an object as appropriate.

Despite their potential usefulness, the simple model of data abstraction does not allow multiple representations to be included in a program, since the specification and representation are in one, textually-combined module. But even where one may separate the representations from the specifications and thereby have a way to write different representations, most systems use the same name for the different representations. Therefore these systems have difficulty in distinguishing one representation from another. To deal with this problem, languages impose a series of restrictions. Initially, a language may prohibit multiple implementations from appearing in a program. For example, Ada [Ichbiah 80] permits only a single package body to be bound to a package specification. But even if multiple implementations are permitted in a language, they may not interact in procedures that use only abstract properties of the object. For example, Low's implementation of sets in Sail [Low 74] prohibits two sets with differing implementations from having intersection performed on them, even though set intersection may be written using only abstract operations of sets. Finally, even when full facilities for multiple representations are provided, there is no way of obtaining information about the different representations to aid in selecting an appropriate representation. The literature contains dozens of different implementations for sets. Each of these implementations is appropriate in a different circumstance. The writer of the implementation should be able to describe the behavior of the implementation so that an intelligent selection is possible.

In addition to the inadequacies of specifications and multiple representations in the simple model, the simple model cannot adequately handle interacting representations. This deficiency occurs in two ways: interactions between different implementations of a specification cannot be defined or used, and a shared implementation for separate specifications cannot be provided.

Even when languages permit different implementations for a single specification, they do not permit a single procedure to use the concrete details of more than one representation. As a simple example, assume that a module implementing complex numbers were specified and that two implementations were written: cartesian and polar representations. Following the simple model, the module for each representation may manipulate either the cartesian representation or the polar representation but not both. It might be useful in a program to write an addition procedure that can work on polar and cartesian representations, yet the simple model does not allow any one representation access to the details of another representation.

Besides the ability to have multiple implementations for each specification, it is desirable to allow a single representation for multiple specifications. Representations are sometimes related even if the specifications are not. For example, a program may manipulate objects that represent disks and drums but it may be necessary that the representations used for data encoding for both devices be identical. The specifications should be separate, since different kinds of operations are performed on disks and drums. But the representations for disks and drums are interrelated because data are transferred between them. While it should be possible to selectively combine representations as necessary, the simple data abstraction method requires a separate representation to be associated with each specification. This adds inflexibility to the program since there is an implicit connection between the modules for disks and drums; a decision made for one module must be reflected in the other.

Although the simple model for data abstraction has limitations, the underlying ideas are sound and are slowly being put into practice. But because of the relative youth of data abstraction techniques in the programming community at large, little work has been done to extend the basic refinement method beyond the simple approach and to explore the implications of those extensions. The initial attempts at creating languages with data abstraction facilities, such as Clu and Alphard, followed the simple model very closely. Some limited extensions, such as generics, are included to try to solve some of these problems, but no general language mechanism has been developed that permits multiple levels of refinement and the retention of abstraction in the final program. This thesis proposes a set of language features base on a type hierarchy that effectively support the data abstraction techniques and allow a more flexible refinement paradigm to be used with data abstraction.

1.2. Summary of Thesis

The theme of this thesis is that type hierarchies are a useful linguistic construct for specifying abstract data types, refining specifications of abstract data types into implementations, and selecting an implementation of an abstract data type for a given specification. The vehicle for exploring this theme is a new programming language, Paragon, which I designed and implemented as part of the research.

There are three main pieces of research. The first part discusses the design of features in Paragon that support specifications of data abstractions and refinements of specifications. The second part presents the features of Paragon that support selection of an appropriate refinement from a collection of possible refinements. The third part describes the implementation of a prototype translator for Paragon that processes the data abstractions and makes selections of refinements for program objects. Together these parts demonstrate how type hierarchies can be used in programming languages to provide a more flexible and useful refinement process for data abstraction.

1.2.1. Data Abstraction Features

There are four basic data abstraction features in Paragon: classes, class inheritance, class nesting and class parameters. Supporting these basic features are the separation of procedure specifications and procedure implementations, multiple implementations of procedures, and a uniform object notation and semantics.

Classes are the basic encapsulation mechanism for modules and contain declarations of procedures that may operate on instances of the class and local state. A class may inherit the declarations of other classes[3] and may add new declarations, such as a procedure implementation for a procedure specification. Such a derived class is considered to be a refinement of the parent classes. When a variable declaration uses a class, the named class defines the abstract properties of the object denoted by the variable. Any refinement of the class used in the declaration may be used as the implementation for the object.

Classes may also contain local class declarations, which give rise to nested classes. When these nested classes are instantiated, they create nested objects. By selective use of class inheritance and class nesting, it is possible to arrange scopes in several useful ways. Two ways are discussed in this thesis. One way permits procedure implementations to be written so they can access different concrete refinements of the same specification. Another way permits a shared refinement to be written for separate specifications.

A class may also have parameters. Parameters permit families of specifications and refinements to be defined. Because the uniform object notation provides different syntax for

---

[3]Since a class may inherit the declarations from more than one class at a time, the classes form a directed acyclic graph of types and not a strict hierarchy. However, the phrase *type hierarchy* is more commonly used in the literature and is used throughout the thesis rather than the technically correct phrase *directed acyclic graph of types*.

denoting a "type"[4] and an object, and because these different syntactic constructions may be used in parameters, Paragon permits the parameters to classes to be used as conventional parameters and as type parameters, eliminating the need for a special generic facility.

To illustrate these data abstraction features, examples in the thesis show how layers of specifications, combined specifications, multiple representations for a specification and a combined representation for multiple specifications, can be expressed in Paragon.

The class features are described in more detail in Chapters 3 and 4.

1.2.2. Representation Selection Features

There are four basic features for selecting representations[5] in Paragon: attributes, a possibility tree, a policy procedure and a feasibility checker.

Attributes are compile-time procedures and variables that a programmer may add to class declarations and procedure declarations. Such attributes are intended to provide information that a selection mechanism could use. For example, each class might contain an attribute *Space* that is a procedure that returns the amount of storage that the class uses, or it may contain a procedure named *Performance_Measured* that returns a boolean value indicating if that particular class keeps track of its performance.

The *possibility tree* is a data structure for organizing the selection decisions made for a program. It resembles an unrolled call graph of the program. Each node represents an instance of a class or an invocation of a procedure. Edges lead from a class instance (or procedure invocation) to instances and invocations within that class instance (or procedure invocation). The tree changes as different representation selections are made for objects and procedure invocations. The presence of such a data structure is an advance over previous representation-selection systems in that it provides a way to make representation selections for local variables in local procedure invocations rather than to make only selections of variables in the program that calls the procedure.

---

[4] Actually, an *indefinite instance*. See Section 3.2.1.

[5] In the context of Paragon, a refinement of a class is a representation of that class, hence the words *refinement* and *representation* are used interchangeably.

The *policy procedure* is a Paragon program that actually performs the representation selection for the user's program. This procedure is interpreted at compile time and operates on the possibility tree, making selections for variables and gathering data about the selection possibilities through the execution of attributes.

Not all choices of representations result in a refined program that can actually execute. For example, it is possible that an incorrect procedure implementation was selected, an incompatible choice of data representations was chosen or that a needed procedure implementation was missing. The translation system contains a procedure that performs a feasibility check of the user's program to guarantee that all necessary representations are present and that the selected representations are compatible. This procedure may be called from the policy procedure as well so that the policy procedure may ensure that its selections result in an executable program.

Selection is completed at compile time. Once the translation process has finished, all choices of procedure implementations and object representations have been determined. No run-time selection is necessary. Further, the translation system can guarantee that no run-time errors will occur because of a missing procedure implementation or an incompatible representation.[6]

To illustrate the utility of these representation-selection features, several example programs have been programmed in Paragon. These examples were drawn from the literature describing multiple representations for a data abstraction. Algorithms that were implemented by previous data structure selection systems have also been programmed as policy procedures.

The representation selection facilities are described in more detail in Chapter 5. Chapter 6 contains a worked-out example program and policy.

---

[6]Unlike, for example, the virtual procedure feature in Simula-67.

1.2.3. Prototype Translator

The motivations for constructing a translator were pragmatic. Since the construction of a translator requires the language to be fully defined, it therefore serves as a way to insure the completeness of the language definition. In addition, the design of the translator illustrates problems that may occur when building compilation systems that use type-hierarchy features, so the prototype serves as a feasibility test. Finally, the operation of the translator can also pinpoint any relations between language features and performance degradations.

The prototype translator written for Paragon processes the entire language. It performs parsing, semantic analysis, policy interpretation and feasibility checking. The translator does not produce object code that runs; as output, it produces a transformed program where all selections of procedures and variable representations are indicated. Because the language definition requires the translator to contain an interpreter for the entire language (to interpret the policies and attributes), an entire run time package does exist and Paragon code can be (and has been) executed. However, there was no effort to produce a final code generator for the translator.

The design of the translator resembles that of conventional compilers, however, it contains three new phases that are not present in current compilers: the possibility tree creator, the policy executor and the feasibility checker. Since these new phases perform analogs of conventional compiler phases, namely call-graph creation, source-language interpretation and type checking respectively, there is no new compiler technology needed to translate type hierarchies in programming languages. Because the translator is an interpreted Lisp program, it runs slowly (about 10 lines of Paragon per minute of Vax 11/780 CPU time). However, its speed is comparable to values for other such prototype systems [Gillman 83].

Details about the design of the translator and its performance can be found in Chapter 7.

1.3. Organization of the Thesis

Chapter 2 outlines the goals of Paragon's design and places them in relation to past work with abstract data type languages and representation selection systems. The next two chapters present the basics of the Paragon language and show how those basics are applied for creating abstract data types. Attributes — which describe implementations — and policies — which guide the selection of representations — are both discussed in the next chapter.

Chapter 6 presents a complete example, showing how an abstract data type, complete with attributes, an application program and a policy, are used together. Then Chapter 7 describes the implementation of a translator for the Paragon languages and its performance on a selection of abstract data types, application programs, and policies. Finally, the last chapter provides a retrospective and a prospective view of the work, analyzing how well the language met its goals and what future areas of research might be explored.

The thesis also contains a number of appendices giving the syntax of Paragon, some additional semantics for Paragon, a glossary of the technical terms used in the thesis, and listings of the programs used for the performance measurements of the translator.

Chapter 2
Goals of Paragon
and
Their Relation to Previous Efforts

There is a great deal of previous work on the design of programming languages, on data abstraction and on selection of data representations. Most of this work has concentrated on one of these aspects, for example, abstract data types in a language or selection of table representations in a database. This current work attempts to synthesize these different efforts into a coherent language design, incorporating the experience gained from the previous efforts. As Paragon represents a synthesis, it has a set of goals that transcend, and sometimes contradict, some specific goals of previous research. To place the past efforts in a proper perspective, it is necessary to understand the specific goals that the design of Paragon is intended to meet, to isolate the goals that past efforts have tried to attain, to consider how the past work has advanced Paragon's goals and to point out the previous limitations that Paragon's design should overcome.

This chapter, therefore, presents an explicit statement of the goals of Paragon's design, including some related but tangential goals that Paragon does not address. Along with Paragon's goals, the goals and methods of two previous approaches to Paragon's overall objectives are considered and compared with Paragon: the design and implementation of abstract data type facilities in languages, and the automatic selection of representations.

2.1. Goals of Paragon

The goals of Paragon can be grouped into four broad classes: abstract data type specification goals, abstract data type representation goals, representation-selection goals and automatic-processing goals. These goals are listed below, followed by a discussion of each:

Abstract Data Type Specification Goals

- Refinements of specifications of abstract data types may be written.

- Related specifications may be combined in a single module.

Abstract Data Type Representation Goals

- Multiple implementations of an abstract data type may be written.

- Several implementations of an abstract data type may be used simultaneously in a program (one implementation per variable).

- If several implementations of an abstract data type are used for different variables, those variables may interact.

- A single implementation may be written for several separate specifications.

Representation-Selection Goals

- An implementation of an abstract data type should contain information describing the implementation without permitting direct, unrestricted access to the implementation.

- Declarations of variables should contain information describing the constraints that an implementation of the variable's type must meet without having to explicitly name an implementation.

- The selection mechanisms should be available to the programmer in a convenient manner.

Automatic-Processing Goals

- Static type checking of all variable declarations (object creations) and procedure calls should be supported.

- The representation information present in abstract data type implementations and variable declarations should be processed automatically, so that a compiler can choose an appropriate implementation of an abstract data type.

- Compile-time checking should ensure that all representation-selection decisions result in a program that can execute without run-time errors.

2.1.1. Refinements of Specifications

Paragon should permit a very abstract specification to be refined into more concrete specifications. Initially, properties of objects may be defined in a very abstract way. Some initial properties might include assignability, hashability, transmissibility over a network, commitment of operations, the ability to be stored in a file system and orderings. Each of these specifications should be able to be refined as a way to add details to the specifications without adding implementation-specific details. For example, a record may be specified as containing a number of fields. The operations on the record might include field selection and record assignment. Then the specification for the record is a refinement of the specification for assignability: fields and field selection have been added.

This goal is partially met by the object-oriented language designs in Simula [Dahl 68] and Smalltalk [Goldberg 81, Ingalls 78, Ingalls 81, Morgan 81, Xerox 81], the use of clusters in Enhanced C [Katzenelson 83a, Katzenelson 83b], the Traits additions to Mesa [Curry 82] and the Flavors facility for Lisp [Weinreb 81]. A similar kind of hierarchy was proposed by Smith and Smith [Smith 77] and in Taxis [Mylopoulos 80] for organizing relations, views and objects in a database. Further, the Program Development System [Cheatham 79] uses a refinement hierarchy for writing system modules. But all of these systems use the refinements only as a way to refine objects or system components however, and not as refinements of specifications with the intention of later refining the specifications into implementations. With the exception of the PDS system, each level of these hierarchies defines both abstract and concrete properties of program objects. There is no intention to provide the absolute separation of abstract and concrete aspects that is required by data abstraction methodology. In some cases, such as the Smalltalk design, there is not even a way to provide this separation. For example, there are no procedure specifications, only implementations. Thus the details for the concrete representation are present where only the abstract details should be allowed. Although the PDS system does separate abstract properties from concrete properties, refinements in PDS may only be performed on modules that contain concrete details. PDS does not intend that the user refine only specifications. Further, PDS is intended to work on system modules and not necessarily on abstract data types, that is, on objects that are declared many times by a programmer and manipulated by an application program.

Program transformation systems represent another approach for adding the refinement paradigm into a language. Some program transformation systems, such as PECOS/LIBRA [Barr 82, Kant 83] and the interactive system developed by Balzer's group [Balzer 81], generate refinements of specifications. However, these systems encode their refining rules in a separate language from the data-type description language and perform the refinement as part of the translation process. In practice, these rules represent ways that a program may be refined rather than ways in which data abstractions may be refined. Therefore these systems are considering a much larger domain than merely specifying data types. In fact, their domain is sufficiently rich that various forms of heuristic search are required to perform the refinement process. In more conventional program development, the user provides some static refinements which can then be used for specifying a program. It is this conventional model of program development that Paragon is supporting. Hence the more static refinement paradigm should be provided by Paragon.

The proposed layers of specifications are a departure from most languages that provide data abstraction facilities. For example, Clu [Liskov 81], Alphard [Shaw 81] and Ada [Ichbiah 80] all use a single level of refinement, the upper level being the abstract specification and the lower level being the concrete implementation. An extension of Simula proposed by Ingargiola [Ingargiola 75] allows, in a very restricted way, layers of specifications. This first goal of Paragon is an attempt to generalize the approaches used in these other languages.

2.1.2. Combined Specifications

When appropriate, related objects should be specified in the same module. One example frequently encountered is a keyboard data type and a screen data type, that is, an input and output device. Logically, the functions of reading and writing may be separate, but for many systems, such as those using half-duplex, local-echo terminal protocols, the specifications of reading and writing are closely coupled. Thus these two objects, screens and keyboard, should be able to be specified in the same module. Hence another of Paragon's goals is to allow a combined specification in a module.

This too is a departure from several data abstraction languages, such as Clu and Alphard, and from object oriented languages such as Simula and Smalltalk, where each module (cluster, form, class and class respectively) specifies a single kind of object. The goal is to emulate the private type facility of Ada or the type facility of Euclid [Chang 78]where a single module (package and module respectively) may contain several specifications for related objects.

2.1.3. Multiple Implementations

Current data abstraction languages focus on the separation of a data type from its implementation. A natural outgrowth of this separation is the ability to substitute one representation for another. Many languages, such as Alphard, force a single implementation to be associated with a specification. One can change the representation only by removing the entire module (form), which contains both the specification and implementation, and by replacing it with a module that contains the same specification and a new implementation. Other languages, such as Ada, permit different implementations (package bodies) of an abstract data type to be written, but only one may be associated with a specification (package specification) for any particular program. One of the goals of Paragon is to eliminate these restrictions and allow multiple representations to be associated simultaneously with a single specification for an abstract data type in a single program.

As explained in Section 1.1.2.2, different representations should be allowed access to additional details about their composition and use. This goal represents a substantial departure from current data abstraction methodology. However, the goal is very similar in concept to the representation selection systems such as the systems built by Low [Low 74], and by Gotlieb and Tompa [Gotlieb 74]. In Low's system, the selection mechanism takes into account the composition of a set's elements. Gotlieb's and Tompa's system performs an initial pass over different table representations to select those that have the necessary operations implemented for the particular use of a table. Therefore these systems can use details about a data type's composition when selecting a representation. But unlike the design of these systems, the design of Paragon strives to integrate the selection of representations with the rest of the language. The selection process is not to be the activity of an extrinsic, representation-selection system.

2.1.4. Simultaneous Implementations

Beyond the ability to define multiple representations in a program, another goal of Paragon is the ability to use multiple representations in a program. Although some language designs permit multiple representations to be present in a source program, they require that each variable in a program be assigned the same implementation. For example, Ada requires that the same representation (package body) be associated with a specification (generic package specification) for each object specified (instantiation of the package). This decision is motivated by implementation complications caused by different representations of an abstract data being passed in the same procedure call, discussed in the next section (Section 2.1.5), since the prohibition of simultaneous, different implementations for a single abstract data type guarantees that the resulting program will have no interacting implementations. The design goals for Paragon differ from these previous design goals. Instead, a Paragon design goal insists that different instances (variables) of the same abstract data type may use different implementations in a single program.

2.1.5. Interacting Implementations

Allowing variables with different implementations to interact is another design goal of Paragon.   But this goal normally presents a problem if two variables with different implementations interact. In general, there is either no guarantee that an appropriate implementation for the interacting operation will exist or there must be an enormous number of operation implementations: for n variable implementations, there needs to be n^2 operation implementations. The use of set implementations illustrates this problem. First, assume that two popular implementations for sets, bit vectors and hash tables, are available to implement set variables. Then suppose that two variables are implemented, one with each of the implementations, and that there exist proper implementations for the intersection operation for each of the two implementations. Although a selection of either representation for all set variables results in a program that has procedure implementations for all calls, there is still no guarantee that there exists an implementation for an intersection operation applied to a hash table and a bit vector. The alternative is to provide procedures for all combinations of set implementations.   Thus the interaction of the differently implemented variables causes problems, which is a reason why many languages exclude this goal. The design of Paragon is intended to solve this problem so that interacting implementations may be used.

Several approaches to the problem have been suggested: automatic conversion from one representation to another; a canonical representation; an implementation of intersection that uses only abstract operations; and the addition of extra implementations of intersection for the different combinations of sets. However, none has ever been incorporated into a complete language design. In fact, previous work tends to ignore this goal explicitly. Low's system, the SETL optimizer [Freudenberger 83] and the Algol-68 extensions proposed by Banatre, et al. [Banatre 81] use variable interactions as a way to decide that different variables should have the *same* representations. One design that permitted interacting representations was an Algol-68 extension designed by Ghezzi and Paolini [Ghezzi 77] but this system requires the programmer to direct explicitly the language system to use different representations. A design goal of Paragon is to remove these restrictions and to provide the facilities that allow different variables to have different implementations of abstract data types, even if they interact in some operation.

2.1.6. Shared Implementations

Distinct abstract data types sometimes have a shared representation. For example, the set facility in SETL uses a combined representation for integers and sets. In this combined representation, there is a single hash table that contains all integers used in a program. Some of these integers are contained in sets; some of these integers are currently assigned to integer variables; some are assigned to both; some are assigned to neither. Each integer in the hash table contains information about its value and all the sets it is contained in. All set variables and integer variables contain specific information for retrieving information from this single hash table (details can be found in the description of SETL's implementation [Dewar 79]). Thus the hash table is part of a combined representation for integers and sets. Besides SETL, this kind of sharing is frequently desirable in memory allocation systems, message transmission systems, file systems and transaction logging systems, where a particular facility needs to have representation control over many kinds of abstract data types. Yet this ability is not provided in data abstraction languages.

Thus another of Paragon's design goals is to support shared implementations for distinct specifications. Related ideas have been proposed by Katz and Rosenchein [Katz 81] and by Rowe and Tonge [Rowe 78] where two distinct data structures are joined into a single data structure and this single data structure is viewed as having two different uses. However, there has been no exploitation of the idea that a single representation may simultaneously implement several specifications. This goal is, therefore, another departure from the usual data abstraction facilities found in most languages.

2.1.7. Distinguishing Implementations

One of the immediate consequences of permitting alternative implementations of abstract data types is that a way to evaluate them must be present. Most representation-selection systems have a way to distinguish representations, such as formulae that indicate a representation's performance. However, these differences are usually not available to the programmer and the programmer may not alter them. In fact, these descriptions are usually external to the language being implemented and instead belong to the translation system or representation selection system.

When a programmer creates a new type, the programmer should be able also to specify the ways in which the representation should be used. Unfortunately, most languages permit the control of different implementations for only predefined types. One such example is Pascal [Jensen 78], which allows the programmer to select a *packed* representation for some of the data types. Other languages fail to distinguish between different representations within the program and create an entirely separate configuration language in which the different implementations can be described [Mitchell 79].

To ameliorate these restrictions, the design of Paragon strives to introduce ways to let the programmer describe and distinguish between the different representations without giving direct access to the details of representation.

2.1.8. Variable Description

To assist in making a representation selection, the programmer should be able to provide the selection system with some kind of information about the variables used in a program. Most languages only permit the programmer to provide some crude, predefined attributes of a variable, such as in Ada, where certain kinds of monitoring of variables can be control by the programmer. Representation-selection systems usually permit the programmer to provide some better information: for example, the PSI system asks the programmer about the program [McCune 77], but the selection of information is still not under programmer control.

Unlike these systems, Paragon should allow the programmer to specify what kinds of information should be provided when declaring a variable and then to describe how that information is to be used by the selection system.

2.1.9. Programmer Accessibility

Representation-selection systems are usually associated with very high-level languages that provide very abstract objects (compared with the level of abstractions provided in typical high-level languages). The representation-selection system provides many representations for these very high-level features but limits the access that a programmer may have to these representations [Schonberg 77], to the descriptions of the representations [Rowe 78] or to the optimization criterion that the representation-selection system is using [Low 74]. These systems further limit the programmer's interference with the selection decisions because only predefined types in the very high-level language associated with representation-selection systems may be used. There are no facilities for user-provided types, user-provided representations or user-provided optimization criteria.

The motivations for these restrictions are the complexity of the data structure that represents the program during representation selection and the complexity of the selection algorithm operating on this data structure. Usually, this data structure is an abstract syntax tree of the program, and the actual representation selection process has the complexity of a compiler phase. Writing a piece of a compiler is thought to be beyond the concern of a typical programmer, hence the lack of programmer-provided, representation-selection mechanisms.

Because a data abstraction language, such as Paragon, is designed to allow programmers to create new high-level abstractions, it should allow programmers to control the representation selection. This programmer control requires programmer-accessible mechanisms for describing the differences between representations and for describing the optimization criteria to be applied. However, the complexity of the resulting mechanism must be limited so that the mechanism is within easy grasp of a typical programmer.

2.1.10. Static Type Checking

Static type checking (checking the compatibility of actual parameters with formal parameters before a program is executed) helps ensure that a program meets its specification and limits the possible kinds of run-time errors. The Paragon design therefore attempts to have all type checking performed during the compilation process and to have no type errors possible during execution.

The goal of static type checking is also a departure from the procedure-call checking performed in typical object-oriented, hierarchy-based systems, such as for Smalltalk's methods and Simula'o virtual procedures. There is a tradeoff in these designs between safety and efficiency, and flexibility. Because the parameter matching for procedure calls can be verified during compilation, static checking is considered safer, and because more is known about the program being checked, a more efficient program should result. Therefore Paragon opts for a safe and efficient language rather than for flexibility.

2.1.11. Automatic Selection of Representation

If a language provides a way to distinguish between representations, then a natural extension of the language should provide some automated way to select an appropriate representation using the distinctions. Since a goal of Paragon is to provide descriptions that distinguish between data type representations, the Paragon language and its translator should also include some mechanisms for automatically selecting a representation for each variable.

There is a problem in defining the term *automatically*. At one extreme, it might mean that the compiler checks the decisions stated by the programmer in the same way that type checking is automatically processed once the program defines all identifiers in declarations. One such example is Mesa [Mitchell 79], which relies on an additional file, called a configuration file, to specify which implementation should be used with each specification (interface module) by naming it. At the other extreme are program transformation systems, such as PSI and Rovner's Sail compiler [Rovner 76], which make a decision by using processes that are internal to the translation system.

Paragon's goal lies somewhere in between. The programmer should be able to describe a method for making selection decisions, for example, to attempt to minimize the time and space product of the variables that the programs use. However, the programmer should not have to state explicitly which implementation should be associated with each variable.

2.1.12. Compile-Time Checking of Program Feasibility

The philosophy of abstract data types dictates that compile-time checking should guarantee that the implementations of an abstract data type can be used when the specification is used. In applying this philosophy to a language with multiple representations of abstract data types, the design of Paragon should allow compile-time checking of implementations, guaranteeing that all variables have a representation. Further the design of Paragon should allow compile-time verification that appropriate procedure implementations exist for the procedure calls using those representations. The idea that this kind of checking be performed independently of the semantic analysis is another departure from conventional language designs.

2.2. Preliminary Design Restrictions for Paragon

Even with the goals that are set forth explicitly, there is still a wide range of choices for the scope of the research. In order to limit this scope, several design restrictions were arbitrarily imposed.

The restrictions were based on a priori guesses about what features might enlarge the scope of the language design. Each restriction could be lifted in order to generate another direction of research that synthesizes abstract data types and representation selection. A brief description and motivation for each restriction follows the list below.

- A type hierarchy will be the basis of the language design.

- An identifier within a scope will have exactly one object bound to it.

- No attempts at automatic creation of representations for abstract data types will be made.

- No attempts at automatic conversion between representations of abstract data types will be made.

- There will be no run-time selection of representations of abstract data types.

- The prototype translator is intended to represent an existence proof of feasibility, not the last word in efficient algorithms.

2.2.1. Use of a Type Hierarchy

This work might have been built on other data abstraction languages, such as Ada, Clu or Alphard, each with its own method of writing the specifications and implementation of abstract data types. Because my thesis is that many levels of refinement are appropriate for specifying and representing abstract data types and because the class mechanism in Simula provides a layering mechanism, I was drawn to Simula-67 as a model. Thus I arbitrarily chose to exploit and explore this particular approach to this problem.

I did not, however, use Simula as my base language design, though the current design of Paragon has many resemblances to Simula. Initially, I wanted to make a clear distinction between types and objects. As a model for this distinction, I used the Red programming language [Nestor 79]. Some initial designs of Paragon resembled a cross between Red and Simula, but these designs were significantly different from Red and Simula that no effort was made to use either language as a base from which to design Paragon.

2.2.2. Single Identifier/Object Binding

Because the eventual translator system needed to select particular implementations for variables and follow their use throughout the program (or block in which the identifiers were bound), I insisted that each binding of identifier to an object, within a block, be immutable. This meant that the choice of representation made for a variable when the variable was created would remain invariant throughout the block. This was an attempt to isolate the object creations to the variable declarations in a block, and hence simplify the analysis of the block for later selection decisions. If one permitted the representation of the object to change at arbitrary places in the program, then one might be unable to determine at compile time which representation a variable might have during a procedure call. Therefore one could possibly increase either the work at compile time to check that an implementation exists or the work at run time to select an appropriate procedure.

2.2.3. Automatic Creation of Representations

A widely pursued research topic is the creation of representations of abstract data types given a formal specification. Although this topic is interesting, a proper treatment of it requires a formal specification language, a processor for that language and some assumptions about the way that data types are implemented. Paragon strives to take advantage of programmer-provided knowledge of representation and not to create new representations. Thus the goal of automatic creation was considered beyond the scope of this work.

2.2.4. Automatic Conversion between Representations

Along with automatic creation of representations, the automated conversion from one representation to another is considered an important research topic. Attempting to pursue this goal raises a large number of problems that have not yet been satisfactorily solved. First, there is the problem of specifying the implementations and their equivalencies. Second a technique must be chosen for the conversion operations: for example, using a canonical representation; using a different conversion routine for each possible conversion between representations; or automatically creating the conversion routines. Third, there is an unsolved question of when to perform the conversion. Because of these issues, the design of Paragon did not explicitly consider automatic conversions between representations, but left the topic open for further research.

2.2.5. Run-Time Selection of Representations

Allowing the run-time selection of representations forces the design of Paragon to answer many additional questions and solve additional problems that were beyond the scope of the research. For example, allowing the run-time selection of representations can hamper the feasibility checking of a program at compile time. Under typical circumstances, every possible implementation must be available at every use of the variable since no compile-time information may be available. Because a goal of Paragon is to guarantee the existence and type correctness of all necessary procedures at compile time, and because allowing run-time selection of representations makes this guarantee difficult to enforce, run-time selection of representation is prohibited. Further, there are open questions about the methods that should be used in making a run-time selection. For example, the cost of making a decisions may be more expensive than the savings from the choice. Finally, there is usually some additional run-time expense in making a selection of a procedure given particular representations for its parameters — an expense I felt that Paragon programs should avoid. Therefore, I limited the scope of this work to compile-time selection.

2.2.6. Prototype Translator

As evidence that the Paragon design was complete and translatable, I constructed a prototype translator. The art of creating efficient translation schemes is another area of research that is logically related to language design, but the creation of an efficient translator was not essential for my demonstration of feasibility. Thus minimal effort was expended to make the translation system efficient, although there was an effort made to ensure that the entire language could be translated and executed. In addition, there was an effort made to ensure that the prototype would show that there are no inherent inefficiencies for processing or executing Paragon.

With these sets of goals and restrictions in hand, I proceeded through several designs of Paragon. The basics of the last version of Paragon are provided in the next chapter, followed by a chapter which illustrates some of the more complex features of the language.

Chapter 3
The Basics of Paragon

This chapter describes the basics of the Paragon programming language. I have assumed that the reader is familiar with algebraic languages such as Pascal or Simula, and with extended BNF notations. No emphasis will be placed, therefore, on describing the exact syntax of various language features or the BNF metalanguage. Instead the discussion will assume that the reader can read the examples without such comments.

Paragon is defined in terms of a process called *elaboration*. Therefore, this chapter starts with a brief description of the three kinds of elaboration that Paragon uses. The basics of Paragon are concerned with the objects and their manipulation, so the notion of object is then introduced along with some examples of how a simple object may be defined and created. Two ways of defining relationships between objects, inheritance and nesting, are also discussed. Then the chapter provides a discussion of how expressions and objects interact through the use of parameters.

Once objects and expressions are introduced, a brief discussion of procedures is presented. Procedures provide a general mechanism for manipulating objects. One special kind of procedure, an iterator, is then described. The discussion of iterators is followed by a description of other control abstractions in Paragon: the usual statements found in an algebraic language.

With this level of introduction, a programmer should be able to read the Paragon programs in this thesis. For the interested, a BNF description of the syntax can be found in Appendix B and additional language details can be found in Appendix A.

3.1. Overview of Elaborations

The semantics of Paragon are defined in terms of elaborations that are performed on a program. Three kinds of elaborations are defined in Paragon: *elaborations with specifications, elaborations with implementations* and *elaborations with realizations*. Although Section 5.1 gives a more complete description of these different kinds of elaborations in Paragon, a brief introduction is needed for understanding this chapter.

Elaborating a program with specifications and implementations can be thought of as performing various kinds of semantic analysis. Thus elaboration of a procedure invocation with *specifications* is the technical way of describing the type checking for a procedure call. When a program cannot be elaborated with specifications, perhaps because of some semantic error, the program is called *ill specified*, otherwise the program is called *well specified*. Elaboration of a procedure call with *implementations* corresponds to feasibility checking. This elaboration checks that an acceptable procedure implementation exists for the procedure call. If an acceptable procedure implementation cannot be found, perhaps because it is never declared, then the program is called *infeasible*. If there are no errors during elaboration with implementations, then a program is called *feasible*. The concept of feasibility checking is described in Section 5.5.5. Finally, elaboration with *realizations* corresponds to the actual running of a program; the term *executing* is used synonymously with the phrase *elaboration with realizations*. A program without run-time errors is called *defined*. A program that generates a run-time error is called *erroneous*. At various times throughout the discussion in this chapter, these terms will be used when a precise statement of Paragon's semantics is required.

3.2. Objects

There is a rich structure to objects that are manipulated by Paragon programs. The parts of the structure are *simple objects, objects, local instances* and *parameters*. Their relationships are discussed below.

Objects in Paragon consist of nested *simple objects*. Some colloquial examples of simple objects include houses, kitchens and refrigerators. An *object* is represented by a list of nested simple objects, such as a house that contains a kitchen that contains a refrigerator. The figure below illustrates this relationship:[7]

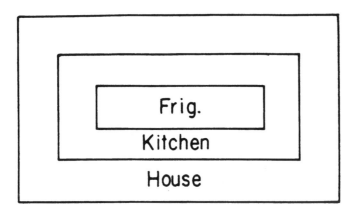

Figure 3-1:   An Object Consisting of 3 Simple Objects

An object is defined in terms of a single nested simple object inside each nested simple object. Many other relationships between simple objects may exist in a program. Most of these relationships have no special value in the definition of Paragon and hence are not named in this thesis. For example, the following figure shows a possible relationship among simple objects in Paragon, but the figure does not represent an object:

---

[7]As discussed in Section 3.2.3 on page 42, a textual representation of the same object would be (*House*, *Kitchen*, *Frig*).

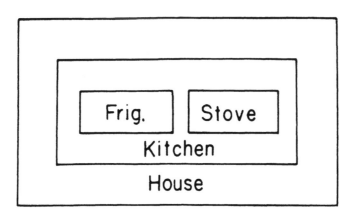

Figure 3-2: Nested Simple Objects that are not an Object

However, the same simple objects may be used in more than one object. For example, the following figure illustrates the same simple objects for *House* and *Kitchen* in a different object than the one shown in Figure 3-1:

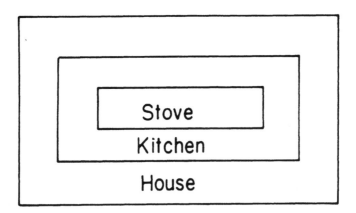

Figure 3-3: Another Object with 3 Simple Objects

This structure permits simple objects to be shared by other simple objects. In particular, an outer simple object can be thought of as a manager or owner of all of the simple objects inside of it. An object can be viewed as the most deeply nested simple object along with its manager(s). This view of "managers controlling individuals" is developed in Chapter 4 and is essential to the definition of abstract data types in Paragon.

As shown above, a simple object may contain other simple objects. Another, unrelated way to analyze simple objects is by considering the local instances and parameters in simple objects.[8] Each simple object contains a set of *local instances* and some *parameters*[9]. Parameters provide a way for one simple object to share objects with another simple object. The details of parameters are deferred until Section 3.4. Each local instance provides some set of properties for the simple object. For example, the kitchen simple object may contain local instances that describe properties of "being something with four walls", "being something with a floor" and "being a place where appliances reside." In programming-language terms, a local instance consists of a set of variables and procedures, where these variables and procedure describe some properties of the simple object. A simple object is illustrated in the figure below:

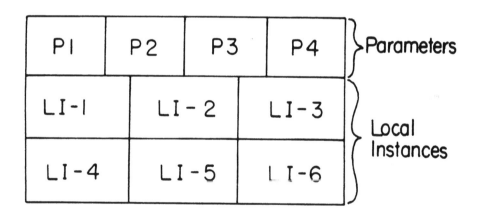

Figure 3-4: A Simple Object with Parameters

So far, simple objects have been described colloquially. Paragon actually defines four

---

[8] There *is* a relationship between local instances, simple objects and objects, but it is far too complex is represent two dimensionally and has no use in this thesis. Therefore, the reader is advised to merely consider the relationship between objects and nested simple objects and the relationship between simple objects and local instances to be unrelated.

[9] A simple object may also have a label if the creating name component is labeled in a parameter. See Section 3.4.1.

different kinds of simple objects. Each simple object can be either *specified* or *realized*, and can be either *definite* or *indefinite*. The first choice of specified or realized is determined by the kind of elaboration that created the simple object. If the simple object results from elaboration with specifications or implementations, then it is *specified*. If the simple object results from elaboration with realizations, then it is *realized*. Thus *specified* can be viewed as a compile-time simple object; *realized* can be viewed as a run-time simple object.

The adjectives *definite* and *indefinite* indicate whether the simple object is considered unique. In a more conventional sense, *indefinite* simple objects are the "types" of *definite* simple objects. In English, *a House* denotes any *House*; it is indefinite. *The House* denotes a particular *House*; it is definite. Similarly in Paragon, it is possible to denote a definite simple object, that is, a particular simple object, and it is possible to denote an indefinite simple object, that is, a simple object that represents some unspecified member of a set of simple objects.

Expressions are elaborated inside of simple objects. The simple objects that enclose the expression contain bindings between identifiers and either procedures, classes or objects. Thus an object is also an *environment*. The two words are used interchangeably in this thesis.

The basic Paragon feature for defining an object is a class. The ways that classes are used to create local instances, simple objects and objects are discussed in the next sections.

3.2.1. Classes and Simple Objects

Classes serve as templates or models of simple objects. Much like classes in Simula, they may contain parameters, declarations and statements. An example is shown below:

```
class Vehicle is              ! A class declaration;
begin
   var Size => IM . new Integer;  ! A variable declaration;
   Size := 0;                 ! A statement;
end;
```

This example declares a class that represents a *Vehicle*. The class contains one declaration, an integer variable *Size*[10], and one statement, that initializes *Size*.

---

[10]Descriptions of variables are deferred until Section 5.2 when distinctions between specifications and implementations are discussed.

Like Algol-68 [VanWijngaarden 69], Paragon uses a kind of generator function on classes in variable declarations to create new, definite simple objects. This generator function is denoted *new* and appears in simple-object creations. For example, the following simple-object creation:[11]

        new Vehicle

creates a definite *Vehicle* simple object. When a simple object is created, one local instance for the class and one for each of its ancestors are created. Because no classes are inherited by *Vehicle*, this simple object consists of one local instance which is the result of elaborating the declarations and statements in the class declaration for *Vehicle*. After creation, the simple object is said to have *Vehicle* as an underlying class.

A simple object (or *instance*) that is formed from a simple-object creation is termed a *definite instance*. There are two other kinds of instances that need to be defined: *indefinite instances* and *any* instances.

An *indefinite instantiation* creates an indefinite instance and merely has the class name without the reserved word *new*. For example,

        Vehicle

represents an indefinite instantiation of *Vehicle*. It too results in a simple object, and as will be illustrated later, is the way in which types are denoted in parameters. The main difference between indefinite instances and definite instances is that the internal declarations and statements of definite instances are completely elaborated, whereas only selected declarations are elaborated in indefinite instances. Like definite instances, indefinite instances have an underlying class, namely the class denoted by the identifier in the expression specifying the instantiation.

A third instance is an *any instance*. The instantiation has the simple representation:

        any

and it results in an indefinite instance of the special *any* class.[12] One can think of this simple object as the most indefinite indefinite object. It is used when a programmer wishes to

---

[11]More properly, object-creation name component, see Section 3.3.1.

[12]For completeness, the underlying class of an *any* instance is defined to be the special *any* class which is otherwise inaccessible to the programmer.

express the notion that some kind of object is present, but does not wish even to specify a class to which the simple object will belong.

3.2.2. Inheritance

Like Simula and Smalltalk, the classes in Paragon may inherit other classes. Inheritance is used to include the declarations and statements from another class. For example, a tank object is a special kind of vehicle and should contain the properties associated with any other vehicle. This is accomplished by inheriting the *Vehicle* class in the declaration for *Tank*, as shown below:

```
class Tank of Vehicle is
begin
    var CrewSize => IM . new integer;
end;
```

A *Tank* simple object has both the properties specified in the declarations for *Vehicle* and the properties specified for *Tank*. More than one parent may be specified and parents are accumulated, that is, inheritance is transitive.[13] This can be illustrated with the following classes that represent ships:

```
class Ship is
begin
    var Displacement => IM . new integer;
end;

class Monitor of Ship, Tank is
begin
    Cannon => IM . new integer;
end;
```

Objects with an underlying class of *Monitor* inherit the properties from both classes *Ship* and *Tank*,[14] and since *Tank* inherits properties from *Vehicle*, *Monitor* inherits *Vehicle's* properities as well.

When a simple object is created, the various classes that are inherited are elaborated, one

---

[13]The set of all inherited parents is called the *ancestors* of the class.

[14]The *Monitor* was among the first class of armor plated ships introduced during the U.S. Civil War.

at a time, starting with the furthest ancestor of the leftmost parent.[15] The order of elaboration matches the order of inheritance. In the example above, the order is *Ship*, *Vehicle*, *Tank* and last, *Monitor*. This order is called *leftmost elaboration order*.[16] The elaboration of each ancestor creates a local instance and the collection of local instances from the elaboration of each ancestor and the class itself are grouped together in the simple object.

It is conceivable that a ancestor class may be inherited more than once. The *Ship* class in the previous example might have been written:

```
class Ship of Vehicle is
begin
   var Displacement => IM . new integer;
end;

class Monitor of Ship, Tank is
begin
   Cannon => IM . new integer;
end;
```

in which case the *Monitor* class would inherit the *Vehicle* class twice, once from *Ship* and once from *Tank*. In this circumstance, only one local instance for the shared class would be elaborated and that elaboration would occur the first time that the shared class is encountered. In this example, the elaboration order of classes for a *Monitor* object creation is *Vehicle*, *Ship*, *Tank* and last, *Monitor*.

Although the semantics for Paragon would be simpler if an ancestor could not be inherited more than once, this feature allows a programmer to refine abstractions one level at a time without having to rearrange an entire tree of refinements. In the example above, the programmer's view of the abstract world is that *Ships* and *Tanks* are special kinds of *Vehicles* and that *Monitors* really are a special kind of *Ships* and *Tanks*. If *Vehicle* could not be inherited more than once, then the programmer would have to change the declaration(s) for either *Tank*, *Ship* or *Monitor*. Although this makes Paragon simpler, this rewriting no longer reflects the programmer's abstract model of the world. Further, in Chapter 4, this same ability is exploited to provided multiple implementation of abstract data types. Therefore, the design of Paragon permits a class to inherit an ancestor more than once.

---

[15] *Leftmost* has been the convention adopted by other languages, in particular Flavors and Traits, and so is adopted by Paragon as well. *Rightmost* would not produce a radical change in the semantics, but since English is read from left to right, there is a slight tendency to examine the parents of a class in the order in which they are read, left to right. If programmers thought like LALR parsers, perhaps rightmost order would make more sense.

[16] Also see leftmost parent order, page 325.

3.2.3. Nested Classes and Objects

In the examples given so far, the only declarations in a class were integer variables. Classes may also be declared in classes which leads to a structure of nested simple objects. For example, nested rooms inside houses might be specified as below:

```
class House is
begin
    class Room is
    begin
    end;
end;
```

An object creation that uses the *House* class, that is *new House*, creates a simple object in which other simple objects may be created, namely *Room* simple objects. The *House* simple object in which a *Room* is created is also called the *environment* for the creation of rooms.

The expressions denoting nested objects are straightforward. For example, a programmer can write the following expressions (which use the *House* and *Room* declarations):

```
var MellonMansion => new House;
var MasterBedRoom => MellonMansion . new Room;
```

The first expression creates a *House* simple object (and the variable declaration causes the identifier *MellonMansion* to be bound to the simple object). The second expression creates a *Room* simple object inside the previous created *House* simple object. Note that a full description of the newly created *Room* requires some reference to the enclosing *House* simple object. Paragon therefore defined the concept of object to mean the simple object along with the environment in which it was created. Thus, an object is a list of simple objects, one created inside another.

In this thesis, a list notation is used to represent objects. Each element of the list denotes a simple object. If the simple object resulting from the first simple object creation is denoted *MM* and the simple object resulting from the second creation denoted *MBR*, then the object denoted by the identifier *MasterBedRoom* is represented by (*MM, MBR*). Rather than always creating a name for every simple object, the class name alone will sometimes be used to represent a definite instance of that class in a list of simple objects. Thus the object denoted by *MasterBedRoom* would be given as (*House, Room*). Since there is only one definite instantiation for each class in the example above, there is no ambiguity about which instantiation of *House* is meant. In cases where some ambiguity exists between definite instances of the same class, the list notation will be abused a little by using the variable identifier associated with the creation name component for the innermost simple object. Thus the object denoted by *MasterBedRoom* might also be represented by (*MellonMansion*, *MasterBedRoom*). This last convention will suffice since definite instances are only permitted in variable declarations, and only one object instantiation is permitted per variable declaration.

3.3. Name Expressions

Name expressions denote actions that are to be performed during elaboration. Each name expression consists of a sequence of *name components* separated by periods (.) where each component performs a single action in a specified environment, and returns another environment in which the next name component is to be elaborated. Such actions include object creation, binding of identifiers to objects and invocation of procedures.

Because no previous component returns an environment for use by the first name component in an expression, it is elaborated in the environment of the object in which it appears. If the *House* class mentioned above were modified a bit as follows:

```
class House is
begin
   class Room is
   begin
   end;

   var Kitchen => new Room;                                    ☜1
end;
```

then the simple object creation for *Room* (notation 1) has as its environment the *House* simple object in which the variable declaration *Kitchen* is being elaborated. Generally, the initial environment for a name expression is the scope in which the first identifier in the name component is declared. In the example, the identifier *Room* is declared in the class *House*, so the environment is the enclosing *House* object. Section A.4 gives a complete description of how this environment is established.

Within its environment, each name component specifies one specific action, such as creation of á simple object, selection of an object, description of an object or invocation of a procedure. The first three kinds of name components are discussed below. The discussion of procedure invocation is postponed until Section 3.6.4 where procedure implementations are discussed.

3.3.1. Generation of Instances

Generation of instances results from the elaboration of an object-creation name component. The syntax for this kind of name component is the reserved word *new* followed by an identifier representing the underlying class for the simple object. Several examples of this kind of name component were shown in previous examples, such as *new Tank*. The environment that results from the creation of a simple object is the environment for the object creation appended by the simple object. In a previous example, *MellonMansion . new Room*, the resulting environment is the resulting object, (*House, Room*).

There are several restrictions on the name expressions that may contain an object creation name component. Briefly, the environment in which the creation takes place may have been neither newly created by another object-creation name component in the same name expression nor the result of a procedure call in the same name expression. The details of these restrictions can be found in Section A.2.

3.3.2. Description of Objects

Paragon provides two kinds of name components to describe an object. Intuitively, these name components provide a way to denote a type.[17] One way uses a class identifier in a name component; this corresponds to explicitly naming a type. The other way uses the reserved word *structure* as a name component; this corresponds to extracting the type of an expression.

More precisely, if a class identifier is used in a component without the reserved word *new*, the class identifier is denoting the creation of an indefinite instance. An example of this kind of name component is shown by the name expression *MellonMansion . Room*. The lack of the reserved word *new* before the class identifier *Room* causes an indefinite instantiation of *Room* and the resulting environment is the list of the definite instance denoted by *MellonMansion* followed by an indefinite instance of *Room*. As a notational convention, an indefinite instance is represented in a list of simple objects as the name of class preceded by the reserved word *any*. Thus the object resulting from the indefinite instance in the previous name expression is (*House, any Room*).

---

[17]Each of these name components results in an object whose innermost simple object is an indefinite simple object.

The reserved word *structure* as a name component uses the current environment to describe an object. The innermost simple object of the current environment is removed and a new indefinite instance of the underlying class of the innermost simple object is created and appended to the remaining environment. The resulting object looks similar to the environment given to the *structure* component except that the innermost simple object has been changed (probably from a definite instance but not necessarily) to an indefinite instance. This can be illustrated by the continuing the example on page 42:

```
... MellonMansion.Room ...
... MasterBedRoom.structure ...
```

The two expressions use the variable declarations of *MellonMansion* and *MasterBedRoom*. These expressions result in similar objects. Both have an outer definite simple object denoted by *MellonMansion*. Both have an inner indefinite simple object denoted by *any Room*. Thus "type" of the innermost simple object is retrieved by the structure name component.

Because descriptions of objects act like types, these descriptions of objects are especially useful in parameters, as will be shown later.

3.3.3. Selection of Objects

When the identifier in a name component is declared as a variable or in a parameter, and the reserved word *new* is absent, the name component is selecting an object. The algorithm for elaboration is simple: the identifier is found and the object bound to it during the declaration elaboration is used as the environment for the next component. This is identical to ordinary field selection in records of Ada and Pascal, and in classes of Simula. This is illustrated by the following continuation of the example on page 38:

```
var MyCar => new Vehicle;

... MyCar.Size ...;
```

Here the integer denoted by *Size* is selected from the simple object denoted by *MyCar*.

3.3.4. Other Name Components

There are several other kinds of name components, some of which deal with attributes and are discussed in Section 5.3.7. The rest are syntactic sugaring for various procedure calls. Their replacements are given here only for completeness. The reader should probably just glance at the left hand column for now and refer back to this chart as necessary in later chapters.

Name Component	Replacement
↑	Value
[s]	Element(s)
L[18]	Literal(&L)

In the above chart, s is any expression, L is any integer literal and &L is the name of a special predefined procedure (see Section 3.3.6).

3.3.5. Other Expressions

There are several other expression besides name expressions. All of them are syntactic sugaring for an equivalent name expression that contains a procedure call. Like the chart above, the reader may wish to just glance at the left hand column and refer back to the chart as necessary while reading later chapters. The following chart gives the translations:

Expression	Replacement
(e1)	e1
e1 := e2	IM.Assign(e1,e2)[19]
e1 = e2	IM.Equal(e1,e2)
e1 + e2	IM.Plus(e1,e2)
e1 - e2	IM.Minus(e1,e2)
e1 / e2	IM.Divide(e1,e2)
e1 * e2	IM.Times(e1,e2)
e1 rem e2	IM.Remainder(e1,e2)
- e1	IM.UnaryMinus(e1)
e1..e2	IM.Sequence(e1,e2)[20]
e1 < e2	IM.LessThan(e1,e2)
e1 > e2	IM.GreaterThan(e1,e2)
e1 <= e2	IM.LessThanEqual(e1,e2)
e1 >= e2	IM.GreaterThanEqual(e1,e2)
e1 and e2	Booleans.LogicalAnd(e1,e2)[21]
e1 or e2	Booleans.LogicalOr(e1,e2)
not e1	Booleans.LogicalNot(e1)

---

[18] This a qualified literal, such as in AppleManager.3, which is interpreted as a three that belongs to the AppleManager. This is how different managers use literals. Managers and their use are discussed in Chapter 4.

[19] Permitted only when the expression is used as a statement.

IM is the predefined Integer Manager (See Section 6.2.6). The syntactic sugaring is only provided for predefined integers and booleans.

[20] Since iterators are only permitted in for statements, this notation is permitted only when the expression is the iterator in a for statement.

[21] Booleans is the predefined manager of booleans. See Section 6.2.3.

$$L^{22} \hspace{5cm} IM.Literal(\&L)$$

where *e1* and *e2* are any expressions, *L* is any integer literal and *&L* is the name of a special predefined procedure (see Section 3.3.6). The parser uses standard arithmetic precedence and association for these expressions. The order of parsing may be changed by parentheses in the conventional way.

3.3.6. Integer Literals

Integer literals may be used as name components and as expressions,[23] though they play an unusual role. Each literal represents an unnameable, predefined procedure that returns a *Word* object (a predefined class, see Section 6.2.7) which contains the appropriate integer value in it. Further, the presence of a literal causes a call to another predefined procedure, *Literal*, to be made. The specification for the *Literal* procedure is

```
procedure Literal(CM.Word)24 return Integer;
```

Literal transforms a word into an integer, using whatever implementation is appropriate. Thus Paragon interprets the name expression *AppleManager.3* as *AppleManager.Literal(&3)* where *&3* is the function that returns a new word with three in it. Therefore a literal first causes a new word of memory to be created and the literal to be placed in it. Then a representation-specific conversion routine is called, *Literal*, which may transform this word into any representation for *Integer* that is desired.

As I explain in the next chapter, Paragon uses an object manager model for data abstraction. One predefined variable is a manager for integers, called *IM* (integer manager). These details are not important yet, except as an explanation of some syntactic sugaring that Paragon provides. Because predefined integers are used so frequently, Paragon has a further transformation of expressions that are only used for integer literals. Specifically, should an integer literal appear as the first (or only) name component, the component *IM* will be prepended to it. Thus the expression *3* is rewritten as *IM.Literal(&3)*.

---

[22] This is an unqualified literal, thus as the replacement shows, it becomes qualified as a predefined integer.

[23] The expressions are transformed into two name components as defined in the previous section.

[24] *CM* is the predefined manager for Computer Memory.

3.4. Parameters

Parameters are objects that are shared with other objects or procedures to provide some flexibility in object creation and procedure invocation. Parameters can be used when declaring procedures, declaring classes, invoking a procedure and instantiating a class. In this section, the basic syntax of parameters is discussed, followed by a description of the way in which parameters are passed. The section concludes with a discussion of how type parameters are provided in Paragon.

3.4.1. Syntax of Parameters

A parameter is a name expression with one restriction and one addition. The restriction is that no definite object may be created in a parameter. Thus the reserved word *new* may not appear anywhere in a name expression used as a parameter. The addition is that name components may be labeled. When comparing two parameters, the identifiers used as labels become bound to objects and these identifiers may be used inside of classes or procedures that declared the labeled parameters. Labels in parameters are defined by placing an identifier followed by a colon (:) before a component. Two labels, one for each simple object in a nested object, are illustrated below:

    H: House . R: Room

Note that more than one name component in a name expression may be labeled. However, only one label per name component is permitted. An identifier that labels a name component is said to be *implicitly declared*.

The only additional semantics for elaborating a parameter describe the effects of a labeling. Most of the semantics concern what happens when two parameters are compared which is discussed in the next section. There are some additional esoteric semantics concerning class inheritance that are not discussed here.[25]

---

[25]When a name component is labeled, the corresponding innermost simple object that results from the elaboration of that name component is also labeled (with the same identifier). The labeling used in the object notation parallels the notation in the name component: the identifier followed by a colon. Thus the object that results from elaborating the previous example is (*H: any House, R: any Room*). This labeling of simple object is used only for ensuring that parameters are properly inherited by subclasses, and that procedure implementations match their specifications.

3.4.2. Comparing Objects

Although comparison of objects is used for many purposes, it forms the basis for parameter passing and so will be discussed here.

A relation called *matching* or *conforming* may exist between an actual object and a formal object. The terms *actual* and *formal* are used in the conventional sense. Unlike the type equivalency relation in many programming languages, this relation is not symmetric. When an actual matches a formal, there is no implication that the formal matches the actual.

Matching is used for comparing parameters. At different times, the same parameter may be used as a formal and an actual. The following table summarizes the kinds of comparisons that occur in Paragon.

Actual	Formal
Procedure Call Parameter	Procedure Specification Parameter
Procedure Call Parameter	Procedure Implementation Parameter
Class Instantiation	Class Declaration Parameter
Subclass Declaration Parameter	Class Declaration Parameter
Procedure Implementation Parameter	Procedure Specification Parameter

3.4.2.1. Simple Object Matching

The basis for matching is the comparison of two simple objects. Intuitively, an actual simple object matches a formal simple object if the underlying class of the formal is a ancestor of, or the same as, the underlying class of the actual simple object. As will be shown in Chapter 4, this permits general procedures[26] to be written and provides a way to write multiple implementations for abstract data types. To ensure compatibility between definite and indefinite instances, one of the following constraints must also be met:

- The formal is an *any* instance,

- The formal is an indefinite instance and the underlying class of the formal is a ancestor of, or the same class as, the underlying class of the actual, or

- The formal is a definite instance and the actual is the same definite instance.

---

[26]Procedures that use only abstract properties of their parameters.

These rules can be illustrated using the following declarations and procedure calls[27]

```
procedure Wash(any);
procedure DriveUninsured(Vehicle);
procedure DriveUnqualified(Tank);
procedure DriveInsured(MyCar);

var YourCar => new Vehicle;

Wash(MyCar);                              ! OK;
Wash(Vehicle);                           ! OK;
Wash(any);                               ! OK;

DriveUninsured(MyCar);                    ! OK;
DriveUninsured(YourCar);                  ! OK;
DriveUninsured(Tank);                     ! OK;

DriveUnqualified(MyCar);                  ! Not OK;
DriveUnqualified(Tank);                   ! OK;
DriveUnqualified(Vehicle);               ! Not OK;

DriveInsured(MyCar);                      ! OK;
DriveInsured(YourCar);                    ! Not OK;
DriveInsured(Tank);                       ! Not OK;
```

In the example above, the procedure *Wash* has an *any* parameter, thus the definite instance denoted by *MyCar* (see page 45), the indefinite *Vehicle* and the *any* instance all match the formal. For the calls of *DriveUninsured*, the formal is an indefinite *Vehicle*, thus definite instances *MyCar* and *YourCar* match because they have *Vehicle* as their underlying classes. Further, the indefinite instance *Tank* matches since it is a subclass of the formal, *Vehicle*[28]. The formal of *DriveUnqualified* specifies that a *Tank* must be passed. Thus the definite instance of *MyCar* and the indefinite instance of *Vehicle* do not match. However, the indefinite instance *Tank* does match since it is the same class as the formal. The final procedure, *DriveInsured* has a definite object in its parameter, denoted by *MyCar*. Therefore, only that definite object may be used as an actual. Thus the actual in the call using *MyCar* matches the formal, the other two do not.

Another set of constraints ensures that parameters in the actual match the parameters in the formal. Thus one of the following must be met for two simple objects to match:

• The formal is an *any* instance without parameters, or

---

[27] Although procedures are not discussed until Section 3.5, I assume that the reader can understand these simple examples.

[28] This is how type parameters are passed.

- The formal is an *any* instance with parameters, the number of parameters in the formal object equals the number of parameters in the actual object, and from left to right, each parameter object in the actual object matches the corresponding parameter object in the formal object, or[29]

- The formal is a definite instance and the actual is the same definite instance, or

- The formal is an indefinite instance, and for each parameter in the formal, the corresponding parameter actual object matches the formal parameter object.[30]

Some examples of these rules are shown below:

```
class CarCarrier(v: Vehicle) is begin end;
var RoadWays => new CarCarrier(MyCar);

procedure RunAnything(any);
procedure RunVehicle(any(Vehicle));
procedure RunRoadWays(RoadWays);
procedure RunMyCar(CarCarrier(Vehicle));

RunAnything(RoadWays)      ! OK;
RunVehicle(RoadWays)       ! OK;
RunVehicle(MyCar);         ! Not OK;
RunRoadWays(RoadWays)      ! OK;
RunMyCar(RoadWays)         ! OK;
```

The class *CarCarrier* has one parameter, so the definite instance *RoadWays* has one parameter. Here, the parameter is the definite instance denoted by *MyCar*. The definite simple object denoted by *RoadWays* is used as an actual in five procedure calls. The first call, *RunAnything* has a formal that is an *any* instance with no parameters. Thus the actual matches the formal by the first rule. The second call, *RunVehicle* is also an *any* instance, but the actual must match the one parameter of the *any* instance, here *Vehicle*. The parameter in the actual, *MyCar*, matches the parameter in the formal *Vehicle*, so actual matches the formal. The third call, also of *RunVehicle*, is not permitted. The formal of *RunVehicle* requires one parameter and the instance denoted by *MyCar* has no parameters. Thus *MyCar* does not match *any(Vehicle)*. The actual in the call of *RunRoadWays* is the same instance as the formal in *RunRoadWays*, thus it matches as stated in the third rule. The formal in the last call requires the parameter to *CarCarrier* to be an indefinite *Vehicle*. Because the parameter in the

---

[29] This is used primarily in pattern statements. See Section 5.5.4.

[30] It is possible that the formal has fewer parameters than the actual and the actual still matches the formal. This fascinating situation requires several class and variables to illustrate it. These cannot be declared with only the knowledge of the current discussion. Thus no example will be illustrated here; I just wanted to point out why the second rule includes a clause requiring the same number of parameters while the last rule only requires "corresponding" parameters to match.

actual, *MyCar*, matches an indefinite *Vehicle*, the actual matches the formal as stated in the fourth rule.

Finally, there is a rule to ensure that labels match:

- If the actual simple object is labeled, then the formal simple object must be labeled with the same identifier.

This rule is used primarily when checking a procedure implementation against its specifications, as shown below:

```
procedure DriveVehicle(v:Vehicle);              ! Procedure Spec.;
procedure DriveVehicle(v:Vehicle) is ... ;      ! OK Impl.;
procedure DriveVehicle(x:Vehicle) is ... ;      ! OK Impl.;

procedure DriveTank(Tank);                      ! Procedure Spec.;
procedure DriveTank(t:Tank) is ... ;            ! OK Impl.;
```

The first procedure specification, *DriveVehicle*, has two implementations. The first is legal because its parameter is labeled like its specification; the second is illegal because its parameter is labeled differently. The second procedure, *DriveTank*, has one implementation. The parameter in that implementation matches the parameter in its specification since the parameter in the specification is unlabeled. As the rule states, the labels must match only if the formal has a label.[31]

The process of comparing simple objects also causes a binding of objects to identifiers to happen. In particular, if the formal simple object is labeled, then a side effect of a successful comparison is a binding of the identifier in the label, to the object which consists of the actual simple object and its environment. In more conventional terms, all binding in Paragon is by reference.

3.4.2.2. Object Matching

For most purposes, an actual object matches a formal object if the two objects have the same number of simple objects and corresponding simple objects match. There are circumstances where an actual object may have more simple objects that a formal, such as illustrated below:

---

[31] Recall that when comparing implementations to specifications, the specification acts as a formal and the implementation as an actual.

```
class House is
begin
   class Furniture is
   begin
      procedure Polish(House . Furniture);
   end;

   class Kitchen is
   begin
      class Refrigerator of Furniture is begin end;
   end;
end;

var MyHouse => new House;
var MyKitchen => MyHouse . new Kitchen;
var MyFrig => MyKitchen . new Refrigerator;

... Polish(MyFrig) ...
```

The formal parameter in the declaration of *Polish* is the object (*any House, any Furniture*)
while the actual parameter in the invocation of *Polish* is the object
(*House, Kitchen, Refrigerator*). Intuitively, the formal object states the requirements for the
procedure's parameter, namely that an object that is a house containing a piece of furniture
(refrigerator) must be passed. Clearly, the actual meets this criterion but it happens to have
some extra structure that procedure *Polish* does not require, the *Kitchen* simple object.
Paragon allows skipping of such simple objects in the actual object. Full details of how simple
objects are skipped during comparison are given in Section A.3 in an appendix.

3.4.3. Type Parameters

Because Paragon represents parameters as merely another object, it is possible to simulate
type parameters by passing a name expression containing indefinite instantiations as an
actual parameter. This is illustrated with the following piece of Paragon:

```
class MyType is begin end;

procedure F(t: any) ... is
begin
   var Local => new t;
   ...
end;

... F(MyType) ...
```

The formal parameter for the procedure *F*, that is, *t*, is later used in an object creation, hence *t*
is used like a type name in most languages. The invocation of *F* has an actual parameter that

is an uninstantiated instance of *MyType* and therefore does not have the definite, object-creation elaborations associated with it. Thus, the object being passed to *F* appears like, and is used as, a type.[32] Through the use of indefinite instances, Paragon permits the structure of classes to be exploited without any definite instances being created, thus Paragon parameters can effectively simulate type parameters.

3.4.4. Parameters to Classes

As alluded to in the beginning of Section 3.4, class declarations may have parameters. Any object creation, whether an indefinite instance or a definite instance, must provide directly or indirectly the same number of actual parameters in the name component as there are formal parameters in the class declaration. The actuals are directly provided if they are explicitly written in the name component between parentheses: for example, *new array(1,100)*. The actuals are indirectly provided if no parenthesized list of expressions is provided in the name component and the identifier in the name component is bound to an object, for example, a variable. This is illustrated below by extending the examples on pages 53 51:

```
    ... F(RoadWays)
```

In this example, the instance denoted by *RoadWays* is used as a type inside of *F* when creating the instance for *Local*. However, the underlying class for *RoadWays*, that is *CarCarrier*, requires a parameter. None is specified in the name component *new T* in *F*, so the parameter comes from the instance denoted by *T*, which is the instance denoted by *RoadWays*. Therefore the parameter becomes *MyCar*. In general, the actuals to be used then come from the innermost simple object in the creation environment that has the same underlying class as the simple object being created. In short, the parameters are copied from the current environment.[33]

A class declaration with parameters may have subclasses, each of which inherits the parameters of the parent and may declare additional parameters. This is illustrated below:

---

[32] Although a definite object may also be passed, to do so is unnecessary. If a definite instance is passed, only its "type" will be used.

[33] A previous version of Paragon permitted default expressions to be declared in parameters. These defaults would be used when actual parameters were indirectly specified. However, it was difficult to define the environment in which the default expressions should be elaborated, so this feature was removed from the design.

```
class ArmyCarrier(v:Vehicle,Tank) of CarCarrier is
begin
end;
```

No example in the main body of this thesis both defines and inherits parameters. However, such parameters are illustrated in Section A.7.

Assuming that a class inherits parameters from at most one parent and does not declare more parameters, then the objects denoted by the subclass parameters must match the corresponding parameters in that one parent class. This is illustrated below:

```
class TankCarrier(v:Tank) of CarCarrier is
begin
end;
```

The parameter in *TankCarrier* matches the parameter in *CarCarrier*, that is, *v:Tank* matches *v:Vehicle*. For more examples, see the class declarations on page 111.

However, it is possible to inherit parameters from more than one parent, even if the parent classes share an ancestor that has a parameter. The process for ensuring that the parameters of the subclass properly match the parameters of the parents is more complicated. To properly discuss the algorithm requires a precise definition of *defined* and *inherited* parameters, and a description of the correspondence between a defined parameter in a class and an inherited parameter in a subclass. For all examples in this thesis, one may use the intuitive concepts of "defined" and "inherited" parameters and assume that "corresponding" means pairwise, that is, the ith parameter in one list of parameters matches the ith parameter in another list. Section A.7 gives all of the details of parameter inheritance, parameter correspondence and parameter matching.

3.5. Procedure Specifications

Procedures in Paragon provide the conventional procedural abstraction associated with high-level languages. Unlike most languages, procedures are separately specified and implemented. This section discusses procedure specifications while the next section (Section 3.6) discusses procedure implementations. Further, Paragon uses procedures to specify and implement iterators but a discussion of iterators is postponed until Section 3.7. Each section gives an overall view of the syntax and semantics of the corresponding feature.

3.5.1. Overall Syntax of Procedure Specifications

Procedure specifications consist of an identifier, some optional formal parameters, an optional specification for a returned or yielded object and some optional constraints. An example of a procedure specification is given below:

```
procedure Compare(L:any,R:any) return Booleans.Bit
     such that L.structure same as R.structure;
```

The specification for the procedure *Compare* states that it takes two parameters which may be any objects at all and returns an object that matches the predefined boolean object. It also has one constraint. Roughly speaking, the constraint states that the two parameters must have the same structure, that is, two *Vehicles* or two *Tanks*, but not a *Ship* and a *Tank*.

More detailed descriptions of each of these pieces of a specification are given in the next sections.

3.5.2. Parameters

The parameters in a procedure specification are name expressions that have neither name components with the reserved word *new* (that is, no definite instantiations) nor any procedure invocations.[34] Intuitively, a formal parameter is supposed to define the structure that actual parameters must match.

3.5.3. Return Expression

The *return* expression is an expression that describes the object that the procedure provides. Like the parameters of the procedure specification, it may not contain definite instantiations or procedure calls. However, it may use identifiers that are used as labels in the parameters of the procedure specification. Such a use is convenient for expressing the fact that a return object has a similar structure to one of the parameters. In the following procedure specification:

```
procedure Copy(A:any) return A.structure;
```

the *return* expression for the *Copy* procedure describes the returned object as having the same structure as the parameter.

---

[34] This means that *array(im.integer)* is permitted but *array(10)* is not permitted, since *10* is an implicit procedure call.

3.5.4. Constraints

Constraints can be used to specify some relationship between parameters. This is necessary because the ordinary parameter passing mechanism does not always provide the appropriate information that a procedure requires. One example of this problem occurs when specifying addition for numbers, as illustrated with the following declarations:[35]

```
class Number is begin end;
procedure Plus(L:Number,R:Number) return Number;
```

The class declaration for *Number* is intended to be used to describe any kind of object that meets some minimal abstract property (in the programmer's mind): for example, the group axioms. The group axioms also define the existence of a binary operation that may be used on elements of the group, here *Plus*.

The programmer may refine *Number* into more precise specifications of real numbers and complex numbers, as shown below:

```
class Real of Number is begin end;
class Complex of Number is begin end;
```

However, this additional level of abstraction has no notion that elements from two different groups should be allowed to interact. Even though *Plus* should operate on two *Reals* and two *Complex* numbers, there is no intention for *Plus* to work on a *Real* and a *Complex* together. To enforce this desire, a constraint is added, as illustrated below:

```
procedure Plus(L:Number,R:Number) return Number
      such that L.structure same as R.structure;
```

Constraints return a truth value, that is, true or false. In this example, the value is determined by elaborating the name expressions in the constraint, that is *L.structure* and *R.structure*, and then checking to see if each matches the other. Thus this constraint ensures that *Reals* may only be added to *Reals*, *Complex* numbers to *Complex* numbers.

Paragon provides for other kinds of constraints, but they are rarely used. The interested reader is referred to Section A.9. All procedure constraints are elaborated only when procedure calls are elaborated with specifications.

---

[35]These declarations are not those used in Paragon for predefined integers.

3.6. Procedure Implementations

A procedure implementation describes how a particular operation should be performed. Each procedure implementation implements a single procedure specification. However, there may be several implementations for each specification in a program. An appropriate implementation will be chosen for each call of the procedure, though a discussion of the selection process is deferred until Section 5.5.5. In this section, the syntax and semantics of procedure implementations and procedure calls will be given.

3.6.1. Overall Syntax of Procedure Implementations

Unlike other declarations, procedure implementations may appear only in the same class as the procedure specification or in any subclass of the class that contains the procedure specification. This ensures that each procedure implementation has a readily identifiable procedure specification that it is implementing.

Syntactically, a procedure implementation resembles a class declaration. The ubiquitous factorial procedure illustrates this syntax:

```
procedure Factorial(IM . n :integer) return IM.integer is
begin
   if n <= 1 then
      return 1;
   else
      return n * Factorial(n - 1);
   fi;
end;
```

The syntax is conventional: There is an identifier followed by optional parameters. A *return* expression, if present, is next, followed by the body of the implementation. The body may have any number of declarations followed by any number of statements.

3.6.2. Parameters

The same restrictions and admissions for parameters in a procedure specification apply to parameters in a procedure implementation. Unlike most languages, the parameters in the implementation need not be identical to the parameters in the specification. All that is required is that the parameters of an implementation match the corresponding parameters of the specification. In the same manner, the *return* expression of a procedure implementation must match the *return* expression of the specification. Either both or neither must have a *return* expression.

No constraints are permitted in a procedure implementation. Unlike procedure specifications, procedure implementations may be intended to work on several different implementations. Since each implementation would have a different structure, a constraint that checked their structures would return false. Thus the constraint would forbid the desired action: a procedure working with different implementations. In retrospect however, the decision to eliminate constraints in procedure implementations may have been unwise. Section 4.6.1 discusses some possible uses of constraints in procedure implementations.

3.6.3. Return Statement

A procedure may contain a *return* statement. The expression in the *return* statement must match the *return* expression. If no *return* expression is present in the procedure implementation, then no *return* statement may contain an expression. Conversely, if the procedure implementation has a *return* expression, then each *return* statement must have a matching expression.

3.6.4. Procedure Invocation

A procedure invocation causes an instance of a procedure to be created, elaborated, possibly suspended (if an iterator, see Section 3.7.1) and eventually terminated. These actions take place for both procedure specifications and procedure implementations, though these invocations occur during different elaborations.[36]

Like the elaboration of all name components, a name component that denotes a procedure invocation[37] starts by locating the appropriate procedure in its environment. During elaboration with specifications, an appropriate procedure specification is found; during elaboration with implementations, an appropriate implementation or specification is found, and during elaboration with realizations, an appropriate implementation is used. Therefore the elaboration with specifications checks that the procedure call meets the procedure's specification, the elaboration with implementations finds a feasible implementation and the the elaboration with realizations uses the implementation chosen during elaboration with implementations as the procedure to actually execute.

---

[36]In particular, invocations of procedure specifications occur only during elaborations with specifications and implementations while invocations of procedure implementations occur only during elaborations with implementations and realizations.

[37]A name component that denotes a procedure invocation is a procedure-invocation name component.

After the appropriate declaration is found, the formal and actual parameters for the procedure invocation are elaborated and compared. Assuming that the parameters match, an instance for the procedure is created and appended to the environment in which the invocation name expression is being elaborated. The body of the procedure, if any, is then elaborated. During elaboration with specifications and implementations, the procedure invocation is terminated when the end of the declaration is reached. Then the *return* expression in the procedure declaration, if any, is elaborated. The object that results from the elaboration of the *return* expression is then used as the environment for the next component. Alternatively, it can be used as the object that results from the elaboration of the name expression for which this invocation is the last component.

These elaborations are illustrated by the following examples:

```
class Example is
begin
   class Inner is begin end;

   procedure Copy(Example) return Example;          ! Spec.;
   procedure Copy(Example) return Example is ...;    ! Impl.;

   procedure Endit(Example);                          ! Spec.;
end;

var v1 => new Example;
var v2 => new Example;
var v3 => new Example;

v1.Endit(v2.Copy(v3).Copy(v1));                       ! Statement;
```

When the statement is elaborated with specifications, the specification for *Endlt* in *v1* is found. The actuals for this call are elaborated with specifications which causes the specification of *Copy* inside of *v2* to be found. During elaboration with specifications, the *return* expression of *Copy* is elaborated (here *Example*) and returned as the environment for the next component, which is another call of *Copy*. This process is repeated, and again the *return* expression *Example* is elaborated with specifications. This results in an indefinite instance of *Example* which is the actual parameter for the call for *Endlt*.

During elaboration with implementations, this process is repeated, except that the implementation for *Copy* is found wherever the specification was found. A search for an implementation of *Endlt* occurs, but none are defined here. Thus the specification is reused during elaboration with implementations. The exact way that an implementation is selected for a procedure call is described in Section 5.5.5.1.

During elaboration with realizations, the invocation is terminated when a *return* statement in the implementation is elaborated. If an expression is present in the *return* statement, it is elaborated with realizations and is used as the environment for the next name component. If the end of the procedure is reached without a *return* statement being elaborated, the procedure is terminated and no object is returned. Under these circumstances, the procedure declaration must not have a return expression.

Like the instantiation of classes, a procedure invocation is said to create a simple object. There is always exactly one local instance, namely the one that results from the elaboration of the declarations and statements in the procedure's declaration. A procedure specification also has a local instance, though it is empty as there are no declarations or statements in a specification. This simple object is appended to the environment[38] in which the procedure call was made to form the environment in which the procedure body is elaborated. This is illustrated below using the declarations for *Example* above:

```
var I_in_V1 => v1 . new Inner;
v1.Copy(...);
```

In the variable declaration, a definite simple object is created inside of the definite simple instance denoted by *v1*. In the procedure call, a definite simple object for the invocation of the *Copy* procedure is created inside of the definite simple instance denoted by *v1*. Both objects consist of two nested simple objects. The innermost simple object for the first came from instantiating a class. The innermost simple object for the second came from invoking a procedure. The local instances for the first come from the ancestors of the class declaration and the class itself. The local instances for the second come from the declaration of the procedure specification. As shown in Section 5.4, the local instances in both simple objects may change. This view of procedure invocations is useful for making representation selections and the pattern matching statement. This last use is discussed in Section 5.5.4.

---

[38]Recall that an environment is an object.

3.7. Iterators

Because iterators are not present is most languages, this section first gives a brief description of iterators and then discusses how they are declared in Paragon. Some special statements that are associated with iterators, *for*, *yield* and *return*, are then described. Lastly, termination of iterators, especially through the use of an *exitloop* statement, is discussed.

3.7.1. Overview of Iterators

An iterator can be thought of as a black box that, once started, produces a sequence of objects on request. The starting of an iterator is termed *invocation* or *call*, and the process of providing the next object in the sequence is termed *yielding*. After the iterator has returned an object, the iterator may be continued, either to provide another object or to terminate. When no more objects are to be yielded and the iterator may not be continued, the iterator has *terminated*. After the last object has been yielded, an iterator may be continued to perform some actions that do not result in the yielding of an object but instead result in termination of the iterator. A terminated iterator may not be continued.

In Paragon, this process only happens in a *for* statement, such as illustrated below:

```
for i in Sequence(1,10) do
    ...
end for;
```

Here the iterator is called *Sequence* and the invocation of the iterator starts when the *for* statement is elaborated. The process of calling an iterator is identical to calling a procedure: a simple object is created, the parameters checked and identifiers bound, a local instance created and added to the simple object, the simple object is appended to the calling environment and elaboration of the declarations and statements within the iterator's body commences.

Unlike a procedure, an iterator may have a *yield* statement which causes suspension of the iterator. The *yield* statement contains an expression which is executed when the *yield* statement is executed. The object that results from the expression is bound to the loop identifier in the *for* statement, for example, *i* in the example above. The statements inside the *for* statement are then elaborated. When the last statement in the *for* loop is elaborated (and assuming that no *exitloop*, *return* or *goto* statement is executed), the previously started invocation of the iterator continues its execution as if the *yield* statement had completed its execution. This cycle continues until one of the following occurs: the iterator executes a *return* statement; the iterator reaches the end of its implementation; a *goto* statement is executed that transfers control out of the loop; or the *for* loop executes an *exitloop* statement.

3.7.2. Iterator Specifications

The specifications for an iterator are identical to other procedure specifications except that a *yield* expression must be present where the optional *return* expression is written. A specification for *Sequence* might be:

```
procedure Sequence(IM.integer,IM.integer) yield IM.integer;
```

Like other procedures, an iterator may have constraints applied to its parameters and its *yield* expression may use identifiers that are bound in the parameters.

3.7.3. Iterator Implementations

The implementations of iterators are identical to other procedure implementations except that the *yield* statement is permitted in an iterator implementation, but not in any other kind of procedure implementation, and that there must be a *yield* expression where the optional *return* expression is written. Like a procedure implementation with a *return* expression, the *yield* expression in the implementation must match the *yield* expression in the specification. A possible implementation for *Sequence* illustrates the syntax:

```
procedure Sequence(IM. low: integer,IM. high: integer)
   yield IM.integer is
begin
   var temp => IM . new integer;
   temp := low;
   while temp < high do
      yield temp;
      temp := temp + 1;
   end;
end;
```

In combination with the previous *for* statement, this procedure yields the integers from *low* to *high* and then terminates, ending the *for* statement. Thus this iterator matches the conventional *for* statement found in most languages.

3.7.4. Yield Statement

The *yield* statement is the way in which an iterator may suspend its operation. The general form of the *yield* statement has two parts: a yielded expression and a conditional statement. This is shown by the following BNF:

yield <expression> { when exitloop <statement> }?[39]

The expression in a *yield* statement denotes the object that the iterator returns. It is bound to the index identifier in the *for* loop that invoked the iterator. This object must match the object denoted by the *yield* expression in the heading of the iterator.

An iterator may be terminated by the execution of an *exitloop, return* or *goto* statement in the *for* statement's body. When this happens, the optional *when exitloop <statement>* permits the iterator to perform some last actions before it is terminated. The statement following the reserved word *exitloop* is usually a *goto* statement which jumps to a part of the iterator that performs some final action. If the statement does not cause any transfer of control, execution after the statement continues just after the *yield* statement. (However, the iterator may not execute any more *yield* statements. It must terminate by executing a *return* statement or by reaching the end of the procedure.) If no optional statement is present and an *exitloop, return* or *goto* statement causes a loop to terminate, then the iterator will be terminated without any further execution.

3.7.5. Return Statement

The *return* statement provides an explicit way for an iterator to terminate itself. Unlike the *return* statement used in other procedures, the *return* statement may not have the optional expression. Thus the syntax is trivial and is simply the reserved word *return*. Recall that an iterator may also terminate itself by reaching the end of its body.

---

[39] The notation { x }? means that x is optional.

3.7.6. For Statement and Iterator Invocations

The *for* statement invokes and continues an iterator, binding an index parameter each time, and executing the statements in its body. An example of a *for* loop is shown below:

```
var i => IM . new integer;
var i2 => IM . new integer;
...
for i in Sequence(1,100) do
    i2 := i * i;
end;
```

This *for* loop calculates the square for each value between 1 and 100.

The object denoted by the index identifier in the *for* loop must match the object that results from elaborating the *yield* expression in the iterator. During execution, the returned object from the iterator is bound to the index identifier, superseding any previous binding to that identifier. During elaboration with specifications and implementations, the processing of an iterator call is identical to the processing of a procedure call except the results from the *yield* expression rather than the *return* expression are used as the result of the expression elaboration. During these two kinds of elaboration, there is no notion of suspension or termination of an iterator. Naturally, the object returned by elaborating the expression following the reserved word *in* must come from an invocation of an iterator.

The *for* loop continues the iterator after each execution of the statements in the *for* loop. If the iterator is continued because an *exitloop*, *return* or *goto* statement was executed in the body of the *for* statement, then the iterator must terminate without yielding any more objects. Failure to terminate under these circumstances renders a program erroneous and continued execution is undefined. If the iterator is continued because the last statement of the *for* loop is finished and the *for* loop is performing the next iteration, then the iterator may yield another object. When an object is yielded, it is rebound of the index identifier and the statements of the loop are reexecuted. However, when the iterator is continued, it may terminate, causing the execution to continue after the end of the *for* loop. When an iterator terminates, all bindings that were set up during its execution are released, thus the index identifier becomes undefined when the iterator terminates.

3.7.7. Exitloop Statement

The *exitloop* statement, whose syntax is shown below, is used to leave an enclosing loop.

    exitloop { <identifier> }?

Although *exitloop* statements may appear inside both *while* loops and *for* loops, only their actions inside *for* loops are discussed here. Section 3.8.3 presents a discussion of *exitloop* statements in *while* loops.

The primary action of an *exitloop* statement is to terminate the loop in which it appears. However, an *exitloop* statement also forces the continuation of the iterator of the *for* loop that contains the *exitloop*. As explained in Section 3.7.6, the execution of the *exitloop* statement causes any optional statement in the iterator's last executed *yield* statement to be executed. However, the iterator may no longer yield any more values; it must terminate.

If an optional identifier is present in an *exitloop* statement, the actions performed by the *exitloop* statement may apply to several loops. The processing of each loop enclosing the *exitloop* statement is performed from innermost loop to outermost, until the loop that is labeled with the identifier is found (see Section 3.8.1 for the syntax of labels.). An example is shown below:

```
Outer =>
   for i in Sequence(1,100) do
      Inner =>
         for j in Sequence(i,100) do
            ...
            exitloop Inner;
            ...
            exitloop Outer;
            ...
         end for;
   end for;
```

In this example, the execution of the statement *exitloop Inner* will cause the inner invocation of the *Sequence* iterator to be continued with the caveat that it must terminate, and then execution continues after the end of the inner loop. The execution of the statement *exitloop Outer* first causes the inner invocation of the *Sequence* iterator to be continued (with the caveat that it must terminate) and then causes the outer invocation of the *Sequence* iterator to be continued, again, with the caveat that it must terminate. Execution would then proceed after the end of the outer loop. In general, after all of the relevant iterators have been terminated because of an *exitloop* statement, execution continues immediately after the end of the labeled (or innermost) loop.

3.8. Conventional Statements

Paragon also contains the usual complement of control structures and facilities which are described in this section.

3.8.1. Labels

Any statement in Paragon may be labeled. The syntax is an identifier followed by = >, and is illustrated below:

```
InnerLoop => while True do ... end loop;
LabelA => LabelB => if True then null; fi;
```

As shown, any number of labels may be prepended to a statement. However, identifiers for all labels within a block of a procedure or class must be unique.

The labels are used in *exitloop* statements and *goto* statements.

3.8.2. Procedure Invocation

The simplest kind of statement is an expression. Perhaps the most common expression used as a statement is assignment, for example:

```
var i => IM . new integer;
var j => IM . new integer;
...
i := j;      ! Really the same as IM.Assign(i,j);
```

No object may be returned by an expression used as a statement.

3.8.3. Conditional Looping

In addition to the *for* loop, Paragon also provides a *while* loop, with a conventional syntax, illustrated in the example *Sequence* implementation in Section 3.7.3. The conditional expression must return an object that matches the predefined boolean object, that is, the object resulting from the expression *Booleans . Bit* where *Booleans* is a predefined variable identifier and *Bit* is a predefined class identifier. Like conventional *while* statements, the statements in the loop will be executed once each time the conditional expression returns an object with a *True* value.[40]

---

[40]Such objects come from the predefined procedure *True*. Similarly, objects with a *False* value come from the predefined procedure *False*.

Transfer of control may also leave a *while* loop if a *goto* statement with target outside of the *while* loop is executed, or an *exitloop* or *return* statement is executed. When such a *goto* statement is executed, execution continues with appropriately labeled statement. When an *exitloop* statement is executed, the execution of the program continues after the end of the loop labeled with the same identifier as present in the *exitloop* statement. If no target label is present in the *exitloop* statement, execution continues after the end of the loop containing the *exitloop* statement.

3.8.4. If Statement

The *if* statement provides a single, conditional execution of a sequence of statements. Through the use of additional clauses, a list of conditions may be expressed. Like the *while* statement, a conventional syntax for *if* statements is used, as defined by the following BNF:

```
    if <expression> then
        { <statement> ; }*⁴¹
{   elseif <expression> then
        { <statement> ; }* }*
{   else
        { <statement> ; }* }?
    fi
```

The conditional expressions following the reserved words *if* and *elseif* must meet the same criteria as the *while* loops' conditional expressions. Any number of statements may be present following the reserved words *then* or *else*, any number of clauses beginning with *elseif* may be present and an optional else clause may be present. Unlike many languages, the *if* statement ends with the reserved word *fi*.

The execution of an *if* statement is also conventional. Each conditional expression is executed until one that has the truth value *True* is found. The statements following that conditional expression are then executed. If no such conditional expression is found, and there is an else clause present, then the statements in the else clause are executed. After the appropriate sequence of statements are executed, and no *goto*, *exitloop* or *return* statement has altered the flow of control out of the clause, execution continues immediately following the reserved word *fi*.

---

[41] The notation { *x* }* means zero or more *x*s.

3.8.5. Goto Statement

The *goto* statement causes unconditional transfer of control from the current statement to the statement labeled by the identifier in the *goto* statement. The syntax is illustrated below:

```
goto End_of_Program;
```

The target of a *goto* statement, that is, the statement that is labeled with the identifier, must be in the same class or procedure declaration as the *goto* statement. Further, the target statement may not be in a loop that does not contain the *goto* statement (though the *goto* statement may be nested inside of a deeper loop), nor may it be in an if clause (if, elseif, else) that does not contain the *goto* statement. However, the converse to these statements is not true. One may write a *goto* statement that transfers control out of a loop or *if* statement.

These conventional statements, along with procedures and classes, describe the basic parts of Paragon, much of whose power lies in the ways that these basic parts can be combined into sophisticated data structures. The next chapter discusses a particular data structure that serves as the basis for writing abstract data types in Paragon, and illustrates how some of goals of Chapter 2 can be realized.

Chapter 4
The Object-Manager Model
and
Its Implementation

The language described in Chapter 3 provides a great deal of flexibility. In this thesis, a particular model of programming, usually termed the *object-manager model*, is used. Nested classes are used in several ways to implement this model: as generalization classes; as specification classes; as implementation classes; and as cross-implementation classes. This chapter describes this model of programming and shows how the simple features of Paragon are applied to implement this model.

4.1. Object Managers and Nested Classes

The object-manager model divides program objects into two categories: *managers* and *individuals*. The manager is created first and contains data and procedures that are shared among all individuals. For each manager, there may be any number of individuals created, and each individual has a single manager. Naturally, each individual may have private data and procedures not shared with other individuals.

As an example of this model, consider integers. Each individual integer can be represented as a word in memory. Further, there exists a procedure, *Addition*, that is shared among all the individual integers, and so this procedure belongs to the manager of all integers.

4.1.1. Classes as Manager and Individuals

Within the Paragon language, classes are used for all objects, and so are used for both managers and individuals. The shared declarations belong to the manager, and to allow access to the shared declarations, the class for individuals is declared inside the class declared for the manager. The integer example is illustrated with Paragon below:

```
class IntegerManager is
begin
   ! Shared data and procedures go here ;
   procedure Addition(Integer,Integer) return Integer;

   ! And the class definition for individuals ;
   class Integer is
   begin
      var Rep => CM⁴² . new Word;
   end;

end;
```

With this model, it is necessary to create a manager before any individuals are created. Thus to use any integers, a program must first create the manager:

```
var MyIntegerManager => new IntegerManager;
```

and only then can it create the individuals:

```
var n => MyIntegerManager . new Integer;
var Size => MyIntegerManager . new Integer;
var Low => MyIntegerManager . new Integer;
```

One uses shared data and operations by selecting them from the object manager. Addition of two integers would look like:

```
... MyIntegerManager.Addition(Size,n) ...
```

This approach offers a great deal of flexibility. For example, it is possible to express that certain kinds of integers may not interact. A frequently cited example of this requirement concerns integers that represent counts of apples and oranges. One wishes the compiler to enforce the rule that apples and oranges do not mix. Using the previous declarations this can be accomplished as follows:

```
var AppleManager => new IntegerManager;
var OrangeManager => new IntegerManager;

var Lisa => AppleManager . new Integer;
var MacIntosh => AppleManager . new Integer;

var Navel => OrangeManager . new Integer;
var Seedless => OrangeManager . new Integer;
```

With these variable declarations, the compiler for Paragon can check the legality of these expressions:

---

[42] *CM* is a predefined variable for Computer memory Manager.

```
... AppleManager.Addition(Lisa,MacIntosh) ...        ! Legal ;
... OrangeManager.Addition(Navel,Seedless) ...       ! Legal ;

... AppleManager.Addition(MacIntosh,Navel) ...       ! Illegal ;
... OrangeManager.Addition(Lisa,Seedless) ...        ! Illegal ;
... AppleManager.Addition(Navel,Seedless) ...        ! Illegal ;
```

Note how the language catches the illegal procedure call of *AppleManager.Addition* with the *MacIntosh* and *Navel* parameters. The expressions for the parameters in the *Addition* procedure are *Integer* which is declared in the *IntegerManager* class. Thus the *Integer* indefinite simple object resides inside of the same simple object as the procedure *Addition*. In the call of *AppleManager.Addition*, the containing simple object is (*AppleManager*), so the object that results from the elaboration of each formal parameter during the procedure call is (*AppleManager,any Integer*). The declaration for *Navel* shows that the definite *Integer* was created inside the object denoted by *OrangeManager*, hence the object denoted by *Navel* — and an actual parameter to this procedure call — is (*OrangeManager, Navel*). According to the object comparison rules in Section 3.4.2.1, two simple definite objects match only if they are the same definite object. *OrangeManager* and *AppleManager* are two different definite instances of *IntegerManager*, so *OrangeManager* does not match *AppleManager*. Since the two simple objects do not match, the two objects do not match and the procedure call is not well specified.

4.1.2. Cross-Implementation Procedures

Under some circumstances, one might want to permit the intermingling of the different integers. One may also specify such procedures in the class for the manager. The *CrossAddition* procedure meets this requirement:

```
class IntegerManager is
begin
  ! Parameters from any manager ;
  procedure CrossAddition(IntegerManager . Integer,
                          IntegerManager . Integer)
     return Integer;

  ! The rest of the declarations are unchanged ;
  ...
end;
```

With such a declaration of *CrossAddition*, one may add apples and oranges. This is because the expressions in the formal parameters now contain an indefinite instantiation for the outer simple object *IntegerManager* instead of the enclosing definite instance of *IntegerManager*.

With the particular declaration given above, the integer returned will belong to the manager from which the procedure was selected. This is illustrated in the following code fragment:

```
... AppleManager.CrossAddition(MacIntosh,Navel) ...
                        ! Returns an AppleManager Integer ;
... OrangeManager.CrossAddition(Lisa,Seedless) ...
                        ! Returns an OrangeManager Integer ;
... AppleManager.CrossAddition(Navel,Seedless) ...
                        ! Returns an AppleManager Integer ;
```

The call *AppleManager.CrossAddition(MacIntosh,Navel)* is now legal because elaboration of each formal parameter results in the object (*any IntegerManager*, *any Integer*), against which the object (*OrangeManager*, *Navel*) now matches.

Paragon also allows for other combinations of managers and individuals. For example, instead of using the manager from which the procedure was selected as the manager of the returned individual, it is possible to select the manager of one of the parameters to explicitly specify the return manager. Such an alternative declaration for *CrossAddition* and its use are shown below:

```
procedure CrossAddition(InManager: IntegerManager . Integer,
                        IntegerManager . Integer)
   return InManager . Integer;

... AppleManager.CrossAddition(MacIntosh,Navel) ...
                        ! Returns an AppleManager Integer ;
... OrangeManager.CrossAddition(Lisa,Seedless) ...
                        ! Returns an AppleManager Integer ;
... AppleManager.CrossAddition(Navel,Seedless) ...
                        ! Returns an OrangeManager Integer ;
```

4.2. The Manager Model in Other Languages

The object-manager model approach to programming abstract data types is supported in many languages. For example, Ada provides a nearly identical facility, where the outer class (that is, the manager) is declared as a generic package and the inner class is declared as a type. Rewriting the examples of *IntegerManager* above in Ada would look like:

```
generic package IntegerManager is
begin
   type Integer is new Standard.Integer ;
   function Addition(L:Integer,R:Integer) returns Integer;
end;

package AppleManager is new IntegerManager;
package OrangeManager is new IntegerManager;
```

```
Lisa: AppleManager . Integer;
MacIntosh: AppleManager . Integer;
Navel: OrangeManager . Integer;
Seedless: OrangeManager . Integer;

... AppleManager.Addition(Lisa,MacIntosh) ...
... OrangeManager.Addition(Navel,Seedless) ...
```

Clu, Alphard and Model [Johnson 76] give similar approaches, though the identifiers are located in different places. In Clu, for example, the name of the inner class (the individual) becomes the name of the cluster (the manager declaration), the reserved word *rep* is used for the individual declaration, and variables are declared with the name of the manager. Shared data among all individuals are declared to be *owned* by the cluster and are semantically identical to variables declared in the outer class. Alphard uses the term *static* for such data in the manager (*form*). Model terms the manager a *space* and the individual a *type*. In nearly all languages that provide data abstraction, there are two separate language features: one for the manager (outer class), and one for the individual (inner class).

Each of these pairs of constructions is similar to but not identical to classes. In particular, there usually are restrictions on the different constructions that eliminate some capabilities. For example, one cannot express the *CrossAddition* procedure in Clu. In Alphard, one can only provide a single inner class declaration where, as we will see later, allowing multiple inner classes permits a programmer to combine abstractions selectively. Model and Ada limit the kinds of parameters and declarations that may be used in the inner classes. In short, each language embodies a certain sets of constraints that programmers are to follow when applying the object-manager model.

These constraints were not unmotivated. One motivation was conservatism. Model had a goal to extend Pascal to include a data abstraction facility while leaving the rest of the language largely intact; Ada had a specific requirement that its design should *not* extend the state of the art. This thesis is intended to explore the object-manager model and type hierarchies as much as possible, so a very general approach is taken.

Other language designs were also motivated by conciseness. In Paragon programs, a rather large number of declarations must be written to declare an integer variable. The restrictions of other languages can eliminate the need to create the manager explicitly (Alphard, Ada), to specify implicitly the manager everywhere an operation is used (Clu) and to eliminate (an explicit) inner declaration (Clu, Alphard, Model). In a production environment, extreme verbosity might cause programmers to shy away from a language, thus it is appropriate that these other languages made such restrictions. As an investigation of the properties of type hierarchies, the Paragon design opted for the verbosity and flexibility.

The subject of the tradeoff between verboseness and flexibility will recur as this model is explored further.

4.3. Hierarchies for Specifications

The integer example on page 72 so far lacks a number of operations that one normally expects for integers, for example, more arithmetic operations, comparison operations, transput operations and simple assignment. In most data abstraction languages, if an abstract data type were to include such operations, they would all be specified in the outer class (form, cluster, model, and so on). Some languages, such as Ada and Clu, do not require certain operations to be named explicitly in the manager's declaration. In Ada, a nonlimited private type automatically has the assignment and equality operations defined for it. In Clu, the presence of certain external representations (*xrep*) imply that *encode* and *decode* operations have been defined for use by the *Transmit* procedure in a *Port* cluster. These special features are not required in Paragon. For example, the special features in Clu can be represented in Paragon as follows:

```
class Transmissible_Type is
begin
   class Internal_Rep is begin end;
   class External_Rep is begin end;
   procedure Encode(Internal_Rep) return External_Rep;
   procedure Decode(External_Rep) return Internal_Rep;
end;

class Port_Manager is
begin
   class Port is
   begin
      procedure Transmit(Transmissible_Type . Internal_Rep);
   end;
end;
```

The *Transmit* procedure in the *Port* class can guarantee that its parameter can use the *Encode* procedure without recourse to additional features in Paragon for the *Encode* procedure or the *Transmissible_Type* class.

In practice, there are many such groups of related operations. In addition to assignment and message passing, one might consider the ability to be ordered, hashed and stored in a file to be properities that may or may not apply to newly declared abstract data types. Rather than select some predefined sets of operations and give them special treatment, Paragon uses the inheritance mechanism for specifying such properties.

4.3.1. Generalizations

By properly defining a set of classes for each set of operations that one might want to inherit later, one can provide the same predefined features that other languages do without limiting the choices of operations. For example, a set of declarations that simulate the concept of nonlimited in Ada is shown below:

```
class AssignableManager is
   class Assignable is begin end;
   procedure Assign(Assignable,Assignable);
   procedure Equal(Assignable,Assignable) return Booleans.Bit;
end;
```

An object manager that inherits the *AssignableManager* class would then define an unlimited type. Extending the previous *IntegerManager* example shows this property:

```
class IntegerManager of AssignableManager is
begin
   ! Shared data and procedures go here ;
   procedure Addition(Integer,Integer) return Integer;

   ! And the class definition for individuals ;
   class Integer of Assignable is
   begin
      var Rep => CM . new Word;
   end;

end;
```

One could then write

```
AppleManager.Assign(Lisa,MacIntosh);
```

just as if one had included an *Assign* procedure specification in the declaration of *IntegerManager*.

By examing the predefined environment for Paragon in Section 6.2, one can examine a number of these prefix classes declared for later use in the program. Classes used in this way — that is, where the programmer intends these classes to be inherited by other specifications — are termed *generalization classes*.

4.3.2. Specifications of Abstract Data Types

In the previous section, a general overview of the object-manager model was provided and a simple example for integers given. In fact, the example illustrates poor practice of data abstraction because the representation of the individuals is visible. For example, there is nothing that prevents a programmer from writing

```
... CM.Plus(Lisa.Rep,Navel.Rep) ...
```

thus directly manipulating the representation and violating the intended separation between implementation and representation. A better declaration would have been:

```
class IntegerManager of AssignableManager is
begin
    ! Shared data and procedures go here ;
    procedure Addition(Integer,Integer) return Integer;

    ! And the class definition for individuals ;
    class Integer of Assignable is begin end;

end;
```

These declarations still allow the programmer to create managers and individuals, and to use the procedures declared in their respective classes. However, the new declarations prevent the programmer, who specifies an integer variable, from manipulating the representation directly. Later, in Section 4.5, I will discuss how to declare the representation for the specification of an abstract data type.

4.4. Problems with Hierarchies for Specifications

Although the type hierarchy can express specifications for data abstractions, it does not capture all the details of refining abstractions that I would like. Several inadequacies are discussed in the following sections.

4.4.1. Constraints in Procedure Specifications

As first shown in Section 3.5.4, constraints must be added to procedure declarations to capture the idea that the use of a subclass in a procedure parameter should be substituted for each use of a class in the original specification. An naive attempt to provide a general specification for the addition operation illustrates this problem:

```
!----------------------------------------;
! A general specification              ;
!----------------------------------------;

class AO_Manager is
begin
   class Addable_Object is begin end;
   procedure Plus(L:Addable_Object,R:Addable_Object)
      return Addable_Object;
end;

!----------------------------------------;
! Two refinements of the specification  ;
!----------------------------------------;

class Number_Manager of AO_Manager is
begin
   class Number of Addable_Object is begin end;
end;

class Matrix_Manager of AO_Manager is
begin
   class Matrix of Addable_Object is begin end;
end;
```

By the rules of parameter matching, one may add *Numbers* and *Matrices*, which was probably not intended by the programmer. The way to solve this problem is by adding constraints to the specification of *Plus*, as follows:

```
procedure Plus(L:Addable_Object,R:Addable_Object)
   return Addable_Object
   such that L.structure same as R.structure;
```

This has the effect of refining the specification of *Plus* along with the classes in its parameters. An unwary programmer would leave out these constraints. The language should provide some other way to refine the procedure's parameters.

4.4.2. Return Objects of Procedure Specifications

But the constraints were not enough for refining the parameters. As the specification is written, the *return* expression specifies that the result of adding any two objects is an object which is an *Addable_Object*. However, if two *Numbers* are added, one expects a *Number* result; if two *Matrices*, then a *Matrix*. Not only must the parameters be refined when the classes mentioned in the parameters are refined, but the *return* expression must also be refined. This is accomplished by using the *structure* name component in the *return* expression, as illustrated below:

```
procedure Plus(L:Addable_Object,R:Addable_Object)
   return L.structure
   such that L.structure same as R.structure;
```

With the specification above, the return object for the *Plus* procedure will reflect the class of one of the parameters. Thus the last specification captures the probable interpretation of the programmer.

A glance at the predefined environment in Section 6.2 shows that this is a rather common situation. An alternative was to provide some kind of renaming rule, such as Ada provides for derived types. In Ada, these renaming rules caused confusion during the test and evaluation period of the language, and took a long time to settle into their final form. Thus it seemed risky to try to conceive of a careful set of rules that easily capture the programmer's desires. Instead, the more explicit method was selected.

4.4.3. Heterogeneous Data Structures

One goal relating to automatic program processing requires that static type checking of all variables declarations (object creations) and procedure calls should be supported. However, the requirement that all checking being performed statically, that is, without any reference to execution of the program, results in a type system that is less flexible than other object-oriented systems, such as Smalltalk. In Paragon, when an object is retrieved from a collection of objects, the most information that can be discerned about the retrieved object is shared information about any object in the collection. In the case of a single procedure call, more information can be gleaned from the parameters of the procedure. This was illustrated in Section 4.4.2 and is repeated below:

```
procedure Plus(L:Addable_Object,R:Addable_Object)
   return L.structure
   such that L.structure same as R.structure;
```

Normally, the *Plus* procedure maps two *Addable_Objects* into another *Addable_Object*. However, by using one of the parameters in the *return* expression, the *Plus* procedure can supply more information, namely that the object to be returned has the same structure as the first parameter. Thus the addition of two *Numbers* will result in a *Number*; two *Matrices*, a *Matrix*. The precise description of the return object can be examined by static type checking since a procedure declaration closely couples the objects used as parameters with the object coming from the procedure.

Frequently, the insertion and retrieval of objects from a collection are not closely coupled in a single procedure call. Then the static type checking cannot determine the precise structure of the retrieved object and a more general description must be used. This situation is shown below, where a symbol table is being defined for use in APL.

```
class APLSymbolTableManager(AO_Manager. t: Addable_Object) is
    class APLSymbolTable is begin end;

    procedure Insert(IM.Integer,t);
    procedure Retrieve(IM.Integer) return t;
end;
```

Identifiers in APL (represented here as predefined Paragon integers) may represent either a number or a matrix, so one should be to create symbol tables that can insert and retrieve *Numbers* and *Matrices*. If the symbol table is used for only *Numbers* or *Matrices*, then the *APLSymbolTableManager* can be instantiated with the appropriate parameter as shown below:

```
var MyMatrixManager => new Matrix_Manager;
var MyMatrix => MyMatrixManager . new Matrix;

var MatrixTableManager =>
      new APLSymbolTableManager(MyMatrixManager . Matrix)
var ST => MatrixTableManager . new APLSymbolTable;

...
ST.Insert(2,MyMatrix);
...
...ST.Retrieve(2)...
```

The underlying class of the returned object for a call of the *Retrieve* procedure can be determined statically by examining the parameter for *ST's* manager, which here is *MyMatrixManager . Matrix*. Thus the call of *Retrieve* will return a *Matrix* object. By the same reasoning, static type checking will permit only *Matrix* objects to be inserted into the symbol table.

But one may wish to include both *Numbers* and *Matrices* in the same symbol table. An instantiation of *APLSymbolTableManager* which provides this capability is illustrated below:

```
var TSO => new APLSymbolTableManager(AO_Manager.Addable_Object);

var ST => TSO. new APLSymbolTable;

var MyNumberManager => new Number_Manager;
var MyNumber => MyNumberManager . new Number;
```

```
var MyMatrixManager => new Matrix_Manager;
var MyMatrix => MyMatrixManager . new Matrix;

...
ST.Insert(1,MyNumber);
ST.Insert(2,MyMatrix);
...
...ST.Retrieve(1)...
...ST.Retrieve(2)...
```

In this example, both calls of *Insert* are well specified, since the both second parameters meet the specification *AO_Manager.Addable_Object*. Unfortunately, when the two calls of *Retrieve* are performed, the structure of the returned object also is specified as *AO_Manager.Addable_Object*, which is the common ancestor of *Numbers* and *Matrices*. However, the program context of the retrieval operation may depend on the specific class of the object that is being retrieved and use some specific information about it, such as inverting a returned *Matrix* object. Another possibility is that the statement which includes the *Retrieve* may wish to test at run time the kind of *Addable_Object* that is returned in order to perform some representation-specific operation. But in Paragon, there is no way to distinguish the kinds of objects that may be returned during elaboration with specifications, so any other procedure calls that require more information about the return object from *Retrieve* will be ill specified. Thus, the general description may be insufficient. Hence the requirement of static type checking in Paragon makes general collection facilities, such as heterogeneous symbol tables, difficult to write.

4.4.4. Adding Classes to an Existing Hierarchy

Besides the inconvenience of carefully specifying procedure specifications, the current design makes a previously defined hierarchy difficult to change. There are two kinds of changes that one might want to make which are difficult: one may want to add another generalization class, and one may want to inherit only part of a class.

In the first suggested change, a new class is added that is intended to provide a property that is inherited by other classes, such as hashing. Then all classes which might inherit this new property, for example, integers, logical values and pointers, must be changed to include the new class. Similarly, all of the implementations of these classes might have to include procedure implementations for the newly inherited specifications, here, probably a hashing function. This is a lot of distributed work that must be performed to add another class to the hierarchy. Because changes to systems should be as local as possible, this effect of changing many classes to add a new feature is undesirable.

The second change suggests that a class may not wish to inherit all of the specifications in a parent class. As a simple example, suppose that an assignment procedure is needed by a new class, but not an equality procedure. Then one might like to add the new class without altering any other class. In fact, one must either inherit the equality procedure specification with the assignment specification or split the class that has the assignment and equality procedures into (in the worse case) three new classes: one class holds the specifications to be inherited, one class the specifications that used to be inherited, and the third class inherits the other two classes so that other classes that used to inherit the original specification can now inherit this new combined class. The two program fragments below (with severely abbreviated procedure declarations) illustrate this transformation:

```
!------------------------------;
! Old form                     ;
!------------------------------;
class Assignable_Manager is
begin
   class Assignable is begin end;
   procedure Assign(Assignable,Assignable);
   procedure Equal(Assignable,Assignable) return Booleans.Bit;
end;
```

After the transformation:

```
!---------------------------;
! New form                  ;
!---------------------------;
class Only_Assign_Manager is
begin
   class Only_Assign is begin end;
   procedure Assign(Only_Assign,Only_Assign);
end;

!---------------------------;

class All_Other_Specs_Manager is
begin
   class All_Other_Specs is begin end;
   procedure Equal(All_Other_Specs,All_Other_Specs)
      return Booleans.Bit;
end;

!---------------------------;
```

```
class Assignable_Manager
   of Only_Assign_Manager, All_Other_Specs_Manager is
begin
   class Assignable of Only_Assign, All_Other_Specs is begin end;
end;
```

With this transformation, one can now specify the new class as inheriting only assignment without inheriting equality as follows:

```
class Strange_Manager of Only_Assign_Manager is
begin
   ...
end;
```

No other classes need to be changed with this transformation, but the breaking of a class into several classes to accomplish the selective inheritance is aesthetically displeasing.

4.4.5. Refinement by Derivation

Actually, the last example is a particular example of commonly used paradigm for creating specifications, which I call *Derivation*. One derives a specification by relating it to other specifications and giving differences. Paragon only permits one to add new specifications, thus restricting the kinds of objects that meet the specification, and does not allow one to remove or alter a previous specification, thus changing the kinds of objects that meet the specification. In the previous example, one wants to specify an object that it just like *Assignable* except that no *Equal* procedure is available. As pointed out by other authors [Lamb 83], this kind of derivation is useful in practice. Unfortunately, Paragon does not provide a complete derivation facility.

Although the previous discussion illustrates that there are some ways of manipulating specifications of abstract data types that are not supported by Paragon, the language does support refinements of specifications and does allow multiple kinds of objects to be specified in a single module.

Starting with generalization classes, a programmer can construct refinements that act as specifications of abstract data types. Such classes are termed *specification classes* since they provide a convenient way to specify abstract data types. The normal scope rules for Paragon give the desired effect of allowing the programmer, who declares variables of a specification class, access only to certain parts of a data object: namely those in the abstract data types specifications. But a working program must have a representation for the abstract data type somewhere. In the next section, one way of writing implementations for a specification is presented.

4.5. Hierarchies for Implementations

As specifications are refined from generalizations, implementations are refined from specifications. This is accomplished through the use of subclasses. Typically, a subclass that is intended to implement an abstract data type contains the implementations for those procedures specified in its ancestors and contains subclasses for the nested classes. Assuming that a full specification and implementation for computer words exists called *CM*, an implementation for the *IntegerManager/Integer* classes is:

```
class WordIntegerManager of IntegerManager is
begin
   !-----------------------------------------------;
   procedure Assign(L:WordInteger, R:WordInteger)
      return WordInteger is
   begin
      CM.Assign(L.Rep,R.Rep);
   end;
   !-----------------------------------------------;
   procedure Equal(L:WordInteger, R:WordInteger)
      return Booleans.Bit is
   begin
      return CM.Equal(L.Rep,R.Rep);
   end;
   !-----------------------------------------------;
   procedure Addition(L:WordInteger, R:WordInteger)
      return WordInteger is
   begin
      return CM.Plus(L.Rep,R.Rep);
   end;
   !-----------------------------------------------;

   ! And the class definition for individuals ;

   class WordInteger of Integer is
   begin
      var Rep => CM . new Word;
   end;

end;
```

The conventional methodology for implementing an abstract data type requires that all operations in the specification must be implemented, that a representation for the object must be described and that there is some way to separate the abstract object from the concrete object. Procedure implementations for *Assign*, *Equal* and *Addition* are declared, the class

WordInteger defines the representation of *Integer* and use of the names *Integer* and *WordInteger* separates the abstract object from the concrete object. Thus all of the requirements for an abstract data type implementation are met in the example above. Classes intended to be used in this way (though not necessarily as complete as this example) are called *implementation classes.*

The example above also illustrates a feasible implementation for *IntegerManager*. In *WordIntegerManager*, procedure implementations are provided for the procedure specifications in all inherited ancestors: here the *Assign*, *Equal* and *Addition* procedures from the *IntegerManager* and *AssignableManager* classes. This is not required by Paragon but does guarantee that this subclass may be used as an implementation anywhere the specification is used. If some operation had been missing, and if a program used that operation on abstract integers, then the implementation subclass for the specification could not be used. An attempt to use such an incomplete subclass in this circumstance would render the program *infeasible*. A more complete discussion of the feasibility of programs can be found later in Section 5.5.5.

The distinction between the abstract use of a object and the concrete use of an object is also illustrated by this example. The example above specifies the class *WordInteger* in all of the procedures' parameters in the *WordIntegerManager* class. This implies that only the *WordInteger* representation of *Integer* can be used with these procedures and provides a boundary between the abstract and concrete representations. Some languages, such as Clu, provide an operation (in Clu called *cvt*) that is supposed to translate between an abstract object and a concrete one. Within the implementation of the abstract data type, one may restrict the implementation to use only the abstract properties of the object by omitting the special operation. Other languages reverse the convention and allow the programmer access to the representation unless the programmer specifies that only the abstract operations should be allowed. Ada uses still another approach by unconditionally permitting access to the representation of an object within the implementation of the abstract data type. Paragon attempts to strike a balance by using the names in the class declarations. Should only the abstract operations be permitted, then the programmer may specify this by writing the name of the specification class in the parameter. If access to the representation is required, then the name of the class used as a representation should be written in the parameter. Because each procedure specifies that *WordInteger* objects may be used as parameters, it may use the details of *WordInteger* objects, such as selecting the *Rep* field. Had the procedures merely required *Integer* objects, then access to the *Rep* field would have been denied, even if an instance of *WordInteger* had been given to the procedure.

The use of names rather than conventions for the abstract/concrete decision permits a greater flexibility in the definition of implementations. This is more fully explored in the next section where some methods for providing multiple implementations of abstract data types are considered.

4.5.1. Multiple Implementations

There are times when a programmer may wish to have more than one implementation for an abstract data type. This can be illustrated with the previously specified *IntegerManager*. Many computers have more than one size of data representation provided by the hardware so it seems reasonable that different integer variables might be able to take advantage of these differences in order to improve a program's performance. Each different sized representation has its own representation class and its own procedure implementations. Most data abstraction languages allow only one representation for each specification. If the one word representation for integers were present in a program, such languages would prohibit the inclusion of a half word integer and a double word integer.

Paragon does not have such a rule. A new representation may be provided by declaring a new set of nested classes. For example, a program might contain the following declarations for integers requiring less than a word of storage:

```
class ShortWordIntegerManager of IntegerManager is
begin
   !------------------------------------------------;
   procedure Assign(L:ShortWordInteger, R:ShortWordInteger)
      return WordInteger is
   begin
      CMSW.Assign(L.Rep,R.Rep);
   end;
   !------------------------------------------------;
   procedure Equal(L:ShortWordInteger, R:ShortWordInteger)
      return Booleans.Bit is
   begin
      return CMSW.Equal(L.Rep,R.Rep);
   end;
   !------------------------------------------------;
   procedure Addition(L:ShortWordInteger, R:ShortWordInteger)
      return ShortWordInteger is
   begin
      return CMSW.Plus(L.Rep,R.Rep);
   end;
   !------------------------------------------------;

   ! And the class definition for individuals ;

   class ShortWordInteger of Integer is
   begin
      var Rep => CMSW . new ShortWord;
   end;

end;
```

The *ShortWordIntegerManager/ShortWordInteger* classes represent another implementation of the integer abstract data type. Two factors are present which allow the second implementation to be declared and included in a program. First, the explicit separation of the specification and implementation of the abstract data type provide a way to bind an implementation to a specification. Many previous data abstraction languages require the specification and implementation to be bound together in single language construction. Thus there is no place to include an additional implementation. Second, the ability to name the representation explicitly circumvents a problem of controlling the access to the concrete object. Languages such as Ada, which give unconditional access to the representation, or Clu, which gives access through representation independent functions *cvt*, *up* and *down*, have no way to distinguish between concrete representations. Without such a mechanism, one concrete representation could manipulate the internal representation of another. This violates the paradigm of data abstraction that permits only the piece of a program defining the representation access to the underlying representation of the objects.

The ability to name explicitly the representations or specifications in parameters permits multiple representations to be used in a more common setting: differing type compositions. Frequently cited examples are set implementations where alternative representations of the set is caused by differing compositions with the element type [Johnson 76, Low 74, Schonberg 77, Wulf 81]. A typical (partial) specification for sets in Paragon appears below:

```
class SetManager(any) is
begin
   class Set is begin end;
   !------------------------------------------------;
   procedure Union(Set,Set) return Set;
   !------------------------------------------------;
end;
```

The element type of the set may be any class. However, certain classes have special properties that an implementation may wish to exploit. For example, if the element type is totally ordered, a B-Tree or discrimination net may be an appropriate implementation. If it can be hashed, a hash table may prove efficient. Sets of a small number of enumerated values are usually represented as a bit vector. Thus one wants the implementation to be able to take advantage of knowledge of the element type.

Other languages, such as Clu and Alphard, do not permit this exploitation in an implementation, or more precisely, they insist that such requirements appear in the specification of the abstract data type. One of the motivations for this insistence is that the additional operations required by the implementation must be provided when using the specification so that those operations may be later used in the implementation. For example, if one wanted to implement sets with a hash table, then the specification of the abstract data type set would include a parameter for the element type and a (procedure) parameter for the hash function. When one uses this abstract data type, one must specify the procedure to be used for hashing so the implementation has a hashing procedure available to it. This seems inappropriate, as such requirements are clearly leaking implementation details to the user of the data type while simultaneously limiting the writer of implementations of the data type to the operations in the specification.

Paragon permits the specification to be as broad as required and the implementation to be as narrow as required by allowing the parameters in subclasses merely to match the parameters in the parent class, and not to be identical. A discrimination-net implementation of the previous *SetManager* could look like the following:

```
class DiscriminationSetManager(OrderedManager.Ordered)
   of SetManager is
begin
   !-----------------------------------------------;
   class DiscSet of Set is
   begin
   end;
   !-----------------------------------------------;
   procedure Union(DiscSet,DiscSet) return DiscSet is
   begin
      ! Impl of Union operation;
   end;
   !-----------------------------------------------;
end;
```

The *DiscriminationSetManager* class may only be used as an implementation for *Setmanager* when the element type of the set is ordered. However, all available information about ordered objects (as expressed in the specification for *OrderedManager*) may be used inside *DiscriminationSetManager* in its manipulation of the set's element type. This use of a subclass in the parameter of the implementation class also eliminates the need for procedure parameters since the composed data type and its operations are combined in a class declaration. Therefore the user can use the abstract data type without needing to consider the constraints required by any particular implementation. Such considerations are automatically processed by the translation system.

Having provided the ability to have multiple implementations, and ways to name the different representations, Paragon further allows some more advanced approaches to implementing abstract data types than those permitted in conventional languages. Two of these approaches, partial implementations and shared implementations, are discussed next.

4.5.2. Partial Implementations

A *partial* or *incomplete implementation* of an abstract data type is an implementation that does not have a procedure implementation for every procedure specification in its ancestors and self. In most languages, an implementation must be able to be used wherever the specification is used. To guarantee such use, every implementation must be complete. However, the existence of an incomplete implementation does not immediately imply that the program cannot execute or more precisely, that the program is infeasible.[43] As long as there

---

[43]As will be explained in Section 5.5.5, the presence of only partial implementations does not guarantee that a program is infeasible, nor does the presence of a complete implementation guarantee that a program is feasible.

is a procedure implementation for each procedure that is used, the implementation may be used. This flexibility becomes important as some representations of abstract data types may take advantage of partial implementations.

A partial implementation of *Set* illustrates the usefulness of partial implementations. One of the more useful operations on a set is enumeration, that is, the generation of all elements in a set. Some languages, such as Sail (with Leap [Reiser 76]) and SETL [Schwartz 73] provide this operation. In both of these languages, several different implementations of sets are possible. Some of these implementations are complete, some are not. The incomplete implementations usually distribute the information concerning sets throughout variables of the element type of the set rather than concentrate the information about the elements in some set storage. For example, if one had a set of integers in the program, every integer value in the program would have two pieces of information: the concrete representation of the actual number and a bit indicating if that value is currently in the set. Integer variables would then refer to this block of information as the representation for the integer variable. When such an approach is taken, a procedure implementation for the "for all elements" iterator is difficult to write:[44] every possible value that can be in the domain of the set must be examined to locate its information regarding set inclusion. In Sail/Leap and SETL, the compiler makes the decision about representations for set variables, knows that certain representations do not have "for all elements" procedures available, and knows if the program uses such an operation. Thus the compiler may reject the incomplete implementation in favor of a complete representation whenever the "for all elements" iterator is used. Data abstraction languages that permit only a single implementation insist that it be complete since no substitutions can be made if a procedure without an implementation is used. Because Paragon allows multiple representations and wishes to allow programmers the flexibility provided by partial implementations, the language does not require all procedure implementations to be present in implementation classes.

---

[44]But not impossible. See the description of SETL's set implementations for a full discussion of this particular problem [Dewar 79].

4.5.3. Shared Implementations

The examples given in the previous sections for integers and sets bring up another topic: the sharing of representations. Because the class mechanism does not restrict the way in which specifications and representations may be combined, several arrangements of classes prove useful in selective sharing between the specifications of abstract data types, between the representations of abstract data types, and between the specifications and the representations of abstract data types. Each of these kinds of sharing is considered in turn.

4.5.3.1. Shared Implementations via Shared Specifications

Selective sharing of specifications is quite common in practice and supported in some languages, such as Ada. This usually takes the form of a single manager being used for several different kinds of individuals. For example, one can consider the keyboard and display of a terminal to be separate individuals but belonging to the same terminal manager (see Section 2.1.2). Another example is a computer memory, as illustrated below:

```
class MemoryManager is
begin
   class Byte is begin end;
   class Word is begin end;
   procedure Read(Byte);
   procedure Write(Byte,IM.Integer);
   procedure LeftByte(Word) return Byte;
   procedure RightByte(Word) return Byte;
end;
```

The single manager *MemoryManager* provides the shared declarations for two related individuals, *Byte* and *Word*. Words and bytes are closely coupled in a memory and should be considered connected in some way. Some languages, such as Clu, have no provisions for this selective sharing. Paragon permits multiple inner classes that are declared in an outer class to denote different kinds of individuals for the same manager.

The implementation of *MemoryManager* could contain further subclasses for *Byte* and *Word* and implementations for *Read*, *Write*, *LeftByte* and *RightByte*, each of which could access the concrete representation for both bytes and words.

4.5.3.2. Shared Implementations via Previous Implementations

Another way of combining classes gives the programmer the ability to write procedure implementations that can access multiple representations. Like the *MemoryManager* example above where one can write a single subclass of the *specification* class that has access to representations of multiple kinds of objects, one can provide a subclass of *implementation* subclasses that permits access to multiple, concrete representations of the same abstract object. This can be illustrated by extending the *IntegerManager* implementations given in Section 4.5.1 (page 87). To include a procedure that can add integers regardless of the implementations of the abstract integer, one can write:

```
class CombinedWordIntegerManager of
   WordIntegerManager, ShortWordIntegerManager is
begin
   !-----------------------------------------------;
   procedure Addition(L:ShortWordInteger, R:WordInteger)
      return WordInteger is
   begin
      . . .
   end;
   !-----------------------------------------------;
   procedure Addition(L:WordInteger, R:ShortWordInteger)
      return WordInteger is
   begin
      . . .
   end;
   !-----------------------------------------------;
end;
```

If *CombinedWordIntegerManager* were to be selected as the implementation for an abstract *IntegerManager* object, then abstract integers could be implemented with either the *ShortWordInteger* or the *WordInteger* subclasses of *Integer*. Regardless of the implementation selected for two abstract integers, there will exist an implementation of the *Addition* procedure that can operate on them. However, as the example is currently written, there is no way to assign between the two different kinds of concrete integers. If one wanted the ability to apply any operation to every combination of operations, then one must either provide an operation that uses only abstract operations on abstract objects, or one must provide a procedure for each combination of concrete representations that are passed as parameters. In practice, it is anticipated that some small number of such interrelated operations will need to be provided, but not all of them.

4.5.3.3. Shared Implementations for Unrelated Specifications

A third way of sharing in Paragon allows an implementation class to be used as an implementation for multiple specification classes. A previous example illustrated this sharing in the SETL system where sets are implemented by altering the representation of the elements of the set (Section 2.1.6 on page 25). This is a unique approach to implementing sets and integers as it requires a shared implementation for two specifications that are not otherwise related: one specification for sets, one specification for the elements of the set. The use of classes and inheritance provides a way to specify this capability as well. Given two separate sets of specification classes, say for integers and sets, one creates a single class that acts as the manager for both and that class contains the representations for the union of the inherited individuals and procedures. An abbreviated illustration is given below:

```
! Specification Classes for Integers ;

class IntegerManager of AssignableManager is
begin
    procedure Addition(Integer,Integer) return Integer;
    class Integer of Assignable is begin end;
end;

! Specification Classes for Sets ;

class SetManager(any) is
begin
    procedure Union(Set,Set) return Set;
    class Set is begin end;
end;
```

With these specifications, one may write the following shared implementation for sets and integers (adapted from [Dewar 79]):

```
class IntegerSetManager(TM: IntegerManager . T : Integer)
    of IntegerManager, SetManager is
begin
   !----------------------------------------------;
   class IntBlock is
   begin
      ! Reps for the integer and set indication ;
   end;
   !----------------------------------------------;
   var RIBM => new RefManager(IntBlock);
   var IntValueList => RIBM . new Reference;
   !----------------------------------------------;
   !----------------------------------------------;
   ! Integer Implementations ;
   !----------------------------------------------;
   class SharedInteger of Integer is
   begin
      var IntValueBlock => RIBM . new Reference;
   end;
   !----------------------------------------------;
   procedure Addition(SharedInteger, SharedInteger)
      return SharedInteger is
   begin
      ! Implementation for Addition operation;
   end;
   !----------------------------------------------;
   !----------------------------------------------;
   ! Set Implementations ;
   !----------------------------------------------;
   class SharedSet of Set is
   begin
      var SetNum => CM. new Word;
   end;
   !----------------------------------------------;
   procedure Union(SharedSet, SharedSet) return SharedSet is
   begin
      ! Implementation for Union operation;
   end;
   !----------------------------------------------;
end;
```

Although the details are missing,[45] the example above shows that representation

---

[45] This combined representation keeps a linked list of all integer values that have ever appeared during the execution of a program. When an arithmetic operation is performed, the values in the appropriate *IntBlocks* are retrieved, the arithmetic performed, an *IntBlock* for the result is found (or created and linked in) and an appropriate *SharedInteger* (containing a pointer to the *IntBlock*) is returned. For set operations, the list of values given by the *IntValueList* variable is examined and the appropriate operations performed. For an operation that spans both types — for example *Membership* — the special representation for the integer gives access directly to the corresponding *IntBlock*, which in turn can be directly examined to determine if the integer value is present in the specified set. In practice, this sort of combined representation has many more details which will not be presented here. For example, the *IntBlocks* are not kept on a list but are hashed. Details of such a representation can be found in an article about SETL [Dewar 79].

combinations of this form can be expressed via the class mechanism whereas most approaches to data abstraction have no way of describing a combined representation.

4.6. Problems with Hierarchies for Implementations

However, the generality of the class mechanism can lead to problems when writing implementation classes. Some of these problems are discussed below.

4.6.1. Incomplete Implementations

The design of parameter matching and inheritance features of Paragon permit a careless programmer to write an incomplete, yet feasible implementation for an abstract data type when a complete implementation was desired. This occurs when a programmer creates a new representation by inheriting a previous representation and does not reimplement all of the necessary procedures. This can be illustrated with the abstract data type *sets*. A specification of sets, followed a single-link list implementation is provided below:

```
!----------------------------------------;
! Specification for Sets                 ;
!----------------------------------------;
class Set_Manager of Assignable_Manager is
begin
    class Set of Assignable is begin end;
    procedure Insert(Set,IM.Integer);
    procedure IsMember(Set,IM.Integer)
        return Booleans.Bit;
    procedure Intersect(Set,Set) return Set;

    procedure Intersect(L:Set,R:Set) return L.structure is
    begin ... end;
end;


!----------------------------------------;
! Single Link Implementation for Sets    ;
!----------------------------------------;
class SingleLinkSetManager of Set_Manager is
begin
    class SingleLinkSet of Set is begin ... end;

    procedure Insert(SingleLinkSet,IM.Integer) is
    begin ... end;

    procedure IsMember(SingleLinkSet,IM.Integer)
        return Booleans.Bit is
    begin ... end;
```

```
   procedure Assign(SingleLinkSet,SingleLinkSet) is
   begin ... ! copy link ; ... end;
end;
```

The implementation above provides implementations for the *Assign*, *IsMember* and *Insert* procedures, and inherits an implementation for *Intersect*, so if a program only requires those four operations, the use of *SingleLinkSet* as an implementation will be feasible.

However, a programmer may decide later to provide a doubly-linked list implementation of sets. One approach to writing the second implementation would be to inherit the *SingleLinkSet* implementation, as shown below:

```
!-------------------------------------------;
! Double Link Implementation for Sets       ;
!-------------------------------------------;
class DoubleLinkSetManager of SingleLinkSetManager is
begin
   class DoubleLinkSet of SingleLinkSet is begin ... end;

   procedure Insert(DoubleLinkSet,IM.Integer) is
   begin ... end;

end;
```

The motivation for deriving the implementation is that some of the previous implementations would still be valid. For example, the *IsMember* procedure may only need one link to walk down the list to search for an element. Thus the doubly-linked list implementation may use the single-linked list implementation of *IsMember* and not write a new one. Because every *DoubleLinkSet* is also a *SingleLinkSet*, the use of the previous *IsMember* implementation is feasible. However, by the same reasoning, every procedure implementation for *SingleLinkSet* is a feasible implementation for *DoubleLinkSet*. In the implementation above, there is no implementation for the *Assign* procedure. Presumably the *Assign* procedure for *SingleLinkSet* will copy only one link, not both. Yet the absence of an *Assign* procedure for *DoubleLinkSet* will cause the Paragon to use the *SingleLinkSet* version, which is feasible but probably not what the programmer wanted. Instead, the programmer probably wanted to include another *Assign* procedure that manipulated both links, for example:

```
   procedure Assign(DoubleLinkSet,DoubleLinkSet) is
   begin ... ! copy both links ; ... end;
```

Thus a feasible program will probably not execute properly, and the programmer will have a very difficult time finding the problem.

One approach to correcting this problem would be to add constraints to procedure implementations. Thus the *Assign* procedure implementation would look like:

```
procedure Assign(L:SingleLinkSet,R:SingleLinkSet)
    such that L.structure same as SingleLinkSet &
              R.structure same as SingleLinkSet is
begin ... ! copy link ; ... end;
```

This constraint requires that both parameters be implemented as *SingleLinkSets*, and not as any subclass of SingleLinkSet. Now a program that used *DoubleLinkSet* and the *Assign* procedure without providing a new implementation for *Assign* would be infeasible and the programmer alerted to the mistake.

4.6.2. Organizing Multiple Implementations

Even where new representations are not derived from old ones, the facilities that Paragon provides for specifying multiple representations can cause some worries for programmers. The problems occur when trying to organize several implementations for use by the selection system and revolves around the need to have a single manager for the shared representations. This is illustrated by the program fragment below:

```
var MySetManager => new SetManager

var Set1 => MySetManager . new Set;
var Set2 => MySetManager . new Set;
var Set3 => MySetManager . new Set;
```

One must pick representations for the three set variables, *Set1*, *Set2*, and *Set3*, but only one object is needed for the manager of all three sets. Thus only one representation is required for *MySetManager*. The problem is how to distribute the possible representations for the sets in possible representations for the set manager. Two general approaches are discussed below in more detail: combine the set representations in a single manager; and provide a single set representation per manager.

4.6.2.1. Using a Single Manager

A typical example of providing multiple set implementations inside of a single implementation of a set manager is shown below:

```
!-------------------------------------------;
! Multiple Implementations for Sets          ;
!-------------------------------------------;
class MultiImplSetManager of Set_Manager is
begin
    !----------------------------------;
    ! First Implementation             ;
    !----------------------------------;
    class SingleLinkSet of Set is begin ... end;

    ! Shared state for SingleLinkSet Manager ;
    ...

    procedure Insert(SingleLinkSet,IM.Integer) is
    begin ... end;

    procedure IsMember(SingleLinkSet,IM.Integer)
        return Booleans.Bit is
    begin ... end;

    procedure Intersect(SingleLinkSet,SingleLinkSet)
        return SingleLinkSet is
    begin ... end;

    procedure Assign(SingleLinkSet,SingleLinkSet) is
    begin ... ! copy link ; ... end;

    !----------------------------------;
    ! Second Implementation            ;
    !----------------------------------;
    class ArraySet of Set is begin ... end;

    ! Shared state for ArraySet Manager ;
    ...

    procedure Insert(ArraySet,IM.Integer) is
    begin ... end;

    procedure IsMember(ArraySet,IM.Integer)
        return Booleans.Bit is
    begin ... end;

    procedure Intersect(ArraySet,ArraySet)
        return ArraySet is
    begin ... end;

    procedure Assign(ArraySet,ArraySet) is
    begin ... ! copy array ; ... end;
```

```
!-------------------------------;
! Third Implementation          ;
!-------------------------------;
class BTreeSet of Set is begin ... end;

! Shared state for BTreeSet Manager ;
...

procedure Insert(BTreeSet,IM.Integer) is
begin ... end;

procedure IsMember(BTreeSet,IM.Integer)
    return Booleans.Bit is
begin ... end;

procedure Intersect(BTreeSet,BTreeSet)
    return BTreeSet is
begin ... end;

procedure Assign(BTreeSet,BTreeSet) is
begin ... ! copy links ; ... end;
end;
```

Using the strategy where all of the representations are in a single manager, the selection mechanism can easily select a representation for the manager, since there is only one available, here *MultiImplSetManager*. Because this outer class contains three subclasses for the individuals, here *SingleLinkSet*, *ArraySet* and *BTreeSet*, a selection of any of these classes is locally feasible for variables specified with the *Set* class.[46] Thus different variables may have different representations. Further, cross-representation procedures may be declared in the one manager, since such procedures can have access to the internal definitions of all of the implementations.

Unfortunately, this strategy results in a manager that contains too much state. For example, a policy may choose the same representation for all of the individuals managed by a manager. Thus each *Set* variable might be implemented as an *ArraySet*. However the manager contains shared declarations needed for all possible representations. The empty tree needed for a *BtreeSet* will still be part of the single manager, even if no sets are implemented as BTrees.

The strategy of using one manager also reduces module separation. The addition of a new implementation should not require the changing of previous implementations, yet this strategy requires the programmer to change an already existing class to add a new implementation for

---

[46]Local feasibility is discussed in Section 5.2.3.

an abstract data type. Thus this strategy violates a notion principle of system building, namely separating program components as much as possible.

4.6.2.2. Using Multiple Managers

The alternative strategy is to provide a different manager implementation for each individual implementation. If multiple implementations are desired, then the implementations should be inherited by another class. As an example, two implementations are declared and then combined in the program text below:

```
!----------------------------------------;
! Single Link Implementation for Sets    ;
!----------------------------------------;
class SingleLinkSetManager of Set_Manager is
begin
    class SingleLinkSet of Set is begin ... end;

    procedure Insert(SingleLinkSet,IM.Integer) is
    begin ... end;

    procedure IsMember(SingleLinkSet,IM.Integer)
        return Booleans.Bit is
    begin ... end;

    procedure Intersect(SingleLinkSet,SingleLinkSet)
        return SingleLinkSet is
    begin ... end;

    procedure Assign(SingleLinkSet,SingleLinkSet) is
    begin ... ! copy link ; ... end;
end;
```

```
!------------------------------------------;
! Array Implementation for Sets            :
!------------------------------------------;
class ArraySetManager of Set_Manager is
begin
   class ArraySet of Set is begin ... end;

   procedure Insert(ArraySet,IM.Integer) is
   begin ... end;

   procedure IsMember(ArraySet,IM.Integer)
      return Booleans.Bit is
   begin ... end;

   procedure Intersect(ArraySet,ArraySet)
      return ArraySet is
   begin ... end;

   procedure Assign(ArraySet,ArraySet) is
   begin ... ! copy link ; ... end;
end;


!------------------------------------------;
! Combined Implementation for Sets         :
!------------------------------------------;
class CombinedSetManager
   of ArraySetManager, SingleLinkSetManager is
begin
end;
```

Again using the variables declarations for *MySetManager*, *Set1*, *Set2* and *Set3*, an implementation must be selected for the manager and then implementations must be selected for the individuals. However, only one implementation may be selected for the manager. For both representations to be available for set variables, the manager must be implemented with *CombinedSetManager*.

However, this strategy of providing a separate manager for each implementation and then combining them into other classes for multiple representations has two drawbacks. First, there are many different combinations of representations that need to be defined and selected. Second, some space in the manager may still be wasted.

If one has many different implementations for an abstract data type and wants to consider all implementation possibilities, there would be an enormous number of possible combinations that would have to be defined. In this small example, only two representations were defined, and they could be combined with a single, extra class declaration. In general, if one had n implementations, then 2^n-$(n + 1)$ additional sets of classes would have to be declared to capture all of the possible ways that multiple representations could be combined.[47] This is far too many to be practical, so representations might be selectively combined.

But selectively combining implementations has the same problems as having one all-encompassing manager, some state for a manager that is not used may be wasted. Suppose that the *CombinedSetManager* were selected as the implementation for *MySetManager* but *ArraySet* were selected as the representation for all three variables: *Set1*, *Set2* and *Set3*. Then the local storage required for the *SingleLinkSetManager* would be unnecessary. In order to obtain a manager that contains all of the desired implementations, a manager that contains additional, unused implementations may have to be selected. Thus a selective combination of implementations may result in a manager that contains unnecessary state.

4.6.3. Sharing a Representation

The last goal for representations of abstract data types is that a single representation should be able to be written for several specifications, and in Section 4.5.3.3, an example was provided showing how a single representation could be written for two specifications: integers and sets. Though the combined implementation may be written, unfortunately it cannot be selected by the selection system described in Chapter 5.

The problem with selecting the combined representation comes from a combination of the manager model and the restriction that every identifier denotes a distinct object. When two separate specifications are used, two different managers are required. This is illustrated below:

```
var MySetManager => new SetManager;
var MyIntManager => new IntManager;

var Set1 => MySetManager . new Set;
var Set2 => MySetManager . new Set;

var Int1 => MyIntManager . new Int;
var Int2 => MyIntManager . new Int;
```

---

[47] Because each combination contains a subset of n implementations, there could be 2^n possible subsets of implementations. But the classes that represent a single implementation are already declared, and the specification serves as the subset where no implementations are declared. Therefore $n + 1$ is subtracted from 2^n.

Although the programmer may provide a single implementation that can serve both *MySetManager* and *MyIntManager*, the selection system will try to make separate object selection choices for each variable. The combined implementation surely can be used for both variables, but such an assignment of implementations would result in two instances of the combined implementation, one for each manager, and not a single shared instance.

One of the difficulties in providing this sharing of objects is providing a rule that states when an object may be shared and where it may not. This raises issues of the proper way to treat intermediate elaborations between the two object instances, as shown below:

```
var MySetManager => new SetManager;
var Problem => new Something(SideEffectFunctionCall);
var MyIntManager => new IntManager;
```

Here, the elaboration of the shared implementation may cause side effects that could interact with the intermediate calculations of *SideEffectFunctionCall*. The criteria that Paragon uses for sharing objects ameliorate elaboration-order effects. (These criteria are listed in Appendix A.8.) However, these criteria were never integrated into the selection system. To do so, the selection system would have to be able to inquire if these criteria were met by some selection of implementations and if so, to then force a sharing of an object.

A related situation comes up when trying to share implementation for the same manager. For example, a programmer may want to use the same implementation for multiple instances of a manager. An example is shown below:

```
var OrangeManager => new Integer_Manager;
var AppleManager  => new Integer_Manager;

var Lisa => AppleManager . new Integer;
var Navel => OrangeManager . new Integer;
```

In this circumstance, one may want to share the *Integer_Manger* object for both the *OrangeManager* and *AppleManager*. Paragon only deals with this problem tangentially by considering the two manager objects to be different specifications and then permitting two different representations of *Integer_Manager* to be combined into a single manager, like *CombinedSetManager* in Section 4.6.2.2. Under these circumstances, a shared instance could be used for both managers. The same criteria given in Appendix A.8 would be used. A future direction of research may consider the entire problem of sharing implementations in more detail than Paragon.

Despite some problems with combining representations, a type hierarchy has been shown to be useful in describing generalization classes, specification classes, implementation classes, shared specifications and shared implementations. A programmer using the type hierarchy would provide several representations for the abstract data types in his program, each tailored for a particular circumstance. The next step in refining a program is the selection of an appropriate representation for each variable and each procedure call in the program. To fulfil this need, Paragon provides a representation selection mechanism that the programmer may use to guide the translator in picking appropriate implementations. This mechanism is discussed in the next chapter.

Chapter 5
Selection of Implementations

The discussion so far has been limited to the use of basic features of Paragon for creating abstract data types. In this chapter, I start to consider the processing of a program. As a large part of the processing is concerned with selection of implementations, this aspect will be described in detail. But first I present some more details about elaborations in Paragon[48]. These details are then used to describe the elaboration of variable declarations. After variable declarations have been described, the three aspects of implementation selection are discussed: class and procedure descriptions via attributes; program representation via a possibility tree; and control of the selection process through a policy procedure. The discussion of implementation features of Paragon completes the description of the Paragon language started in Chapter 3.

5.1. Elaborations

A program is processed in four stages:

- The entire program is elaborated with specifications;

- A policy procedure makes implementation selections for variables;

- After the policy procedure finishes, the entire program is elaborated with implementations;

- Finally, the entire program is elaborated with realizations.

Each of the these stages is outlined below.

---

[48] Section 3.1 provides an overview of elaborations.

5.1.1. Elaboration with Specifications

Initially, a program is *elaborated with specifications*. In other languages, this corresponds to having the semantic analysis and type checking performed. During this phase, the objects that are created and manipulated by the program are specified by the class identifier used in the program text. Thus, a variable declared with the class *Set* will have a simple object created that has the underlying class *Set*. In addition to performing parameter checking, elaborating a procedure invocation with specifications causes a simple object to be created that contains one local instance: namely, the local instance created by elaborating the declaration of the procedure specification. These simple objects created by elaborating name components that denote definite instantiations and procedure invocations are collected in the containing simple object (or environment) for later use. If elaboration with specifications is successful, that is, no object mismatch or other semantic error is encountered,[49] then the program is said to be *well specified* otherwise the program is *ill specified*.

5.1.2. Implementation Selection

After a program is elaborated with specifications, a policy procedure (see Section 5.5.1) makes implementation selections for the variables in the program. An implementation choice for a variable, or more precisely, for the innermost simple object being instantiated in the object-creation name component in the variable declaration, is made from the subclasses of the specified class.[50] For example, if the class *Set* has a subclass *ArraySet*, then a variable declared with the class *Set* may use *ArraySet* as an implementation. After this selection, the innermost simple object that the variable denotes has the underlying class *ArraySet*.

5.1.3. Elaboration with Implementations

After all selections of variable implementations have been made, elaboration of the program with implementations occurs. When elaborating name components that denote object instantiations, the translation system processing the program verifies that the selected implementation is feasible (see Section 5.2.3). When elaborating a name component that

---

[49]Some semantic errors that are not related to object matching are finding an undefined identifier or a misplaced goto label.

[50]The subclass relation is meant to be reflexive here, so the class itself may be used as its own implementation. Such a selection is said to be *self-implementing*.

denotes a procedure invocation, an appropriate implementation for a given procedure is chosen (see Section 5.5.5.1). If elaboration with implementations is successful, the program is said to be *feasible*. Should a procedure implementation be missing where required or should a selected implementation class not conform properly to its environment or parameters, then the program is *infeasible*.

5.1.4. Elaboration with Realizations

After a program is elaborated with implementations, it is *elaborated with realizations*. This corresponds to conventional program execution. The implementations for objects and procedures used during this phase come from the decisions made during elaboration with implementations. If the program attempts to perform some action not permitted in the language, the program is termed *erroneous*, otherwise the program is considered to be *defined*.

These definitions may appear unmotivated without the context of the selection process, but as they are applied to different pieces of the program during representation selection, the interactions and the motivations should become clear.

5.2. Variable Declarations and Object Creations

This thesis has been using variable declarations in examples without explaining their syntax or interpretation. In this section, a description of variable declarations is given as well as an explanation of how the different elaborations process these declarations.

A variable declaration is used to bind an identifier to an object. The simplest form of a variable declaration is an identifier, followed by = >, followed by an expression that has a definite object creation as its last name component. This can be illustrated by using the previous class declarations for *Vehicle*, *Tank*, *Ship* and *Monitor* in Section 3.2.2, for example:

```
var i => new Vehicle;
```

When the declaration above is elaborated with specifications, the identifier *i* will be bound to a new definite *Vehicle* object. Informally, this object is referred to as the *type* of *i*. Since an implementation is a subclass of the class specified in the variable declaration, a subclass of *Vehicle* may be used to implement *i*. To select an implementation for *i*, the policy procedure will associate a subclass of *Vehicle* with the *Vehicle* simple object created during elaboration with specifications. For example, if *Tank* is selected as the implementation, all of the classes that form *Tanks* but that are missing from *Vehicles* will be elaborated with specifications and added to the local instance set for the simple object associated with *i*. Finally, if this variable declaration is elaborated with realizations, a new simple object will be created by elaborating, with realizations, the expression following the = >. However, this elaboration will assume that the implementation class was written where the specification class was written, that is, substituting *Tank* for *Vehicle*.

The description above of how an implementation for a simple object is processed is simplified. Some of the complicating problems deal with changes of parameters when selecting an implementation and with changing an already selected implementation. These become important since a program may be elaborated with implementations many times, at the discretion of the policy. All that Paragon guarantees is that after the policy procedure is finished, the entire program will be elaborated with implementations to check the program for feasibility.

In each of the next three sections, some details will be given about the selection of a variable implementation, the checking of a variable declaration for feasibility, and the elaboration of a variable declaration with elaborations.

5.2.1. Selecting a Variable Implementation

For purposes of selecting an implementation and of describing the different elaborations, simple objects have two varieties. The first kind of simple object results from elaboration with specifications, the second results from elaboration with realizations. In this section, only the first kind is discussed. The other is considered in Section 5.2.4.

Like all simple objects, simple objects created during elaboration with specifications contain a set of local instances, and in addition, have a (possibly empty) set of currently unused local instances.[51] The local instances in a simple object come from two sources:

1. The elaboration of the name component containing a definite-object instantiation.

---

[51]These unused local instances are created as different implementations are selected for a variable. See page 114.

2. The selection of an implementation for a variable.[52]

When either of these actions is performed, the set of local instances and the set of unused local instances in a simple object may change. Each of these actions is discussed below.

When a simple object is created during elaboration with specifications, the set of local instances that results from elaborating both the class declarations of the ancestor classes and the specified class are added to the simple object. Initially, the set of unused local instances is empty.

When the implementation of a simple object is changed, the sets of local instances may also have to be changed. This can be illustrated by considering the following class declarations:[53]

```
!-------------------------------------------------;
! This is a generalization class;
!-------------------------------------------------;
class AssignableManager is
begin
   class Assignable is begin end;
end;
!-------------------------------------------------;


!-------------------------------------------------;
! This is a specification class;
!-------------------------------------------------;
class ListManager(any) of AssignableManager is
begin
   class List of Assignable is begin end;
end;
!-------------------------------------------------;
```

---

[52]Paragon permits name components that denote object creations only as the last name component in the expression of a variable declaration. Further, this last component must be a definite-object creation. Therefore there is a bijection between definite-object creations and variable declarations. Thus the discussion will interchangeably associate an implementation with the variable and with the definite object creation.

[53]These declarations are somewhat strange for purposes of illustration.

```
!-----------------------------------------------------;
! The next two classes are implementation classes;
!-----------------------------------------------------;
class ArrayListManager(type:Tank) of ListManager is
begin
   class ArrayList of List is begin end;
end;
!-----------------------------------------------------;
class LinkedListManager(type:Vehicle) of ListManager is
begin
   class LinkedList of List is begin end;
end;
!-----------------------------------------------------;

!-----------------------------------------------------;
! The following variables use the above classes;
!-----------------------------------------------------;
var MyListManager => new ListManager(Tank);
var List1 => MyListManager . new List;
var List2 => MyListManager . new List;
!-----------------------------------------------------;
```

In this example, there are four classes that act as managers: *AssignableManager*, *ListManager*, *ArrayListManager* and *LinkedListManager* along with four classes that act as individuals: *Assignable*, *List*, *ArrayList* and *LinkedList*. The three variable declarations first create a manager for lists of *Tanks* and then create two such lists.

As in the previous description of elaborating variable declarations with specifications, the elaboration with specifications of the variable declaration for *MyListManager* causes a new simple object to be created and two local instances to be elaborated with specifications and then to be added to the simple object: one for *AssignableManager* and one for *ListManager*. The simple object creation for *List1* is similar. After elaboration with specifications, the simple object contains two local instances: one for *Assignable* and one for *List*. Both simple objects have empty unused local instance sets. Once elaboration with specifications is completed, selection may proceed.

When an implementation is selected for a variable, it must first be checked for local feasibility, then the local instance sets may be modified. Each step is discussed below and then illustrated with the example above.

Checking for *local feasibility* is a combination of elaborating the definite instantiation with specifications and with implementations. The following five steps are taken:

1. The environment in which the creation is to take place is searched for the

selected implementation class[54]. If the class is not found, then the selection is not locally feasible.

2. The parameters in the declaration for the implementation class are elaborated with implementations.

3. The objects that are associated with the simple object are compared with the objects that result from the elaboration above. If the comparison is successful, then all resulting bindings of identifiers to objects replace the old bindings in the simple object. If the comparison is not successful, then the selection is not locally feasible.

4. If the selection is still locally feasible, then a new set of local instances is created to replace the current set of local instances. This is done by placing all of the local instances from the old local instance set into the unused local instance set and then moving, in leftmost elaboration order, local instances for the implementation class from the unused local instance set to the new local instance set. If a local instance for a class is not available in the unused local instance set, it is created, its body elaborated with specifications, and then added to the local instance set. (The local instances in the unused local instance set may be later retrieved if an implementation that uses them is later (re)selected.)

5. All constraints in the variable declaration are executed (elaborated with realizations). If any *False* object is returned by a constraint, then the selection is not locally feasible, and the old set of local instances is restored (as well as the old parameter bindings). Variable constraints are discussed fully in Section 5.2.2.

This process of selecting an implementation can be illustrated with the variable declarations for *MyListManager* and *List1*. The discussion starts v. ı the details of elaborating those declarations with specifications. Then a series of locally-feasible implementation selections for *MyListManager* and *List1* are examined. Finally, the actions that result from some locally infeasible implementation selections for these variables are considered.

Like all object instantiations during elaboration with specifications, each new simple object contains a set of local instances. The new simple object for *MyListManager* is created and has two local instances corresponding to the classes in the leftmost elaboration order: one for *AssignableManager* and one for *ListManager*. In a corresponding manner, the new simple object for *List1* is created in the environment of *MyListManager* and has two local instances: one for *Assignable* and one for *List*. Neither simple object has an unused local instance.

Now consider the effects of implementing *MyListManager* with the *LinkedListManager* class.

---

[54] The search takes place in leftmost parent order.

The check for local feasibility (step 1) first ensures that the *LinkedListManager* class is available in the environment. Since the class *LinkedListManager* is visible where the variable declaration is written, the class is available in the environment.   The parameter for *LinkedListManager* is elaborated with implementations (step 2) which yields an indefinite *Vehicle* object. The actual parameter that has already been elaborated, an indefinite *Tank* object, is then compared with the formal object, a *Vehicle* object. The comparison succeeds, and as a result of the comparison, a binding between *type* and the indefinite *Tank* object in the actual object is added to the simple object (step 3). As the last step (step 4), the local instances in the simple object for *MyListManager* (which are *AssignableManager* and *ListManager*, as mentioned above) are moved to its unused local instance set, and for each class in the leftmost elaboration order for *LinkedListManager*, the corresponding local instance is moved from the unused local instance set to the local instance set. For a simple object with the underlying class of *LinkedListManager*, the leftmost elaboration order is *AssignableManager, ListManager, LinkedListManager*.   Note that one necessary local instance is missing: the local instance for *LinkedListManager*.   Therefore, the selection of *LinkedListManager* as the implementation for *MyListManager* will cause a new local instance of *LinkedListManager* to be created and elaborated with specifications, and then added to the local instance set for *MyListManager*.   There are no constraints to be elaborated, so the selection process is complete and *MyListManager* has the representation *LinkedListManager*.

It is possible to change the implementation of *MyListManager* from *LinkedListManager* to *ArrayListManager*. As before, the environment is checked, the parameters elaborated and compared, and all of the local instances moved to the unused local instance set. Similarly, a new local instance for *ArrayListManager* will be added eventually to the local instance set of the simple object for *MyListManager*. Unlike all the previous examples, the resulting unused local instance set is not empty. It contains a local instance for *LinkedListManager*. Should the implementation change from *ArrayListManager* back to *LinkedListManager*, the local instance for *ArrayListManager* would be present in the unused local instance set and the previously unused local instance for *LinkedListManager* would be in the local instance set of *MyListManager*. Thus no new local instances would be created under these circumstances.

So far, all of the implementation selections have been locally feasible. Next, two locally infeasible selections are illustrated.   They result from an improper environment and mismatched parameters.

One kind of infeasibility results from the violation of the first rule which requires that the implementation be found in its creation environment. Suppose that the selection of LinkedListManager has been made for MyListManager and a selection of ArrayList is about to be made for List1. As required in the first step for local feasibility, the creation environment for List1 is examined for the implementation class. Here the creation environment for List1 is the object denoted by MyListManager, a LinkedListManager. ArrayList is available in ArrayListManager, not in LinkedListManager, thus an attempt to assign ArrayList as the implementation for List1 is not locally feasible.

Another possible impediment to local feasibility is a parameter mismatch. Assume for a moment that the declaration for MyListManager is

```
var MyListManager => new ListManager(Vehicle);
```

If a selection of ArrayListManager were made for MyListManager, the comparison of the indefinite Vehicle object would not match the indefinite Tank object specified in ArrayListManager. Thus the choice is not locally feasible. However, LinkedListManager may accept a Vehicle parameter and so may be selected as a feasible implementation for MyListManager.

One should note that an implementation being locally feasible does not guarantee that the implementation is feasible. It is trivial to change one implementation that would render another selection infeasible. For example, if MyListManager were first assigned the LinkedListManager class, then List1 were assigned the LinkedList class, and then the implementation for MyListManager were to be changed to the ArrayListManager class, the choice of LinkedList for List1 would not be feasible though it was locally feasible. The reason is the class LinkedList is not in the environment for List1 which is now an ArrayListManager, not a LinkedListManager as it was during the selection of LinkedList for List1. Although the notion of local feasibility of an implementation selection is similar to elaboration with implementations, it is not identical. A more complete description of elaborating an object creation with implementation is considered in Section 5.2.3. However, the program does have some ability to control local feasibility through the use of variable constraints, which are considered next.

5.2.2. Constraints on Variables

One form of control that a programmer has over the feasibility of a variable implementation is a variable constraint. This section provides an overview of this feature.

The syntax of a constraint expression in a variable declaration consists of the reserved words *such that* followed by any expression. An example is given below:

```
var MyList => MyListManager . new List
    such that desc (MyList) . IsDebugging return (Booleans.Bit);
```

This example shows how a variable declaration can use an attribute procedure in its implementation to check for a particular feature. (The use of attribute procedures is discussed later in Section 5.5.3.) Here, the constraint attempts to ensure that the implementation for *MyList* has debugging capabilities.

The semantics of a variable constraint are designed to permit the programmer to control the feasibility of an implementation selection beyond the methods provided by the type hierarchy. The constraints of a variable declaration are elaborated with specifications after the expression containing the object instantiation is elaborated with specifications. However, the constraints are elaborated with realizations during two circumstances: when the expression containing the object instantiation is elaborated with implementations and when an implementation choice for the variable declaration is checked for local feasibility. The constraint expression must return an object that matches the predefined boolean object, that is *Booleans.Bit*, and if a *False* object is returned during elaboration with realizations, the variable declaration is considered infeasible.

5.2.3. Checking the Feasibility of Variable Declarations

Elaboration with implementations is used to check that all necessary implementation decisions have been made and are compatible with one another. There are two facets to this checking: making sure that object instantiations are compatible with one another and making sure that an appropriate procedure implementation exists for each procedure invocation. In this section, only the means for elaborating an object instantiation with implementations will be described. Section 5.5.5 will discuss how an appropriate procedure implementation is found.

Elaboration of object instantiation with implementations differs from elaboration with specifications in two significant ways. First, the selected implementation class is used instead of the class specified by the name component that contains the reserved word *new*. Second, all related elaborations are carried out with implementations and not specifications. In detail, this means:

1. If the last assignment of an implementation for the object instantiation was locally infeasible, then the object instantiation is infeasible.

2. The environment in which the instantiation is taking place is searched for the selected implementation class of the simple object. If the implementation class is not found, the object instantiation is infeasible.

3. The parameters in the name component for the object instantiation are elaborated with implementations. If any of these elaborations are infeasible, then the instantiation is infeasible.

4. The parameters in the declaration of the selected implementation class are elaborated with implementations. If any of those elaborations are infeasible, then the instantiation is infeasible.

5. The objects that result from the elaboration of the actual parameters are compared with the objects that result from the elaboration of the formal parameters. If the comparison fails, then the instantiation is infeasible. If the comparison succeeds, the actual parameters and any bindings that result from the comparison replace the parameters and the bindings that exist in the simple object.

6. In leftmost elaboration order of the selected implementation class, each local instance in the local instance set is elaborated with implementations. A local instance is elaborated with implementations by elaborating each of its (nonattribute) variable declarations with implementations, and then each of its statements with implementations. If any of these elaborations are infeasible, the object instantiation is infeasible.

There are four aspects of this elaboration that deserve more discussion: the reuse of definite simple objects, the applicability only to definite simple objects, the finality of locally infeasible implementation selections and the elaboration of the local instances making up the object.

None of the steps above directs the creation of a new definite simple object during the elaboration of an object instantiation name component with implementations. All of the necessary local instances have been created when an implementation for a variable is selected, so no new local instances are necessary during elaboration with implementations. Each time an object instantiation is elaborated with implementations, and it may be so elaborated many times during a compilation, the same simple definite object is used.

Only *definite* instances have an elaboration different with implementations than with specifications. The elaboration of *indefinite* instances with implementations is defined to be identical to their elaboration with specifications. Since these indefinite objects act as representatives of definite objects, they may take any implementation. Thus for feasibility, an implementation that assumes the least information about them is used. Such an implementation is the specification itself. In addition, since there is no way of assigning a particular implementation to an indefinite instance, there is no need to maintain the local instance set between assignments of implementations in an unused local instance set. Therefore, the expedient of equating the elaboration of specifications and of implementations for indefinite simple objects is adopted.

The fact that an implementation selection is locally infeasible, if it is not changed by another implementation selection for the same simple object, forces the object creation to be infeasible whenever the creation is elaborated with implementations. This unchangable status of infeasibility could be counterintuitive when a later selection makes the originally infeasible selection into a feasible selection, as illustrated by the following circumstance.

In the previous example, assume that *MyListManager* has the *LinkedListManager* implementation selected and then *List1* had the *ArrayList* implementation selected. Clearly, this second choice is locally infeasible. However, one may change the implementation of the *MyListManager* to *ArrayListManager*. The selection of *ArrayList* for *List1* now seems reasonable. The language defines this circumstance to result in an infeasible program, primarily for ease of language definition. If this rule were not included in Paragon and a once locally infeasible selection could become feasible through a change in its environment, any implementation selection for an object in an environment could cause a reanalysis of all the selection decisions made for objects created in that environment. This is potentially a large amount of complicated checking. Further, because some of these elaborations might cause side effects (see Section 5.3.2), some order of the rechecking would have to be provided and reelaboration prevented when necessary (or reasonable). As a practical matter, this situation is unexpected. Because Paragon requires variables to be declared before they are used, it seems reasonable to expect that the implementations of variables will be selected before those variables are used in further object creations. Thus a changing environment for an already implemented individual is not expected to occur, and in fact, never occurs in any example in this thesis. However, if Paragon were to permit such a situation, the language would require extra rules and complications. Hence Paragon adopts the rule that a locally infeasible implementation selection causes the object creation to be infeasible.

The last important aspect of elaborating object instantiations with implementations is the recursive nature of the check. When checking an instantiation for feasibility, all of the local instances that make up the simple object must also be checked, which includes all of their variable declarations. This differs from the check for local feasibility which is concerned primarily with the parameters for the implementation and the relation between the implementation and its environment. Thus local feasibility is seen as a heuristic measure of the feasibility of an implementation selection and not as a guarantee of feasibility.

Once all choices in a program are made and the program has been checked for feasibility, it may be elaborated with realizations. The details of this kind of elaboration of object creations is discussed in the next section.

5.2.4. Elaboration of Object Creations with Realizations

Elaboration with realizations is intended to capture the effects of execution. Definite objects are newly created in the same way as objects are created during elaboration with specifications. The difference between the two is that the classes used when elaborating the creation with realizations are determined by the last elaboration with implementations. Elaboration with realizations is defined only if a program is well specified and feasible. A brief outline of the actions that occur during this elaboration for object instantiation are as follows:

1. If any simple object in the creation environment is an indefinite instance, then the creation is erroneous.

2. A new simple object is created.

3. The parameters in the name component for the object creation are elaborated with realizations.

4. The parameters of the implementation class for this variable are elaborated with realizations.[55]

5. The corresponding objects from the parameter elaborations are compared and the resulting binding of objects to identifiers is saved in the new simple object.

6. In leftmost elaboration order of the implementation class, each ancestor class of the implementation is elaborated with realizations and added to the new simple object.

---

[55]As a practical matter, because Paragon does not allow definite object creations or procedure invocations in formal parameters, no action is needed to perform this step in compiled Paragon code. All of the information necessary for determining the results of later steps is available from information gathered during elaboration with implementations. However, this list defines what the effects should be, not how they are accomplished.

Elaboration of indefinite instances is similar except that no elaboration of local instances is performed and the creation environment may contain indefinite instances. Once the parameters have been saved, the process of creating an object is finished.

Conventional translation systems perform elaborations with specifications, implementation selection and feasibility analysis before creating the translated program. Then elaboration with realizations is confined to the program created by the translation system. In Paragon however, certain pieces of a program are elaborated with realizations during elaboration with specifications and implementations, and also during policy execution. One feature that is elaborated with realizations before the program as a whole is called an attribute, and is discussed in the next section.

5.3. Describing Classes and Procedures — Attributes

Attributes are the primary feature that Paragon provides for describing classes and procedures. An introductory discussion is followed by descriptions of how attribute variables and attribute procedures are defined in classes and procedures. Then some uses of attributes in expressions and variables are illustrated. The use of these attributes in policy procedures is deferred until Section 5.5.3.

5.3.1. Purpose of Attributes

Attributes are unlike much of Paragon in that there is no clear analog between attributes in Paragon and features in other languages. In some sense, attributes are a generalization of compile-time switches, pragmata, hints and compiler options that other translator systems employ. Unlike other systems, the definitions of attributes are completely under the control of the programmer. The distinction can be illustrated with some examples from other languages.

The Pascal language defines certain reserved words, like *packed*, that a programmer may use to inform the compiler that a particular data structure should use a space efficient representation. Ada provides a host of information for the compiler via the *pragma* construct. In both of these cases, the programmer is providing some limited information to the compiler about the way certain parts of the program should be behave. Unfortunately, there is no way of generalizing this property. For example, Pascal does not allow a programmer to inform the compiler to pick a time efficient representation for a data structure. Thus current systems strongly relate the ways that the programmer can provide information to the compiler with the kinds of information that the compiler will process. The attribute facility in Paragon is intended to provide a flexible way to give information to the compiler and to provide as few restrictions as possible to the ways in which the information may be used.

Simply, one may view attributes as describing differences between one class and another, and between one procedure and another. The examples in the previous paragraph illustrate such differences as time efficiency of a representation and space efficiency of a representation. Some other distinctions one typically encounters are the amount of debugging assistance provided, the amount of error detection provided, the amount of performance monitoring provided, a tradeoff between time and space, and the choice of interface to other languages. Some of these distinctions will be illustrated in the next chapter.

Paragon provides two kinds of attributes: attribute variables and attribute procedures. These can be viewed as compile-time variables and procedures that are provided by the programmer. Before illustrating their uses, a description of the syntax and interpretation of attribute variables and procedures is needed; this is provided in the following sections.

5.3.2. Attribute Variables

The syntax for attribute variable declarations is nearly identical to that for variable declarations: the presence or absence of the reserved word *attribute*. But there are two important semantic differences: the order of elaborations and the ability to use procedure invocations. The syntax and semantics are considered below.

The syntax for declarations of attribute variables resembles variable declarations, except that it contains the reserved word *attribute* before the reserved word *var*, as illustrated below:

```
attribute var Total_Space_Used => IM . new Integer;
```

Like a variable declaration, an attribute variable declaration causes an identifier, here *Total_Space_Used*, to be bound to an object, here a definite *Integer* object. The primary difference lies in when the different elaborations of this declaration occur. The expressions in variable declarations are elaborated with specifications, implementations and realizations when the enclosing class or procedure declaration is elaborated with specifications, implementations and realizations respectively. The expressions in attribute variable declarations are elaborated only with specifications and realizations. These two elaborations of the expressions happen in tandem when the attribute variable declaration is elaborated with specifications. No action is taken when an attribute variable declaration is elaborated with implementations or realizations. In a colloquial sense. therefore, attribute variables exist only during the compile-time processing of the program.

A secondary, but important difference between attribute variable declarations and nonattribute variable declarations is the ability of the former to include a name component that denotes a procedure invocation in the expression. For example, one may write:

```
attribute var Expected_Size => 10;
```

while one may not write:

```
var Expect_Size => 10;
```

since the literal *10* is an implicit procedure invocation (see Section 3.3.6).

Paragon attaches no predefined meaning to any identifier declared as an attribute variable. Although the examples shown here use predefined integer and boolean objects, nearly any kind of object may be present. More precisely, any class that is *self-implementing* may be used. The notion of self-implementing is discussed further with policy procedures (see Section 5.5.2).

5.3.3. Attribute Procedures

Attribute procedures provide a way to attach more sophisticated information to classes and procedures. Attribute variables denote a single value but attribute procedures may be as complex as any other procedure in Paragon. As will be discussed later (Section 5.4.3), an attribute procedure has access to a representation of the entire program. Thus an attribute procedure may provide information based not only on local information in the attribute procedure, but also on the structure of the program as well. In this section, only the syntax and semantics of attribute procedures will be discussed. A description of attribute procedure invocations is postponed until Section 5.5.3.

The syntax of attribute procedures resembles procedure implementations, though like attribute variables, the semantics of using attribute procedures differ from procedures. These differences are described below.

The syntax of an attribute procedure is like a procedure implementation except that the reserved word *attribute* must precede the reserved word *procedure*, and there must be a *return* expression present. A simple example is shown below:

```
attribute procedure Total_Time return IM . integer is
begin
   return 100;
end;
```

As one might expect, this parameterless attribute procedure will always return *100*.

Unlike nonattribute procedures, attribute procedures do not have any specifications. Their invocations provide any necessary specifications which must be met by the attribute procedure.

The semantic differences between nonattribute procedure and attribute procedures involve the ways in which they are called. A more detailed discussion of how attribute procedures are invoked is provided in Section 5.5.3.

5.3.4. Attributes in Classes

Adding an attribute declaration to a class is identical to adding any other kind of declaration to the class: one merely adds the declaration in the declaration list. An example is shown below:

```
class ListManager(t:any) is
begin
   attribute var Maximum_List_Size => 100;

   class List is
   begin
      attribute var Average_List_Size => 50;
      ...
   end;

   ...

end;
```

The *ListManager* class has an attribute variable describing the maximum list size for individual lists from this manager, and the inner class, *List*, has one describing the average size of those lists. Naturally, all such interpretations of attribute variables are provided by the programmer.

5.3.5. Procedure Respecifications

The notion of refinement has been used extensively in this thesis, but most of the emphasis has been on refinements using subclasses. Many levels of subclasses may be used to refine an abstract data type. But the only refinement for procedure specifications discussed so far has been procedure implementations. Paragon provides another refinement for procedure specifications, namely *procedure respecifications*.

A procedure respecification lies between a procedure specification and a procedure implementation. The syntax of a procedure specification looks like a procedure implementation except that the reserved words *specified with* appear before the reserved word *begin* and no statements, classes or nonattribute variables or procedures may be declared. Thus like a procedure specification, a procedure respecification contains a description of the interface for calling the procedure and like a procedure implementation, a procedure respecification may have different expressions for its parameters, so long as the parameters match the specification. A somewhat contrived example of a procedure specification, respecification and implementation is shown below:

```
! Three classes that form a list of specifications ;

class General is begin end;
class Middle of General is begin end;
class Lowest of Middle is begin end;

! A procedure specification that uses the ;
! most abstract level of the tree ;

procedure f(General);

! A procedure respecification that uses the ;
! first refinement of General;

procedure f(Middle) is specified with begin end;

! A procedure implementation that uses the ;
! final refinement of General;

procedure f(Lowest) is begin ... end;
```

The motivations for including the procedure respecification are based on the ability to add attributes to procedure declarations. The way this may occur is discussed in the next section, which also contains a more realistic example of the procedure respecifications.

5.3.6. Attributes in Procedures

In all three kinds of procedure declarations, it is possible to annotate the declaration with attributes. One may add attributes for several reasons: to a procedure specification to provide some initial description of the procedure; to a procedure respecification to change and refine the initial description based on some more information about possible procedure calls; and to a procedure implementation to refine further the description based on the final, chosen implementation. In this section, the ways that attributes are added to procedure specifications, respecifications and implementations are discussed.

As it is possible to add attributes to any class, attributes in procedures are declared in the block between the *begin* and *end* reserved words. In the case of a procedure specification, where no block is normally present, a dummy block is used which is prefixed with the reserved words *specified with*, just like a procedure respecification. Such a procedure specification is shown below:

```
procedure Insert(L:List, E: t) is
specified with begin
   attribute var Checks_Parameters => True;
end;
```

Only attributes may be declared in such dummy blocks. No other declarations and no statements are permitted.

The use of the reserved words *specified with* to denote both procedure respecifications and procedure specifications (with attributes) can be confusing.[56] Usually, a block in a procedure declaration that starts with the reserved words *specified with* denotes a procedure respecification. As illustrated above, it may be used as a procedure specification. The choice is determined by context. If there exists a procedure specification with the same identifier as the procedure respecification in the current class or procedure, in an enclosing class or procedure or in one of the ancestors of the current (or an enclosing) class, then the presence of a *specified with* prefix indicates a procedure respecification, otherwise a procedure

---

[56]Perhaps another revision of the language design would eliminate this ambiguity by introducing different syntax for respecification and initial specification. Another change would permit a procedure implementation to act implicitly as a procedure specification if no specification was present.

specification.[57] An illustration of this circumstance is shown below:

```
! Specification for Table objects ;
class Table is
begin
   attribute var Average_Size => 100;
   procedure Insert;    ! Specification for Insert ;
end;

! Two general implementation approaches: Arrays and Trees ;

class Table_with_Arrays of Table is
begin
   procedure Insert is
   specified with begin
      attribute procedure Time return im.integer is
      begin
         return Average_Size;
      end;
   end;
end;

class Table_with_Trees of Table is
begin
   procedure Insert is
   specified with begin
      attribute procedure Time return im.integer is
      begin
         return log2(Average_Size);
      end;
   end;
end;

! Some specific array implementations ;
```

---

[57]This rule makes the hiding of procedures difficult if one wants to provide initial attributes. In particular, to guarantee that the procedure declaration will be interpreted as a specification and not as a respecification while still providing initial attributes, the following ruse must be coded:

```
! New specification;
procedure foo;
! New respecification with same signature to hold attributes ;
procedure foo is specified with
begin
   ! Add attributes here ;
end;
```

The first declaration ensures the specification hides previous specifications; the second guarantees the presence of the initial attributes.

```
class Table_with_Arrays_Impl1 of Table_with_Arrays is
begin
   procedure Insert is
   begin
      attribute procedure Time return im.integer is ... ;
      ...
   end;
end;

class Table_with_Arrays_Impl2 of Table_with_Arrays is
begin
   procedure Insert is
   begin
      attribute procedure Time return im.integer ... ;
      ...
   end;

| More specific array and tree implementations .... ;

end;
```

The class *Table* serves as a specification for objects that are tables. There is one procedure in table objects, *Insert*, which is specified in the *Table* class. The *Insert* procedure has a single attribute, *Time*, which reports the amount of time the procedure requires to execute. Given a particular implementation of *Table*, it is possible to select the appropriate implementation or respecification of *Insert* for each of its invocations, and to invoke its corresponding *Time* attribute procedure.

If one merely picked a complete implementation for *Table*, say *Table_with_Arrays_Impl2*, then the *Time* attribute procedure associated with the *Insert* procedure implementation would be used. But one may use a stepwise-refinement technique, similar to the one in PECOS [Barstow 79], for selecting an implementation. Thus one would first consider whether to use arrays or trees to implement tables and select either *Table_with_Arrays* or *Table_with_Trees* as the interim implementation of *Tree*. Such a selection would also cause the respecification of *Insert* in the selected class to be used as a refinement of the specification of the *Insert* procedure. With this technique, one can ask about the time that an *Insert* procedure might take with each approach and receive a linear time with arrays and a log time with trees.[58] Such information, when combined with data on other implementations and the frequency of operations, could be used to decide whether to pursue further refinements of tree implementations or array implementations.

_____

[58] Only for the sake of argument. The examples are necessarily simple so that they can be easily understood.

5.3.7. Attribute Variables in Expressions

Since attribute variables denote objects that exist only at compile time (although they are run time in nature), attribute variables may be used in expressions that exist only at compile time. Thus they may be used only in expressions in the statement parts of attribute procedures and in expressions of other attribute variable declarations. Their use in a name expression is syntactically identical to the use of a nonattribute variable: merely the identifier. This is demonstrated below:

```
class List is
begin
    attribute var Average_List_Size => 50;
    attribute procedure Get_Size return IM.integer is
    begin
        return Average_List_Size;
    end;
    ...
end;
```

When the attribute procedure *Get_Size* is called, it will obtain the current (realized) value of *Average_List_Size* and return that object. However, *Average_List_Size* may not appear in the statement list of the *List* class since those statements would be executed at run time when *Average_List_Size* no longer denotes an object.

5.3.8. Variables with Attributes

Another way to manipulate attribute variables is available through the use of *attribute associations*. As attribute variables represent some information about the object being created, it is reasonable to allow a programmer to alter the attribute variables on an instance by instance basis. For example, a programmer may wish to indicate that the average size for a particular list is not the *100* specified by the *Average_List_Size* attribute variable in the class declaration for *List*, but is rather *50*. This altering can be done by the *attribute association* feature of variable declarations.

Each association has the syntax *attribute identifier* = > *attribute value* where the attribute identifier is any identifier and the attribute value is any expression (also called the *value expression*). A list of associations is preceded by the reserved word *where*. An example that changes the *100* for *Average_List_Size* to *50* is shown below:

```
! First create a manager for integer lists ;
var MyListManager => new ListManager(IM . integer);
```

```
var MyList => MyListManager . new List
   where Average_List_Size => 50;
```

The process by which the new object replaces the old object is a bit complicated. In short, there is a check made to ensure that the new object is somehow the same "type" as the old, and then the object replacement is made. The details for the example above are provided below.

When the declaration for *MyList* is elaborated with specifications, the classes associated with *List* will be elaborated with specifications and any attribute variables in those classes will also be elaborated with realizations. After the classes are elaborated with specifications, each attribute association is elaborated as follows:

1. The attribute identifier is located in the object returned for the object instantiation expression of the variable declaration.

2. The attribute value expression in the attribute association is elaborated first with specifications and then with realizations.

3. The object bound to the attribute identifier has its innermost component altered to an indefinite instance if it is a definite instance.

4. The object returned by the elaboration of the attribute value expression with realizations is compared with the altered object originally bound to the attribute identifier.

If all of the previous elaborations are well specified, feasible and defined, and if the comparison is successful, then the object returned by elaborating the value expression with realizations is bound to the attribute identifier in the newly created definite instance. The previous binding is discarded. If the elaborations are ill specified, infeasible or erroneous, or if the comparison between objects fails, then the variable declaration containing the attribute association is ill specified.

The use of attribute variables to attach information to classes and procedures, and the use of attribute procedures to provide values based on calculations using attribute variables, provide a powerful way to distinguish different implementations of an abstract data type as they are used in a program. In fact, the attributes serve as decorations on a tree structure, called the *Possibility Tree*, that resembles the program. Because of the pervasiveness of this data structure, it is described next.

5.4. Representing the Implementation Choices — The Possibility Tree

After a program has been elaborated with specifications, each variable declaration and each procedure invocation has been associated with some set of local instances. The structure of these variable declarations and procedure invocations form a tree, with each node of the tree being a simple object associated with a variable declaration or a procedure invocation and each edge leading to local variable declarations and procedure invocations of the parent node. This tree, called a *Possibility Tree*, is the data structure that the policy procedure operates on. In this section, a detailed description of the possibility tree for a program is given.

5.4.1. Abstract Possibility Trees

Throughout this section, a rather contrived, but illustrative program will be used to show how possibility trees are constructed and changed. The beginning of this program is shown below, followed by its initial possibility tree.

```
class MainProgram is
begin
   class Generality is begin end;

   class Specification of Generality is
   begin
      procedure MyProc;          ! This is the specification ;
   end;

   class Implementation1 of Specification is
   begin
      procedure MyProc is     ! This is implementation # 1;
      begin
      end;
   end;

   class Implementation2 of Specification is
   begin
      procedure MyProc is      ' This is implementation # 2;
      begin
      end;
   end;

   class Implementation3 of Specification is
   begin
                               ! No MyProc implementation;
   end;

   var x => new Specification;
   var y => new Specification;
   x.MyProc;                    ! Procedure call #1 ;
   y.MyProc;                    ! Procedure call #2 ;
end;
```

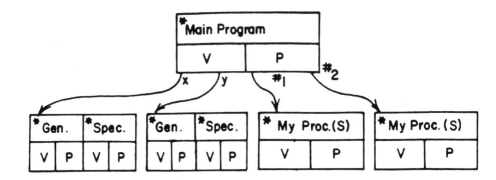

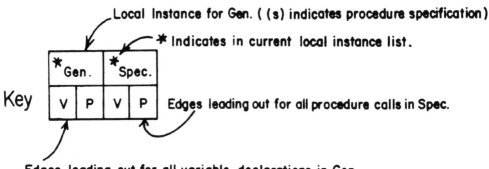

Figure 5-1: Simple Possibility Tree

This diagram illustrates several of the previous terms. There are five *nodes* in this tree: one for the instance of the main program, one for the simple object that *x* denotes, one for the simple object that *y* denotes, and one for each procedure call in the main program. Each node consists of a set of local instances. Each local instance consists of three parts: a name (for identification); some indication about whether that local instance is in the simple object's local instance set (* present) or unused local instance set (*missing); and edges to other instances — one for each variable declaration and procedure invocation in that instance.

Parts of the structures of the program and its objects are also illustrated by Figure 5-1. The simple object for the main program has only one local instance, hence the single local instance for *MainProgram*. There are two edges for variables, one for *x* and one for *y*, which lead to simple objects with *Specification* as an underlying class. Note that such simple objects have two local instances, one for the *Generality* class and one for the *Specification* class. There are no variable declarations in *Specification* or *Generality*, so no edges for variables lead from those local instances. The local instance for the main program also has two edges leading to nodes for the two procedure calls. The edges are labeled with the number of the procedure call in the parent instance since there is no separate identification of each call. Initially, the node for each call contains a local instance for the procedure specification (denoted by the parenthesized S).

A possibility tree is not a static structure. It represents in part, a flow graph of the program, in part, an abstract syntax tree, and in part, a dependency graph. Thus as implementation decisions are made, the flow graph of a program is changed and the possibility tree changes. The exact way that the possibility tree changes depends on the kind of node of that is being processed. The changes for the two kinds of nodes, object instances and procedure-invocation instances, are in considered in turn.

When a node in the possibility tree represents an object instance, it is changed by selecting a new implementation for the object. As explained in Section 5.2, new local instances may have to be created or some local instances may have to be moved between the local instance set and the unused local instance set. These changes are reflected in the possibility tree. When a new local instance is created for addition to the local instance set, the new local instance is added to the simple object node and marked with an asterisk. Local instances that were previously in the unused local instance set but which moved to the local instance set are also marked with an asterisk. Conversely, local instances that are moved from the local instance set to the unused local instance set are so marked by removing any asterisk.

Continuing the example that is shown in Figure 5-1, the implementation for x is set to Implementation1, so a new local instance for the class Implementation1 would be created, appended to the simple object for x and marked as in the local instance set. This is shown in Figure 5-2.

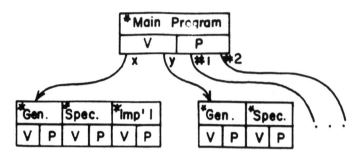

Figure 5-2: Selecting *Implementation1* for *x*

Should the implementation of *x* be changed back to *Specification* (that is, no choice of implementation), then the local instance for *Implementation1* would no longer be marked as being on the local instance set, but it would not be removed from the possibility tree. Only the asterisk in the local instance for *Implementation1* would be removed. If the *Implementation1* were reselected, then the possibility tree would return to the one shown in Figure 5-2.

Changing the implementation of *x* from *Implementation1* to *Implementation2* causes similar changes. First, the local instance associated with *Implementation1* is marked as no longer being in the local instance set. Then a new local instance for *Implementation2* is created and added to the local instance set. The resulting tree is shown in Figure 5-3. Note that the local instance for *Implementation1* is still present, though marked as being in the unused local instance set.

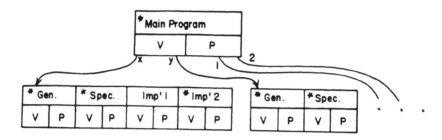

Figure 5-3: Changing *x* to *Implementation2*

Should *Implementation1* be selected again, then the local instance for *Implementation2* would no longer be marked as being in the local instance set and the local instance for *Implementation1* would be remarked. Should the *Specification* be selected as the implementation — that is, the class implements itself — then the local instances for both *Implementation1* and *Implementation2* would be moved to the unused local instance set.

A similar process occurs when a procedure implementation (or specification or respecification) is selected for a procedure-invocation instance during elaboration with implementations. To illustrate this, assume that the implementation *Implementation1* has been initially selected for *x* and *Implementation2* has been selected for *y*. After elaborating the main program with implementations, a selection of implementation 1[59] will have been made for the call *x.MyProc* and a selection of implementation 2 will have been made for the invocation *y.MyProc*. The resulting possibility tree is shown in Figure 5-4.

---

[59]Procedure specifications, respecifications and implementations have the same name, so to distinguish them, they are given numbers in comments next to the declarations.

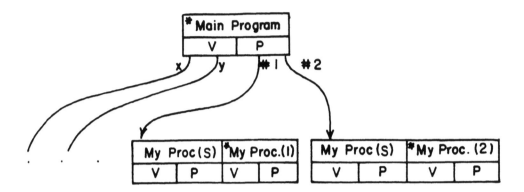

Figure 5-4: Adding Procedure Implementations to the Possibility Tree

In this possibility tree, a local instance for implementation 1 is part of the simple object node for x.MyProc and a local instance for implementation 2 is part of the simple object node for y.MyProc. Note that the local instances for the specifications of the procedure are no longer considered to be part of the simple objects' local instance sets but are considered part of the unused local instance sets.   Should the implementation for the procedure invocation x.MyProc change, say because Implementation3 was selected for x and the main program was reelaborated with implementations, then the specification could again be associated with the procedure invocation and be moved to the local instance set from the unused local instance set. This situation is illustrated below in Figure 5-5.

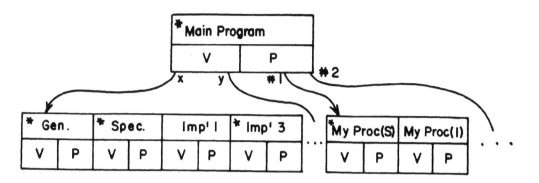

Figure 5-5: Reusing old Procedure Local Instances in a Possibility Tree

The saving of previous local instances preserves implementation decisions that were made for local instances in case those local instances are needed again. This feature is not readily visible in the previous possibility trees because the example classes had no local variables or procedure calls. To expand the example, consider the following additional class declarations:

```
! Some classes for use as local variables ;
! in further implementations ;

class LocalVariable is begin end;
class LV1 of LocalVariable is begin end;
class LV2 of LocalVariable is begin end;

! Some more implementations for the class Specification ;

class Implementation4 of Specification is
begin
   var MyLocal => new LocalVariable
end;
```

If the only implementation selection made in the main program were *Implementation4* for the variable *x*, then the resulting possibility tree would appear as follows:

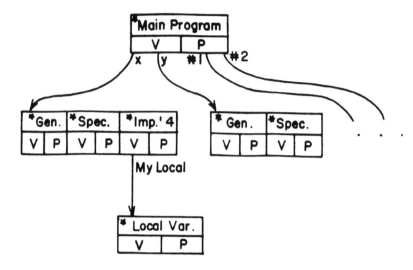

Figure 5-6: A Possibility Tree with only *Implementation4*

Note that the local variable for the instance of *Implementation4* is also present. It is possible that the next implementation decision be a selection of *LV1* for the variable *MyLocal*. Thus the possibility tree would look like the following:

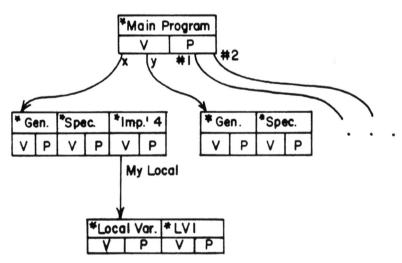

Figure 5-7: A Possibility Tree with *Implementation4* and *LV1*

Some effort has been expended to make the choice of *LV1*. Some time later, however, a different decision for *x* may be made — say to use *Implementation3* instead of *Implementation4*. The resulting tree would then appear as follows:

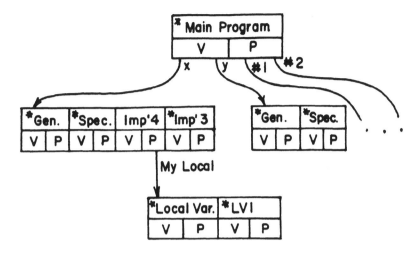

Figure 5-8: Picking *Implementation3* after *Implementation4*

Although the local instance for *Implementation4* is in the unused local instance set, the choices made for its local variables are unchanged. Should *Implementation4* be reselected as the implementation for *x*, the decisions made for the variable *MyLocal* are also preserved, saving the effort that was used to make that selection.

The instances in the possibility tree have been described as abstract nodes that are manipulated by the programmer. Actually, the tree is composed of instances of Paragon classes. The details of the predefined classes that make up the possibility tree are described in the next section.

5.4.2. Instances and *Instance Classes*

In this section, the predefined classes used to describe possibility trees are described. In one sense, possibility-tree nodes are like any other object realization[60] in the language. There is a class that defines them and they are manipulated like other Paragon class instances. But they are different in that they are created by the underlying translation system and not by the program that uses them. Possibility-tree nodes also correspond to specified objects in addition to being realized objects. For each realization of the *Instance* class (called an *Instance* object), there is a simple object that resulted from the elaboration of a class or procedure with specifications. This simple object is called the *doppelganger* of the realization

---

[60]An *object realization*, or a realized object, is an object that was created when elaborating expressions with realizations. A *specified object* is one that was created when elaborating expressions with specifications.

of the *Instance* object. Thus a tree node in the possibility tree simultaneously represents two objects instantiations: a realized instance of the class *Instance* and a specified instance of a variable declaration or procedure invocation. The realized *Instance* object and its doppelganger are always manipulated together, though the policy procedure usually manipulates the realized version while attribute procedures manipulate the doppelganger. The discussion in this section starts with a presentation of how the realized versions may be manipulated. In Section 5.4.3, a brief discussion of the manipulations of the doppelganger will be provided.

5.4.2.1. Realized *Instance* Objects

Each node in the possibility tree is a realized instance of the predefined class *Instance*. The declaration of this class is given below:

```
class Instance(IM. NumV: Integer, IM. NumP: Integer) is
begin
    var VarDecls => VAM⁶¹ . new array(1,NumV);
    var ProcCalls => PAM . new array(1,NumP);
    procedure BindProcs return Booleans.Bit;
end;
```

The meaning of most of the identifiers in the class corresponds to the pictorial representation of a tree node. *NumV* is the number of variable edges from all of the local instances in the local instance set (but not from any unused local instances). *NumP* is the number of procedure invocation edges from all of the local instances in the local instance set (but not from any unused local instances). *VarDecls* and *ProcCalls* are arrays of pointers to the instance realizations that represent the corresponding variable and procedure-invocation simple objects. The elements in the *VarDecls* array are ordered by appearance of the variables in the leftmost elaboration order of the current implementation of the simple object. Similarly, the elements in the *ProcCalls* array are ordered by appearance of the procedure calls in the leftmost elaboration order of the current implementation of the simple object.

---

[61] The identifiers before arrays and reference instantiations in class declarations for possibility-tree nodes represent managers for these arrays and references. The declarations of these managers are:

```
var VAM => new ArrayManager(VarDecl);
var OAM => new ArrayManager(ObjDecl);
var PAM => new ArrayManager(ProcCall);
var CDRM => new RefManager(ClassDecl);
var CDRAM => new ArrayManager(CDRM.Reference);
```

Arrays and references are discussed in Sections 6.2.8 and 6.2.9.

In addition to the structure of the possibility tree, the class *Instance* also defines *BindProcs* which is one of two procedures that control the elaboration of the program with implementations. The second predefined procedure, *CheckFeasibility*, is not defined in any class; that is, it is a global procedure, and it has the following declaration:

```
procedure CheckFeasibility return Booleans.Bit;
```

Both procedures cause pieces of a program to be elaborated with implementations. The former, *BindProcs*, causes the doppelganger of the instance object to be elaborated with implementations without elaborating the procedure implementations used for the procedure invocation in the instance. The *CheckFeasibility* procedure causes the entire program to be elaborated with implementations. Both procedures return a logical object. If *True* is returned, then the program part that was elaborated with implementations is feasible. *False* is returned if some part of the program being elaborated with implementations is infeasible.

One consequence of elaborating an instance with implementations is that the implementation of some procedures may change, thus changing its local instance set. In the simplest case, an implementation is selected where a specification was previously used. As procedure specifications have no variable declarations or procedure invocations, the parameters *NumV* and *NumP* are initially bound to zero and the corresponding arrays are empty. However, most procedure implementations have local variables and local procedure invocations, so these bindings must change. After elaborating an instance with implementations, the translation system will alter the *Instance* objects bound to these identifiers (and their corresponding arrays) so that they correctly represent the local instance set in the possibility tree.

The possibility tree that is accessible via the *Instance* objects represents only the last choice made for each variable or procedure. There is no way for a programmer to manipulate the local instances in the unused local instance list. These local instances were omitted from the tree since identifiers in these local instances may refer to parameters in the specified object which ceased to exist when the implementation was changed.

Although the class *Instance* defines the basic structure of the possibility tree, it does not fully represent the nodes. There are therefore three additional subclasses that are used to provide a more detailed description of the tree: *ObjDecl*, *VarDecl* and *ProcCall*. Each of these classes is discussed in turn.

5.4.2.2. Object Instantiations

The *ObjDecl* and *VarDecl* classes are used to define nodes that represent class instances. As a practical matter, there are no *ObjDecl* instances that are not also instances of *VarDecl* and so the discussion will assume that every *ObjDecl* object is also a *VarDecl* object.[62] These two classes are declared below:

```
class ObjDecl(IM. NumV: Integer, IM. NumP: Integer)
   of Instance is
begin
   procedure GetSpec return CDRM.Reference;
   procedure GetImpl return CDRM.Reference;
end;

class VarDecl(IM. NumV: Integer, IM. NumP: Integer)
   of ObjDecl is
begin
   var ImplSet => IM . new Integer;

   procedure SetImpl(CDRM.Reference);
   procedure LocallyFeasible(CDRM.Reference)
      return Booleans.Bit;

   ImplSet := 0;
end;
```

No more tree structure is introduced by these classes, only some more procedures and a variable *ImplSet*. The procedures are used to examine and set the implementations of the variables as appropriate. Since these classes inherit the class *Instance*, variable objects naturally have arrays of pointers to the *Instance* objects for local variables and procedure invocations.

The procedures declared in the *ObjDecl* and *VarDecl* class manipulate the implementations for the variables associated with the instance objects. These implementations are denoted by pointers to objects that represent the class declarations in the program. To explain the procedures, it is useful to consider the representation of class declarations as well.

Each class in the program, including predefined classes, is represented as an instance of a predefined class *ClassDecl* which has the following declaration:

---

[62]In an earlier design, *Instance* objects also contained an array of pointers to parameters of the simple object. Each pointer referred to instances of the *ObjDecl* class. Because actual parameters could be indefinite instances, these *ObjDecl* objects were not necessarily also instances of *VarDecl*. This would have permitted policies and attribute procedures to get information from attributes in parameters being used as type parameters. Since this was never fully completed, only the remnants of the design in the form of the class declaration *ObjDecl* remains.

```
class ClassDecl(IM. NumC: Integer, IM. NumP: Integer) is
begin
   var Children => CDRAM. new Array(1,NumC);
   var Parents => CDRAM. new Array(1,NumP);
end;
```

The form is similar to the *Instance* class declaration, only the two arrays contain pointers to instances of *ClassDecl* for the immediate parents and immediate children of the denoted class declaration. When the *GetSpec* and *GetImpl* procedures are invoked, they return pointers to *ClassDecl* objects for the classes used as the specification and the current implementation of the variable. Initially, the class used as the implementation of a variable is the same as its specification. By using the *Children* and *Parents* arrays in *ClassDecl* objects, it is possible to denote different implementations for a variable and to set the implementation of the variable by passing the appropriate pointer to the *SetImpl* procedure.

The *SetImpl* procedure can cause other effects in the possibility tree besides changing the implementation of variable. For example, if the designated class is not a locally feasible implementation for the variable, the variable is marked as infeasible and no change is made in its implementation. Even if the class is locally feasible, the change in the local instances may cause the *NumV* and *NumC* values to change with corresponding changes to the arrays *VarDecls* and *ProcCalls*. Note however, the objects will not change, only the internals of those objects. Thus if those objects were passed as parameters to another class or procedure, the class or procedure will also see the change in the possibility tree and the objects in the *Instance* class in which *SetImpl* has been invoked.

Unfortunately, some selections of children of a specification class may not result in a feasible program. Many times, this can be determined by checking only the local feasibility of a variable declaration, as defined in Section 5.2.1. The *LocallyFeasible* procedure provides the facility to check if an implementation choice is locally feasible for a variable declaration before selecting that particular implementation for a variable. If the passed parameter denotes a class that is not a locally feasible implementation for the variable, the procedure will return *False*, otherwise it will return *True*. In neither case will the current implementation of the variable be changed.

The last declaration in *VarDecl* is for the variable *ImplSet*. This integer variable has no special meaning to the translator system. It is provided as a kind of limited tree decoration for use by the programmer writing a policy. However, the single *ImplSet* variable is sometimes not enough.

Typically a compiler records a large information about the program directly on the internal form of the program (usually termed "decorating the tree"). This is a very convenient tactic for organizing any information that is collected about the program. The analogous operation for a policy procedure would be to decorate the possibility tree with information it gathers from the execution of attributes. Unfortunately, the predefined classes for *VarDecl*, *ObjDecl*, *ProcCall*, and *ClassDecl* do not permit any additional information to be recorded with the exception of the special integer variable *ImplSet* in *VarDecl*. Thus a programmer must devise some other mechanism for recording program information, such a tree parallel to the possibility tree.

For this problem, an earlier design of Paragon did contain a solution. The policy manipulated the same classes, but the currently predefined classes were prefixes of programmer-provided classes used for the policy. For example, the following declarations were used for the possibility tree:

```
|------------------------------------------;
| Instance Declarations                    ;
|------------------------------------------;

class InstancePrefix(IM. NumV: Integer, IM. NumP: Integer) is
begin
    var VarDecls => VAM . new array(1,NumV);
    var ProcCalls => PAM . new array(1,NumP);
    procedure BindProcs return Booleans.Bit;
end;

class Instance(IM. NumV: Integer, IM. NumP: Integer)
    of In  incePrefix is
begin
! programmer provided declarations and statements;
end;
```

```
|----------------------------------------;
! ObjDecl Declarations                    ;
|----------------------------------------;

class ObjDeclPrefix(IM. NumV: Integer, IM. NumP: Integer)
   of Instance is
begin
   procedure GetSpec return CDRM.Reference;
   procedure GetImpl return CDRM.Reference;
end;

class ObjDecl(IM. NumV: Integer, IM. NumP: Integer)
   of ObjDeclPrefix is
begin
   ! Programmer provided declarations and statements ;
end;

|----------------------------------------;
! VarDecl Declarations                    ;
|----------------------------------------;

class VarDeclPrefix(IM. NumV: Integer, IM. NumP: Integer)
   of ObjDecl is
begin
   procedure SetImpl(CDRM.Reference);
   procedure LocallyFeasible(CDRM.Reference) return Booleans.Bit;
end;

class VarDecl(IM. NumV: Integer, IM. NumP: Integer)
   of VarDeclPrefix is
begin
! Programmer provided declarations and statements ;
end;

|----------------------------------------;
! ProcCall Declarations                   ;
|----------------------------------------;

class ProcCallPrefix(IM. NumV: Integer, IM. NumP: Integer)
   of Instance is
begin
   procedure AlreadySeen return Booleans.Bit;
   procedure Frequency return IM.Integer;
   procedure IsImplementation return Booleans.Bit;
end;

class ProcCall(IM. NumV: Integer, IM. NumP: Integer)
   of ProcCallPrefix is
begin
! Programmer provided declarations and statements ;
end;
```

As before, when the possibility tree is created, appropriate instances of *Instance* would be created, each of which would contain the information from *InstancePrefix* (filled in the by the translator) and the information from *Instance*, to be manipulated by the policy procedure. The reason for the elimination of this scheme was size. It requires twice as many classes as before, half of which need to be provided by the programmer. During testing of the translation system, the need to provide extra class declarations seemed very inconvenient, thus they were eliminated. Thus the *ImplSet* variable is a compromise to let the programmer add some programmer-defined decorations to the possibility tree. If Paragon were to be used in a production system, then it might be reasonable to keep this strategy and automatically to provide empty *Instance*, *ObjDecl*, *VarDecl* and *ProcCall* subclasses should the programmer leave them out.

5.4.2.3. Procedure Invocations

Just as the special subclasses for object instances provide procedures for manipulating variable declarations, so the *ProcCall* subclass declares procedures for manipulating procedure invocations. The declaration of *ProcCall* is shown below:

```
class ProcCall(IM. NumV: Integer, IM. NumP: Integer)
    of Instance is
begin
    procedure AlreadySeen return Booleans.Bit;
    procedure Frequency return IM.Integer;
    procedure IsImplementation return Booleans.Bit;
end;
```

Again, no more tree structure is defined by the class, only some procedures are defined. However, some relations between this procedure invocation and others are provided by the *AlreadySeen* and *Frequency* procedures.

The *AlreadySeen* procedure provides a way for the programmer to determine if a recursive call has already been encountered in the call chain. The algorithm used by the translation system for pruning a possibility tree is performed to verify if the corresponding procedure invocation is a recursive call of a similar procedure invocation. The appropriate *True* or *False* object is returned. The details concerning *similar procedure invocations* are postponed until a general discussion of feasibility in Section 5.5.5.

The *Frequency* procedure is used to provide some measure of how often the invocation is elaborated during the execution of the program. Normally this would be tied to some kind of performance-evaluation scheme, such as simulation results suggested by Low [Low 74] or a performance verifier suggested by Shaw [Shaw 79]. Because this thesis does not intend to address the ways in which such data are collected, the implemented translation system causes an invocation of this procedure to ask the user what value should be returned.

The third procedure in the *ProcCall* class, *IsImplementation*, returns *True* if the local instance for the simple object is an instance of a procedure implementation. It returns *False* if the local instance is an instance of a procedure specification or respecification. Thus this procedure provides an analog to the *LocallyFeasible* procedure in the *VarDecl* class in that it is a heuristic approximation of feasibility.

5.4.3. Bridging *Instance* Objects and Doppelgangers

Each *Instance* object in the possibility tree corresponds to a specified simple object that results from an object instantiation or a procedure invocation. Since the underlying class declaration or procedure declaration of the doppelganger might contain attribute declarations, it is desirable to gain access to the doppelganger from an *Instance* object to use the attribute procedures. But an attribute procedure must be invoked in an *Instance* environment (see Section 5.5.3) so it is also desirable to gain access to an *Instance* object inside of a doppelganger. One half of the bridge, from *Instance* objects to doppelgangers, is provided by attribute procedure invocations. The other half of the bridge, from doppelgangers to *Instance* objects, is discussed below.

Since attribute invocations take place inside *Instance* objects, the nonlocal identifiers they refer to must also be *Instance* objects. This is illustrated below:

```
class Example is
begin
   var Temp => new MyClass;
   attribute procedure Get_Time is
   begin
        ... Temp ...
   end;
end;
```

When the attribute *Get_Time* is being executed, the reference to *Temp* is a reference to an object that exists only as a result of elaborating the variable declaration with specifications. There should be a way to access the *Instance* object associated with *Temp* — that is, the *Instance* object which has as its doppelganger the object denoted by *Temp* — and *description name components* are the Paragon facility for doing so.

The description name component is used to bridge between doppelgangers — that is, objects elaborated with specifications — and *Instance* objects. The syntax of a description name component is simply the reserved word *desc* followed by a parenthesized expression. An example is given below:

```
desc (IM.integer)
```

The semantics of the description name component are quite simple. When a description name component is elaborated with specifications, the parenthesized expression is elaborated with specifications and then an instance of the *any* object is returned as the resulting environment. When a description name component is elaborated with realizations, the parenthesized expression is still elaborated with specifications, which results in the doppelganger of some *Instance* object. Then that *Instance* object is returned as the environment for the next component. Elaborating a description name component with implementations causes the program to be ill specified.

With attributes, possibility trees and descriptions, the programmer has all of the tools needed to describe different pieces of a program and represent some selection of implementations. As yet, there is no way for the programmer to specify how the selections should be made. The mechanism for specifying such decisions is called the policy procedure and is discussed in the next section.

5.5. Making the Implementation Choices — The Policy Procedure

Global manipulation of the possibility tree is performed by a *policy procedure*, which is described in this section. The policy procedure makes further use of some special features of Paragon, such as invocations of attributes, pattern matching of nodes in the possibility tree and feasibility checking, also described in this section. With these mechanisms, a programmer may specify the criteria that should be applied when making decisions about implementation selections.

5.5.1. Syntactic Properties of the Policy Procedure

The policy procedure is a user provided procedure that is executed (elaborated with realizations) at compile time and selects the implementations for variables in the user's program. It is written in Paragon and is interpreted by the translation system. The Paragon specification for the policy procedure is:

```
procedure Policy(i:Instance);
```

and the user procedure must use the same header for the provided policy procedure implementation. Although the language permits multiple implementations of a procedure specification, only one implementation of *Policy* is permitted in a program.

The parameter to the policy procedure is an *Instance* object for the main program. When the policy procedure finishes execution, that is, returns, the entire program is elaborated with implementations to check for program feasibility (in case the policy procedure made infeasible implementation selections). After elaboration with implementations, a transformed version of the program can be given to a code generation system. This transformed version has all procedure invocations associated with particular procedure implementations and all variables associated with particular implementation classes. The current prototype merely writes out a stylized version of the program along with all of the implementation decisions.

The goal of this design of a policy procedure is to give the programmer a mechanism with which the programmer can enforce any selection policy. The mechanism for implementation selection is merely a procedure written in Paragon. Thus most data structure selection algorithms that are expressed in other algebraic languages can be expressed as policies for Paragon. In Sections 6.5 and 6.9, sample policy procedures are given that implement the following strategies:

- Any set of implementations that makes the program feasible.

- Minimum product of time and space for a feasible program.

- Low's Heuristic (Hill Climbing time/space product) for a feasible program [Low 74].

- Ramirez's Dynamic Programming Algorithm (Minimizing Cost function along with time and space constraints) [Ramirez 80].

- Branch-and-Bound search for a feasible implementation selection that minimizes a cost function [Winston 77].

The primary differences between other data structure selection systems and Paragon's policy procedures are the method in which program specific information is provided and the control of the algorithm that uses the program specific information. Typically, this information is specially coded in a table or set of rules known to the translation system (along with the translator system's internal representation of the program). This is sufficient for specific, predefined data types, such as associative stores, and specific selection methods, such as hill climbing heuristics. However this method does not integrate well with abstract data type methodology.

5.5.2. Executing a Policy Procedure

Like all Paragon programs that are executed, variables and procedures in the policy procedure and the attribute procedures must have implementations. Normally, such implementations are chosen before elaboration with realizations by the policy procedure, but that clearly leads to an infinite regression of selection decisions. To avoid making implementation selections in policy and attribute procedures, Paragon insists that all classes used in policies and attributes be *self-implementing*.

A self-implementing class is one where the implementation class is the same as the specification class and where all procedure specifications have the necessary procedure implementations. More precisely, a class is self-implementing if it is a predefined class, or if for every procedure specification in the class and for every procedure specification in the class's ancestors, there is exactly one procedure implementation declared in the class (not in the ancestors of the class).

To ensure that a policy can execute, Paragon insists that every object creation in a policy procedure, attribute procedure or attribute variable use the class given as the specification for the implementation. At a practical level, therefore, there is no separation of specification and implementation of user-defined types for the policy procedure.

Procedure invocations during policy execution are handled much like elaborations with implementations. When a procedure invocation is elaborated, the environment is searched for the unique procedure implementation for the specified procedure. If exactly one such implementation is found, then that implementation is used for the invocation. Should this implementation be infeasible for this invocation (and thereby cause an error during elaboration with realizations), then the program being processed is considered infeasible. If the underlying class of the environment is predefined, then the translation system will provided an appropriate implementation. For example, any use of a predefined integer object (*IM.new integer*|) with the predefined *Assign* procedure will be implemented by the translation system, but any user-provided subclass of *Assignable* must include an implementation of the procedure *Assign* for the class to be self-implementable and hence usable in a policy or attribute.

Paragon attempts to provide sufficient mechanisms of program description as primitive operations so that policy procedures may implement a wide range of criteria for its selection decisions.   Most of these mechanisms were discussed in this chapter and include the possibility tree, user provided attribute procedures and variables that provide information about implementations, and some predefined procedures that provide information about the feasibility of the program. Two additional mechanisms are attribute procedure invocations and a predefined iteration construct for matching certain patterns in the possibility tree. These additional mechanisms are considered next.

5.5.3. Attribute-Procedure Invocations

Attribute procedures are invoked by a special kind of name component. Both the syntax and the semantics of this name component differ markedly from other procedure invocation name components.

The syntax of an attribute-procedure invocation component contains a specification of the return object that the attribute should return. Like other invocations, first the name of the attribute procedure is given followed by the parameters for the invocation. For an attribute procedure, the reserved word *return* is then written followed by a parenthesized expression. This expression describes the object to be returned by the attribute. A typical attribute procedure invocation is given below:

```
Time return (IM.integer)
```

When the *Time* attribute procedure terminates, it will return an object that matches the expression *IM.integer.*

The semantics of an attribute-procedure invocation component differ from other procedure invocations in three main ways: the invocation environment is implied and possibly changing; the return object is specified by the name component describing the invocation and not by the declaration of the invoked procedure; and only elaborations with specifications and realizations are defined. These interrelated differences are discussed below.

When an attribute-procedure invocation is elaborated with specifications, the environment in which the invocation is to take place is ignored. Thus the identifier in the name component is not searched for in any environment. However, the parameters are elaborated with specifications to ensure that they are well specified. But since there is no declaration found in the environment, the resulting objects are not compared with any other objects. Finally, the expression following the *return* reserved word is elaborated and used as the environment for the next name component.

If an attribute-procedure invocation is elaborated with implementations, then the program is ill specified. This check ensures that no compile-time facilities of Paragon are present during the actual execution of the user's program.

An attribute-procedure invocation may be elaborated with realizations only in the environment of an *Instance* object; that is, the environment must be an object that has an instantiation of the predefined class *Instance* in its local instance set. Recall that *Instance* objects are associated with a class instance or a procedure call in a Paragon program called the *doppelganger* of the *Instance* object. When an attribute invocation occurs in the environment of an *Instance* object, the doppelganger of the *Instance* object is searched for the attribute procedure. If the identifier cannot be found, or if the identifier does not denote an attribute procedure, then the program is erroneous.

The searching of the doppelganger is what makes invocation of attribute procedures very different from other procedure invocations. Normally, a procedure invocation causes the environment, which resulted from elaboration with specifications, to be search for an appropriate procedure specification. Although the implementation of the object used as the environment changes, the procedure specification denoted by the name component does not change. However, as the implementation of the object changes, some attribute procedures may be added and others hidden or eliminated. Thus each attribute-procedure invocation must search for an appropriate attribute procedure in its doppelganger. In many ways, this process resembles the invocation of Simula virtual procedures or Smalltalk methods.

Once an attribute procedure is found, the actual parameters and return expression in the name component are elaborated with realizations and the formal parameters and return expression of the attribute procedure are elaborated with realizations. The resulting actual objects are compared with the corresponding formal objects. If a match occurs, then the attribute procedure is elaborated with realizations. The object that is returned by the attribute procedure is used either as the environment for the name component following the attribute-procedure invocation or as the result of the expression. If any of the elaborations of parameters or return expressions are ill specified or erroneous, or if the comparison of objects fails, then the attribute-procedure invocation is erroneous.

Because of the possibility that an attribute-procedure invocation can be erroneous through a parameter mismatch (which for nonattribute procedure invocations are checked during elaboration with specifications and not during elaboration with realizations), the *check name component* is provided. This component is a modification of the name component used for attribute-procedure invocation. The syntactic difference between these two components is that the reserved word *check* appears before the identifier for the attribute in the name component. This is illustrated below:

```
check Time return (IM.integer)
```

This check name component effectively checks to see if an appropriate *Time* procedure is available in the calling environment.

There are some small, semantic differences between a check name component and an attribute-procedure invocation name component. A different method is used for determining the resulting object of the name component. For a check component, the new environment is an instance of the predefined boolean object: that is, the object that results from elaborating the expression *Booleans.Bit* with specifications. Normally, the returned object results from elaborating the return expression in the name component.

Another difference occurs when elaborating with realizations. Initially, the same actions are performed for check components as for attribute-procedure invocation components, till the time when the actual elaboration of the attribute procedure with realizations occur. If the elaboration is well specified and defined until that time, then a realized object from the *True* procedure is returned as the environment for the next component and the elaboration of the check component is finished. If the actions preceding the actual elaboration of the attribute procedure are ill specified or erroneous in any way, then a realized object for the *False* object is returned as the environment for the next component.

Typically, checks would be used in tandem with an actual attribute-procedure invocation, as illustrated below:

```
if check Time return (IM.integer) then
    totalTime := Time return (IM.integer);
else
    totalTime := DefaultTime;
end if;
```

In the example above, the program ensures the existence of a *Time* attribute procedure before using it. If the attribute for calculating the *Time* of an object exists, then its value is used in the calculation, otherwise some default value is used.

5.5.4. The Pattern Matching Statement

The pattern matching statement provides a special kind of predefined iterator for use by policy and attribute procedures. The syntax resembles ordinary *for* statements and is defined below:

```
let <identifier> match <expression> in <expression> do
   { <statement> ; }*
end let
```

Following the reserved word *let* is an identifier that denotes a particular *ProcCall* instance and is called the *index* identifier of the pattern matching statement. Like all identifiers, it must be declared before it is used, but unlike other variable declarations, it is declared with an indefinite instance of the *ProcCall* class, as illustrated below:

```
var Call => ProcCall;
```

The expression following the reserved word *match* is called the *pattern expression* and represents the pattern that should be searched for. The expression following the reserved word *in* is called the *target expression* and represents the *Instance* class in which the search should be carried out.

After elaborating pattern and target expressions, the object that results from elaborating the pattern expression is compared with each procedure invocation instance in the *Instance* object (that is, the *ProcCall* instances referenced by the *ProcCalls* array in the *Instance* object) that resulted from elaborating the target expression. All of the matching instances are saved. Then, one at a time, each matching instance is bound to the index identifier and the statements after the reserved word *do* in the pattern matching statement are elaborated.

A typical use of the pattern matching statement is shown below:

```
class SetManager(T: any) of AssignableManager is
begin

   attribute procedure ManagerTime(i:instance)
      return IM.integer is
   begin
      var TotalTime => IM . new integer;
      var call => ProcCall;
```

```
            TotalTime := 0;
            let call match desc(this63 SetManager) in i do
              if call.check Time
                              return (IM.integer) then
                  TotalTime := call.Frequency * call.Time
                              return (IM.integer) + TotalTime ;
              fi;
            end let;
            return TotalTime;
        end;
    end;
```

The pattern statement in the example above performs a search of the *Instance* object that is passed to the attribute. Through the use of the description expression, the corresponding *Instance* for the enclosing *SetManager* can be found in the pattern expression. Thus the passed tree node of the possibility tree is searched for any procedure calls that occur in the particular *SetManager* that contains the attribute procedure being called. Because matching of objects allows holes in objects, this iterator effectively provides a list of all procedure calls in *i* that use *this SetManager* as an environment. Similar kinds of use of the pattern matching statement can retrieve all the uses of particular data abstraction in some part of the program for further analysis.

The use of attribute invocations and pattern matching statements provide some local information about the program to the policy procedure. Information about a global property of the program, feasibility, can also be deduced and given to the program. This is discussed in the next section.

5.5.5. Feasibility of a Program

Feasibility is a property that a program has where all of the selection decisions that have been made for variables and procedure invocations result in a program that can be executed. The details of feasibility checking for variable declarations were provided in Section 5.2.3. In this section, the checking of feasibility for procedure invocations will be discussed.

---

[63] *This* refers to the object in which this attribute is being elaborated.

5.5.5.1. Selecting a Procedure Invocation

Unlike variable implementations which are selected explicitly by the policy procedure, procedure implementations are selected implicitly by the translation system during elaboration with implementations.   The process is similar to elaboration of procedure invocations with specifications (see Section 3.6.4) and consists of four steps.   First, the environment is searched to gather up all available implementations of the procedure, then each of the implementations is examined for feasibility until an appropriate one is found, third, the selected implementation is elaborated with implementations and finally the return expression of the implementation, if any, is elaborated with implementations and used as the environment for the next name component.

When a procedure invocation is elaborated with implementations, the environment in which the invocation occurs has also been elaborated with implementations and thus reflects the implementation choices made for previous components of the name expression. This environment is searched for all procedure implementations that implement the procedure specified in the name component. For this purpose alone, procedure respecifications and specifications also implement the specification.   There may have been other procedures specified in the implementation environment with the same identifier, but only the procedures that implement the procedure originally specified are considered.   These procedure implementations are placed in a list, where implementations that occur in different classes are listed in leftmost parent order while implementations in the same class are listed in reverse declaration order, that is, bottom up in the class declaration. This is illustrated by the following example:

```
class Parent is
begin
   Procedure P;                                 ! Specification ;
   Procedure P is begin end;                    ! Implementation 1;
end;

class Implementation1 of Parent is
begin
   Procedure P is begin end;                    ! Implementation 2;
   Procedure P is specified with begin end;     ! Implementation 3;
end;

class Implementation2 of Parent is
begin
   Procedure P is begin end;                    ! Implementation 4;
   Procedure P is begin end;                    ! Implementation 5;
end;
```

```
class Both of Implementation1, Implementation2 is
begin
    Procedure P is begin end;                    ! Implementation 6;
end;
```

If a procedure invocation of P takes place in an instance of Both, then the implementations for P would be examined in the following order: 6, 3, 2, 1, Spec, 5, 4.

Once a list of possible implementations is constructed, the implementations are examined in order until one with an appropriate set of parameters is located. Before the examination may occur, the parameters in the procedure invocation name component (actual parameters) are elaborated with implementations.   Then for each implementation in the list, the (formal) parameters are elaborated with implementations and compared with the objects that resulted from elaborating the actual parameters with implementations. If the comparisons are successful, then the implementation being considered is selected as the appropriate implementation and the search is terminated. Because the specification of the procedure is in the list of implementations to be checked, there is a guarantee that some implementation (if nothing else, the original specification) will match.

Once an implementation has been selected, elaboration of the procedure invocation continues by elaborating the declarations and body of the procedure implementation with implementations. This is done to ensure that local variables and procedure invocations are also feasible. Should any local declarations or procedure invocations not be feasible, then the program is also infeasible.

After the procedure Implementation has been elaborated with implementations, the return expression in the declaration is used as the environment for the next name component or as the result of the expression in which the procedure invocation occurs.

Like the choosing of an implementation for a variable, the selection of a procedure implementation may cause changes both in the local instance set and the unused local instance set of the simple object for the procedure invocation. Before any choice is made, the local instance for the current selection (usually the specification) is moved from the local instance set to the unused local instance set. If the selected procedure implementation has been previously selected, its local instance is moved from the unused local instance set to the local instance set. If the selected procedure implementation has never been previously selected for this invocation, then a new local instance for this procedure declaration is created, elaborated with specifications and added to the local instance set. Note that the simple object for a procedure invocation always has exactly one local instance in its local instance set: the last selected procedure implementation.

Although the programmer can explicitly control the selection of implementations for variables, the programmer has no way to chose among feasible implementations for procedures. Instead the system will select a feasible implementation based on its way of searching for a procedure implementation. This division of labor between the programmer and the translation system was created to limit the amount of processing done by the programmer. If the policy had to chose an implementation for each procedure call then the amount of time the policy requires would be a function of the number of procedure calls in a program rather than the number of variable declarations and the policy would require too much time for execution. Thus a special, relatively fast method of finding a procedure implementation is built into the system.

An interesting feature of elaboration with implementations is that it closely resembles elaboration with realizations. Procedure invocations actually have their declarations and bodies elaborated rather than merely returning as during elaboration with specifications. This presents no problems for variables, since Paragon prohibits recursive instantiations of classes. However, recursion in procedures is quite natural and permitted in Paragon. Unlike execution, there is no conditional procedure invocation; all invocations must be checked for feasibility.   Thus the elaboration of a recursive procedure implementation with implementations will never terminate.   Fortunately, an infinite recursion of procedure invocations is not necessary for feasibility checking. Instead, procedure invocations that are similar to previous invocations need not be checked since they have already been checked. The exact meaning of "similar" is considered in the next section.

5.5.5.2. Limiting the Size of the Possibility Tree

As described in the previous section, the possibility tree that results from the selection of a recursive procedure implementation is a possibly infinite data structure. A program that can generate such a tree is illustrated below:

```
class MainProgram is
begin
   procedure Recur;
   procedure Recur is
   begin
      Recur;
   end;

   Recur;
end;
```

If the main program were to be elaborated with implementations without any concern for recursion, the tree would continue forever, expanding the specification for the procedure *Recur* into the implementation of *Recur*. The initial part of this tree is shown below:

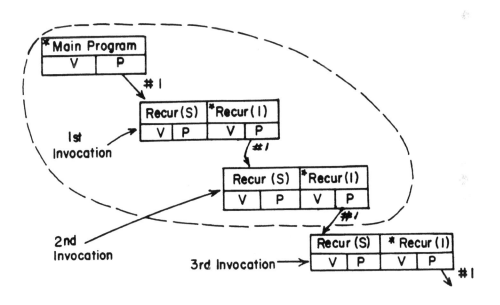

Figure 5-9: Part of an Infinite Possibility Tree

This recursion is ended when elaborating a program with implementations when the elaborator finds a procedure invocation that is *similar* to a previous procedure invocation in the call chain, that is, on a path from the root of the possibility tree to the current invocation. If the invocation is similar to a previous invocation, then it is assumed that the decisions made for that previous invocation should be made for this invocation and no further elaboration with implementations is done. Two procedure invocations are *similar* if the same procedure implementation is invoked, if the objects passed as parameters for both invocations are similar, and if the environment of both invocations are similar. Two objects (environments) are *similar* if each of their simple objects are similar, and simple objects are *similar* if they have the same underlying class, have similar parameters and have similar objects bound to all variables defined in those objects.   In Figure 5-9, the circled part of the tree is all that is elaborated with implementations. The third invocation of *Recur* is similar to the second invocation of *Recur* and so elaboration with implementations would not be performed for the simple object for the third invocation of *Recur*.

Note how the checking for similarity of procedure invocations guarantees that appropriate implementations exist for the recursive call of a procedure. The only objects that may be referenced by a procedure are those in its parameters and in its environment. Based on the implementations for these objects, certain procedure implementations must be guaranteed in the implementation of the procedure. Assuming the previous invocation is feasible, then the same selections of procedure implementations and variables can be made for the recursive invocation of the procedure with the knowledge that the resulting procedure implementation is feasible. If the previous invocation is not feasible, then the program is will not be considered feasible and there is no sense in wasting resources checking another invocation of the same procedure. Further, since there is a finite number of procedure implementations, parameters, class declarations and scope nesting (which corresponds to the maximum number of levels in an object), there are a finite number of possible procedure invocations and so there must eventually exist a similar procedure invocation in an infinite call chain. Thus the feasibility check is guaranteed to terminate.

Although the method used for elaborating procedure invocations with implementations can guarantee the feasibility of a program, there are subtleties when performing the processing. Three subtle facets, determining the return object of a procedure call, hidden implementations, and stopping infinite recursion, are discussed below.

5.5.5.3. Selecting the Implementations of Return Objects

Typically there is no problem to determine the return object of a procedure call, since the procedure implementation explicitly names the return implementation, as illustrated below:

```
procedure Intersect(SingleLinkSet,SingleLinkSet)
    return SingleLinkSet is
begin ... end;
```

The return object for this implementation of *Intersect* has the structure *SingleLinkSet*.

However, this information is not generally available in general procedure implementations. In a general implementation for *Intersect* that uses only abstract operations on *Sets*, the *return* expression (typically) specifies only *Set*, as shown below:

```
procedure Intersect(L:Set,R:Set) return Set is
begin ... end;
```

Assuming that the result of the *Intersect* procedure will be used in another procedure call, more information about the implementation of return object will be needed to guarantee feasibility of the next procedure call.

Two alternatives were considered for determining the implementation of the return object: explicitly and implicitly.

The explicit method uses the *return* expression to provide explicitly the implementation of the return object. For the general procedure implementation, the *return* expression usually is an expression containing one of the parameters, in analogous way that procedure specifications specify their return object when used for subclasses in Section 4.4.3. This is illustrated below:

```
procedure Intersect(L:Set,R:Set) return L.structure is
begin ... end;
```

The example above specifies that the implementation of the return object will be the same structure as the implementation of the first parameter, *L*.

The implicit method, which was rejected, determines the return object by examining all of the *return* statements in a procedure implementation. When elaborating a call of a procedure implementation with elaborations, the expression in each *return* statement will be elaborated with implementations. All of the resulting objects are collected and each is used in turn as the return object for further elaboration of the expression containing the procedure call. The further elaboration of the expression would be considered feasible only if all of the resulting objects would result in a feasible elaboration of the expression.

The implicit method was rejected for two reasons. First, the implicit method requires more processing during elaboration with implementations. If only two return statements were found in a procedure and four levels of procedure nesting were present, as for example:[64]

---

[64] Recall that literals create an implicit call of *Literal*.

```
x := Square(2) + 3; ! Really: IM.Assign(x,IM.Plus(Square(2)),3);
```

then the expression would have to be elaborated with implementations 2^4 or 16 times.

Second, the implicit method would add run time costs to the compiled code. With the explicit method, exactly one procedure implementation is associated with each procedure call. Thus the compiler can generate code to call that one procedure at the call site. With the implicit method, the returned object has to be examined to determine which procedure implementation will be used next. Because the language design attempts to reduce run-time checking, the implicit method for determining a return object's implementation was rejected.

Nevertheless, run-time selection of procedure implementations has value in a general-purpose programming language. Although Paragon was not intended to be a complete, production language, it already contains the rudiments of dynamic procedure selection in the attribute-procedure mechanism. If one were to permit attribute procedures to exist after representation selection, and also allow attribute call expressions to be elaborated with implementations, that is, permit attribute calls in the user's program, then attribute procedures could be used in circumstances where a dynamic selection of a procedure is desired.

One result of the design that emerged from the above considerations is a rather baroque way of ensuring that implementations exist when using type parameters. The underlying problem is that no implementation is selected for an indefinite instance, so any return object that is expressed in terms of an indefinite instance is nearly always infeasible. This occurs in the symbol table example in Section 4.4.3. The creation of the table manager and a use of the table is shown again below:

```
var TSO => new APLSymbolTableManager(AO_Manager.Addable_Object);
...
...ST.Retrieve(1)...
```

During elaboration with specifications, the return object for *Retrieve* is *AO_Manager.Addable_Object*, which is adequate for many purposes. But no representation selection is ever performed for *AO_Manager* since it is an indefinite instance. In this declaration, *AO_Manager* contains no implementations for any operations. Thus during elaboration with implementations, the returned object for *Retrieve* has a manager that contains no implementations. More than likely, such an object will prove to be infeasible when the next operation is applied to it, as for example, when the result of the *Retrieve* procedure is assigned to a temporary variable. A Paragon programmer can solve this problem by creating a variable whose sole purpose is to be used as a type parameter. This is illustrated below:

```
var FakeManager => new AO_Manager;
var FakeIndividual => FakeManager . new Addable_Object;

var TSO => new APLSymbolTableManager(FakeIndividual.structure);
...
...ST.Retrieve(1)...
```

During elaboration with specifications, the use of *FakeIndividual.structure* takes the place of the underlying class *Addable_Object*, yet is still an indefinite instance. However, the policy will make an implementation selection for *FakeIndividual* and during elaboration with implementations, that choice will be propagated when reelaborating the variable declaration for *TSO*, thus providing the *Retrieve* procedure with an object that has an implementation.

This problem clearly indicates that types should not be treated as object expressions as Paragon attempts to do. Another approach is suggested in Section C.2.

5.5.5.4. Hidden Implementations

Because of the way that procedure implementations are selected, it is possible that some operations may be hidden. This occurs when using the multiple manager strategy discussed in Section 4.6.2.2. Recall that implementations for a procedure are considered in a leftmost parent order, and that specifications are included in the list of implementations to ensure that every procedure call is associated with some procedure declaration during elaboration with implementations. However if a class has multiple parents that have a common ancestor, a leftmost parent search uses declarations in the common ancestor before the declarations in a second parent. This was first demonstrated in Section 5.5.5.1. A more compelling example can be generated by the declarations in Sections 4.6.1 (page 96), 4.6.2 (page 98) and 4.6.2.2 (page 101). If the *CombinedSetManager* were chosen for *MySetManager* and *SingleLinkSet* were chosen for *Set1* and *Set2*, and a call on *Intersect* were made with *Set1* and *Set2*, the general implementation of *Intersect* in *Set_Manager* would always be selected before the *ArraySet*-specific implementation in *ArraySetManager*. Worse, a call of the *Insert* procedure made with *Set1* would always be matched with the specification of *Insert* in *Set_Manager* and never with the implementation in *ArraySetManager*, thus always rendering the call infeasible.

This last problem results from implementations being considered in leftmost parent order.

This decision was casually made based on the observation that other languages with multiple inheritance, such as Flavors/Lisp [Weinreb 80]   and Traits/Mesa [Curry 82] used this order for searching for procedure implementations. However, both of these systems were looking only for a single implementation and not necessarily trying to locate an appropriate implementation out of a set of possible implementations. Thus they do not suffer as does Paragon. There are two alternatives to a leftmost parent order search. The first would merely take the list of implementation choices as generated by the leftmost parent order list, extract the specifications and place them last. This eliminates the problem where no call of *Insert* would be feasible, but does not effectively place the representation-specific implementation for *Intersect* before the general implementation. Further, this alternative does not properly place procedure respecifications in the list of implementations. The second alternative is to abandon the leftmost parent order and instead use a reverse leftmost elaboration order of classes for conducting the search. Then the specific implementation would be used before the general implementation, and the general implementation before the specification. This change would be adopted if Paragon were to undergo another design iteration.

5.5.5.5. Another Way to Terminate Recursive Procedure Calls

Although Paragon defines the notion of *similar* procedure calls which is used to terminate mutually recursive calls, there are two ways in which similar procedure calls could be applied. The adopted choice requires that a similar procedure call exist in the call chain of the procedure call under examination. The rejected alternative was to permit the similar procedure call to exist anywhere else in the possibility tree. Initially, this approach seems better since I believe fewer procedure calls would have to be elaborated with implementations. Only one recursive call of a procedure would have to be kept; all others would be similar to it.

The alternative above was rejected because the translation system should guarantee that the call that was *similar* would not be altered by later elaboration with implementations. If the translation system requires only that some other call be similar, then a later elaboration of the procedure call with implementations might choose a different implementation for that call, thus invalidating the motivation for omitting the feasibility checking of the call under consideration. However, a call in the call chain already has its selection made and cannot be changed: the call under consideration is reached only by the previous selection in the call chain. Therefore the first alternative is used as the termination criterion for elaborating procedure calls with implementations.

In this chapter, the various mechanisms that Paragon provides for describing and selecting appropriate implementations for variables and procedure in a program have been discussed. In the next chapter, a full example using all of these mechanisms will be presented as an illustration of the useful of the features.

Chapter 6
A Complete Example Using Paragon

This chapter illustrates the processing of an example program which demonstrates all of the features presented in the previous chapters. The chapter starts with a description of the structure of a program, and then gives the parts for a typical program: the predefined environment, a specification for an abstract data type, an implementation for an abstract data type, an application program that uses the abstract data type, and a policy for making representation selections. After these descriptions, some pieces of the transformed program are provided, showing the results of processing the program.

Following the simple example, the processing for a more complicated example is presented, and some alternative policies are described.

Frequently, the program text in this chapter is abbreviated to conserve space, and make the examples manageable. The full text for all examples is reproduced in Appendices E and F.

6.1. Program Structure and Processing

Programs in Paragon are a single class, called the *Universal_Environment*. Inside of the universal environment are the predefined classes, variables and procedures for Paragon, programmer-provided declarations for specifications and implementations of abstract data types, a programmer-provided policy procedure and the programmer's application program. The application program is a parameterless, parentless class declared as *MainProgram*.

The elaboration with specifications consists of elaborating the declaration for *Universal_Environment* with specifications. The policy procedure is executed by elaborating the *Universal_Environment* with realizations, creating a call to the *Policy* procedure, and then elaborating the call with realizations. When the policy procedure terminates, the *MainProgram* class declaration is elaborated with implementations. A file containing all of the decisions made for the user's program is then written, though in a production system, the transformed program would be retained internally and used for final code generation.

6.2. Predefined Environment

The predefined environment contains declarations for the objects one normally expects in a general purpose algebraic language, such as integers, booleans, arrays and pointers. The specific declarations for these facilities are presented below.

6.2.1. Input and Output

Objects that are capable of being read or written may inherit the generalization classes for *TransputManager*. Many of the predefined objects, such as integers, also inherit this class, providing Paragon with primitive terminal input and output capabilities. The actual declarations are shown below:

```
class TransputManager is
begin
    class Transportable is begin end;
    procedure Read(Transportable);
    procedure Write(Transportable);
end;
```

6.2.2. Assignment

A frequently used capability is assignment, and Paragon provides the generalization classes for assignment, as shown below:

```
class AssignableManager is
begin
    class Assignable is begin end;

    procedure Assign(L:Assignable, R:Assignable)
        such that L.structure same as R.structure;
    procedure Equal(L:Assignable, R:Assignable)
        return Booleans.Bit
        such that L.structure same as R.structure;
end;
```

Note that the *Assign* procedure specifies that the two objects passed to it must have the same structure. This prevents variables declared with two different specification classes from being used in an assignment operation. The same comment applies to comparing two objects with the *Equal* procedure. Since these constraints are only applied during elaboration with specifications, two objects may be implemented differently and still have assignment performed from one to the other. However, there must be an *Assign* procedure implementation available for the relevant procedure call.

6.2.3. Logical Objects

Paragon also provides class, procedure and variable declarations for truth (or logical or boolean) objects, called *Bits*. *Bits* inherit *Assignable* and so may have assignment performed on them as well as the usual logical operations declared in their manager, *BitManager*. The language provides an implementation for *Bit* objects, though it is not written in Paragon, and so is not shown here. The actual text for the declarations of *Bits* is given below:

```
class BitManager of AssignableManager is
begin
   class Bit of Assignable is begin end;

   procedure LogicalAnd(b1: Bit, b2: Bit)
      return b1.structure
      such that b1.structure same as b2.structure;
   procedure LogicalOr(b1: Bit, b2: Bit)
      return b1.structure
      such that b1.structure same as b2.structure;
   procedure LogicalNot(b: Bit)
      return b.structure;
end;

var Booleans => new BitManager;
! var PredefinedBooleans => Booleans.Bit;

procedure True return Booleans . Bit;
procedure False return Booleans . Bit;
```

Bits provide the first opportunity to illustrate some predefined declarations of variables. The *Booleans* variable defines the manager for all predefined logical values that Paragon uses when logical values are needed, for example, in *if* statements, *while* statements, *Check* expressions and variable constraints. The variable *PredefinedBooleans* defines the precise object that is used in these circumstances, but as the declaration for *PredefinedBooleans* is not legal Paragon, it is shown here as a comment.[65]

---

[65] Recall that the last component of the expression in a variable declaration must be an object instantiation. Here it is an indefinite instance.

6.2.4. Ordered Objects

A third kind of generalization class that is predefined by Paragon is *Ordered* objects. These are objects that can be compared and are totally ordered. The usual relational operations are provided, as declared below:

```
class OrderedManager of AssignableManager is
begin
    class Ordered of Assignable is begin end;

    procedure LessThan(L: Ordered, R: Ordered)
        return Booleans.Bit
        such that L.structure same as R.structure;
    procedure GreaterThan(L: Ordered, R: Ordered)
        return Booleans.Bit
        such that L.structure same as R.structure;
    procedure LessThanEqual(L: Ordered, R: Ordered)
        return Booleans.Bit
        such that L.structure same as R.structure;
    procedure GreaterThanEqual(L: Ordered, R: Ordered)
        return Booleans.Bit
        such that L.structure same as R.structure;

end;
```

Because *OrderedManager* inherits *AssignableManager*, the *Equal* procedure is also available for *Ordered* objects.

6.2.5. Hashable Objects

A fourth generalization class provided by Paragon declares objects on which a hashing operation may be performed. This class illustrates the general way that a particular kind of procedure, here hashing, can be provided in a generalization class. Particular specification or implementation classes for an abstract data type may inherit this generalization class as a way to indicate that the specification or implementation class can perform the generalized procedure (and naturally, the implementations also provide an implementation for the generalized procedure). One such use, for hashing, occurs for predefined integers, shown in Section 6.2.6.

The declarations for *Hashable* objects are shown below:

```
class HashableManager of AssignableManager is
begin
    class Hashable of Assignable is begin end;
```

```
    procedure Hash(H: Hashable)
        return IM.Integer;
end;
```

6.2.6. Integer Objects

Paragon provides predefined integers through the declarations of the *DiscreteManager* class, the *Discrete* class and the *IM* variable. The usual operations, except for exponentiation, are declared as well. Two iterators are also provided: *Sequence* for counting upwards from one integer value to another, and *ReverseSequence* for counting down. Together with the *for* statement, these two iterators provide the usual indexed *for* loops found in many languages.

The manager class also contains two procedure declarations that are used for transformations between abstract integer objects and machine words: *Value* and *Literal*. The use of *Literal* was described in Section 3.3.6. The *Value* procedure is intended to provide an inverse function as necessary, though it is not used in any example in this thesis.

The actual text of these declarations is provided below:

```
class DiscreteManager of
    OrderedManager, TransputManager, HashableManager is
begin
    class Integer of Ordered, Transportable, Hashable is
    begin
    end;
```

```
    procedure Plus(L: Integer, R: Integer)
       return L.structure
       such that L.structure same as R.structure;
    procedure Minus(L: Integer, R: Integer)
       return L.structure
       such that L.structure same as R.structure;
    procedure UnaryMinus(L: Integer)
       return L.structure;
    procedure Times(L: Integer, R: Integer)
       return L.structure
       such that L.structure same as R.structure;
    procedure Divide(L: Integer, R: Integer)
       return L.structure
       such that L.structure same as R.structure;
    procedure Remainder(L: Integer, R: Integer)
       return L.structure
       such that L.structure same as R.structure;
    procedure Sequence(Lower: Integer, Upper: Integer)
       yield Lower.structure
       such that Lower.structure same as Upper.structure;
    procedure ReverseSequence(Lower: Integer, Upper: Integer)
       yield Lower.structure
       such that Lower.structure same as Upper.structure;

    procedure Literal(CM . l: word )
       return Integer;
    procedure Value(i: Integer)
       return CM.word;

  end;

  var IM => new DiscreteManager;        ! IntegerManager ;
```

The translation system guarantees an implementation for the *DiscreteManager* and *Integer* classes, as well as for all procedures visible in *DiscreteManager*.

6.2.7. Word Objects

The basic storage element that is predefined in Paragon is a *Word*. In fact, implementations for *Bits* and *Integers* have been written in terms of *Words*, but for efficiency, the implementations for these two categories of objects were built directly into the translation system. In principle, however, one could insist that only *Word* objects be provided and write implementations for *Bits* and *Integers* in terms of *Words*. The Paragon declarations for defining *Words* are shown below:

```
class WordManager of AssignableManager, TransputManager is
begin

   class Word of Assignable, Transportable is begin end;

   procedure Plus(L: Word, R: Word)
      return L.structure
         such that L.structure same as R.structure;
   procedure Minus(L: Word, R: Word)
      return L.structure
      such that L.structure same as R.structure;
   procedure Times(L: Word, R: Word)
      return L.structure
      such that L.structure same as R.structure;
   procedure Divide(L: Word, R: Word)
      return L.structure
      such that L.structure same as R.structure;
   procedure Remainder(L: Word, R: Word)
      return L.structure
      such that L.structure same as R.structure;
end;

var CM => new WordManager;    ! CM = Computer Memory. ;
```

In the original design of Paragon, the operations for *Word* objects were supposed to be implementable by a single instruction on a machine. Because the final code generation phase in the prototype was never constructed, this supposition remains untested.

6.2.8. Arrays

Arrays form one of two sets of class declarations that are intended to be used as type constructors, the other being pointers (see Section 6.2.9). The classes that provide the array facility are shown below:

```
class ArrayManager(Elt: any) is
begin
   class Array(IM . LowerBound: Integer,
               IM . UpperBound: Integer)  is
   begin
      procedure Element(IM. Index: Integer)
         return Elt.structure;
   end;
end;
```

Arrays are declared in a two step process. First, the element type of the array is established by creating a manager with the appropriate parameter, then individual arrays are created. For example, to declare integer arrays, one would create the following manager:

```
var IntArrayManager => new ArrayManager(IM.Integer);
```

Once the manager of the array has been declared, individual arrays may be declared like any other individual object, for example:

```
var MyArray => IntArrayManager. new Array(1,10);
var BigArray => IntArrayManager. new Array(1,1000);
```

Elements of arrays are selected by the predefined procedure *Element*. Without any syntactic transformations, one can refer to an element of an array by calling *Element*, for example *MyArray.Element(1)*. Note that this predefined *Element* procedure does not belong to manager, but instead belongs to individual array objects. This is because elements belong to arrays, and are not shared among all arrays.

Because programmers are not used to using a procedure call notation to select an element of an array, Paragon provides the transformation of *[]* to *Element()* , thus a programmer may write *MyArray.[1]* instead of *MyArray.Element(1)*.

Some example programs use unexpected type parameters when creating array managers. Frequently, an actual object will be used to represent the element type to the manager instead of an indefinite instance. For example, the following code might be present to declare the manager for integer arrays:

```
var FakeInteger => IM . new Integer;
var IntArrayManager => new ArrayManager(FakeInteger.structure);
```

This is done to aid selection analysis. The reasoning behind this seemingly baroque code is provided in Section 5.5.5.3. In short, the implementation of Paragon guarantees an implementation for array objects if there is an implementation for the passed type parameter.

6.2.9. Pointers

The second type constructor provided by Paragon is used to create typed pointers which are called *References*. The declarations are shown below:

```
class RefManager(Elt: any) of AssignableManager is
begin
   class Reference of Assignable is
   begin
      procedure Value return Elt.structure;
   end;
```

```
        procedure Allocate return Reference;
        procedure Free(r: Reference);
        procedure Nil return Reference;
    end;
```

The use of pointers is very similar to arrays. One first creates a manager that defines the type of object that the references will point at, then one can create pointer variables.

Through the use of the *Allocate* and *Free* procedures, one can dynamically create and release objects. Paragon guarantees an implementation for pointers, but the implementation of the referred object matches the implementation used for the parameter to the manager. For this reason, an expression containing a definite instance is usually used, just like for arrays.

The manager for *References* also provides a special *Reference* that can be used to point at no object, namely a *Reference* returned by the procedure *Nil*.

Unlike arrays, *References* inherit *Assignable*, and so may be assigned and tested for equality.

6.2.10. Selection Facilities

The classes and procedures used for the selection facility are also declared in the *Universal_Environment* class, and are elaborated along with the rest of the predefined environment. Since these declarations were discussed Chapter 5, they will not be repeated here.

The first declarations in *Universal_Environment* are for predefined identifiers; user defined abstract data types are declared next. A typical abstract data type is discussed in the next section.

6.3. An Abstract Data Type: List

The application program in Section 6.4 uses two programmer provided abstract data types: Lists and Sets. In this section, part of the specification for lists is presented and discussed. Later in this section, an implementation for lists that uses arrays is presented and discussed. The complete text for the list abstract data type can be found in Appendix E.2.

6.3.1. A Specification for Lists

This section provides a brief specification for lists. The complete specification is not given here; only those operations actually required by the application program, *Clear*, *Length*, *GetIndex*, *AddBeforeIndex* and *Members* are given. The text for the declaration follows below (the discussion continues on page 179). In the text, there are some numbers against the right hand margin that are used in the following discussion.

```
class ListManager(TManager : AssignableManager . T : Assignable)
   of AssignableManager is
begin
   attribute procedure ManagerTime(i:instance)                    ☜1
      return im.integer is
   begin
      var TotalTime => im . new integer;
      var call => ProcCall;

      TotalTime := 0;
      let call match this ListManager in i do                     ☜6A
         if call.check Time return (im.integer) then
            TotalTime := call.Frequency *
               call.Time return (im.integer) +
               TotalTime ;
         fi;
      end let;
      return TotalTime;
   end;  ! of attribute procedure ManagerTime ;

   !----------------------------------------;

   attribute procedure Time(i:instance)                           ☜2A
      return im.integer is
   begin
      return 1;
   end;

   !----------------------------------------;

   class List of Assignable is
   begin
```

```
attribute var ListSize => 100;                              ☞3
!------------------------;
attribute procedure Space return IM.Integer is             ☞4
begin
   return ListSize * 100;
end;
!------------------------;
attribute procedure GetSize return IM.Integer is           ☞5
begin
   return ListSize;
end;
!------------------------;
attribute procedure Time(i:instance)                       ☞2B
   return im.integer is
begin
   var TotalTime => im . new integer;
   var Call => ProcCall;
```

```
            TotalTime := 0;
            ! List operations have one, two and three parameters;
            let call match any(this List, any) in i do              🖙6B
               if call.check Time return (im.integer) then
                  TotalTime := call.Frequency *
                               call.Time return (im.integer) +
                               TotalTime ;
               fi;
            end let;
            let call match any(any, this List) in i do
               if call.check Time return (im.integer) then
                  TotalTime := call.Frequency *
                               call.Time return (im.integer) +
                               TotalTime ;
               fi;
            end let;
            ! "Charge" each List object half to avoid double;
            ! counting of binary operations;
            TotalTime := TotalTime / 2;
            let call match any(this List) in i do
               if call.check Time return (im.integer) then
                  TotalTime := call.Frequency *
                               call.Time return (im.integer) +
                               TotalTime ;
               fi;
            end let;
            ! When 3 parameters, lists are only in first position;
            let call match any(this List,any,any) in i do
               if call.check Time return (im.integer) then
                  TotalTime := call.Frequency *
                               call.Time return (im.integer) +
                               TotalTime ;
               fi;
            end let;
            return TotalTime;
         end; ! of attribute procedure Time ;
      end; ! of class List ;

      !-----------------------;
      procedure AddBeforeIndex(L: List, IM. Position: Integer,
                              T. NewElt: Structure) is
      specified with begin                                          🖙7
         attribute procedure Time return IM.Integer is
         begin
            return desc (L) . GetSize return (IM.Integer) * 100;    🖙8
         end;
      end;
```

```
    !-----------------------;
    procedure Clear(L: List) is
    specified with begin
       attribute procedure Time return IM.Integer is
       begin
          return 100;
       end;
    end;

    !-----------------------;
    procedure GetIndex(L: List, IM . Position: Integer)
       return T.Structure is
    specified with begin
       attribute procedure Time return IM.Integer is
       begin
          return desc (L) . GetSize return (IM.Integer) * 100;
       end;
    end;

    !-----------------------;
    procedure Length(L: List) return IM.Integer is
    specified with begin
       attribute procedure Time return IM.Integer is
       begin
          return 100;
       end;
    end;

    !-----------------------;
    procedure Members(L: List) yield T.Structure is
    specified with begin
       attribute procedure Time return IM.Integer is
       begin
          return desc (L) . GetSize return (IM.Integer) * 100;
       end;
    end;
    !-----------------------;
end; ! of class ListManager ;
```

This specification illustrates how attributes interact with the class facility and policy procedures through the use of redundant attributes, abstract description of space requirements, analysis of object usage and default attributes for procedures.

6.3.1.1. Redundant Attributes

Notations 1, 2A and 2B refer to redundant attributes that describe time requirements of the abstract data type. The three attribute procedures, *ManagerTime*, *Time* and *Time*, are intended to be used with two different policy strategies. The first strategy does not take advantage of the manager model in programming abstract data types, and so uses the attribute *Time* for determining the amount of time required by each variable in the program, regardless of whether the variable is being used as a manager or individual. Thus both manager and individual classes must contain attributes for *Time*. In this circumstance, the time required by the manager is merely the time object creation takes. For simplicity, the value *1* is returned. The time required for an individual list is calculated by the *Time* attribute procedure in the *List* class, which contains a number of pattern matching statements which will be discussed later.

The second strategy exploits the manager model. Only those variables that are used as managers will have attributes called for describing possible implementations. For a policy designed to exploit the manager model, a second attribute procedure called *ManagerTime* is provided. This attribute understands how that particular data type can be used and so can report data on all uses of individuals in that manager.

In general, there may be many attributes describing an abstract data type that are redundant. The exact attributes to be provided depends on the strategy that the policy will use. To use Paragon effectively, policies and attributes must be coordinated.

6.3.1.2. Attributes that Abstract Representation Differences

Notations 3, 4 and 5 illustrate how attributes can interact to provide some abstract information about representation properties. These three attributes, *ListSize*, *Space* and *GetSize*, attempt to provide information about the abstract number of elements in a list and provide a measure of the space that these elements will require. The use of an attribute variable permits a variable declaration to change the attribute value as appropriate while the use of procedures allows representations to change the procedure declaration associated with the identifier to provide a more accurate analysis of the data. Thus a policy may get information about the space required by a representation without having to examine the internal details of the implementation. Further, the programmer using the abstract data type may provide necessary information, via the attribute variables, that act as parameters to the attribute procedures. Together, these declarations provide an abstract way to describe the hidden details of a representation. Naturally, if no representation is chosen, the attribute procedures in the specification class, here *List*, will be used as default values. In this example, the default is an estimate of the size required by a list representation: 100 units per element.

6.3.1.3. Gathering Usage Data

Notations 6A and 6B refer to places where attribute procedures use a pattern matching statement to gather data about an object's usage. At 6A, an environment is searched for the use of a manager as a container for procedure calls; At 6B, the environment is searched for the use of an individual as a parameter. These represent two common uses of pattern statements.

When a manager is looked for, no particular procedure call is mentioned. Instead, any procedure call that starts with the manager is found by the match. This is possible because a procedure invocation results in the creation of an object where the innermost simple object is an instance of the procedure. The outer classes in such an object are the manager (and its enclosing environment). All of the procedure calls in an *Instance* object are such objects. In this example, the object that results from elaborating the pattern expression is merely the manager with no inner simple object. During elaboration of the pattern statement, the objects for the calls are compared with the object that results from elaborating the pattern expression. The call objects are larger, because they have the innermost simple object for the call. Because the innermost simple object may be discarded when comparing two objects when the actual object (call) has more simple objects that the formal object (pattern expression), the innermost simple object for the call can be discarded during object comparison. Therefore calls within a manager will match a pattern expression that contains only the manager. In this example, all procedures declared by the manager's implementation will be examined during execution of the pattern loop. As is illustrated at 6A, the resulting pattern loop is quite simple.

In contrast, the use of pattern loops after 6B is more complex. Here, no manager is specified in the pattern to be matched. Instead, all uses of the individual as a parameter are found. Thus there may appear uses of the individual outside of the manager. For example, if this attribute procedure were present in the *Integer* class instead of the *List* class (and the pattern expression were *any(any,this Integer)* instead of *any(this List,any)*) a call of the attribute procedure would find all calls where the integer was used in a list operation, as well as in an arithmetic operation.

For this strategy to be effective, all combinations of the individual must be searched for. Thus one loop has the individual as the first parameter, another loop has the individual as the second parameter, followed by an assignment that attempts to prevent double counting across all individual Lists.[66] In some sense, the value calculated by this attribute is more accurate than the value calculated by the manager oriented strategy, but this attribute procedure is also more complicated.

6.3.1.4. Default Attributes

Notation 7 indicates a default attribute for a procedure. Since the procedure specification will be placed in the possibility tree whenever an implementation is not available for a procedure call, this default attribute will be available if no procedure implementation is available. Thus this attribute procedure may be called by the policy to provide some limited kinds of information about the procedure without having a specific implementation available.

Note that this default attribute can use some information about the specific call, and perhaps, about implementations already chosen for the containing procedure's parameters. Notation 8 illustrates how the *Time* attribute can base its calculation of the size of the first parameter. The key feature is the use of the *Desc* facility to gain access to the node in the possibility tree for the first parameter. This feature is used throughout attributes in the example abstract data types, and so represents a typical way that information about the possibility tree is gathered by attribute procedures.

6.3.2. An Implementation of Lists with Arrays

Each class that is not self implementing should have a representation class declared for it. In this section, such an implementation of lists using arrays is discussed. Like its specification, the representation is abbreviated, with procedure implementations provided for only the procedures that were specified in ancestor classes. Noteworthy parts of the representation are indicated by the notation at the right margin. (The discussion continues on page 185.)

```
class ArrayListManager(TManager:AssignableManager.T:Assignable)
    of ListManager is
begin

    var MaxArraySize => IM . new Integer;                    1
    var AM => new ArrayManager(T . structure);
```

---

[66]This guarantees that the total time counted by executing this attribute over all *List* individuals does not count the same call of a binary operation twice. Otherwise the pattern would match the call on two *Lists* twice, once when executing the attribute for the first *List* (in the first loop), once when executing the attribute for the second *List* (in the second loop).

```
class ArrayList of List is
begin

   attribute procedure Space return IM.Integer is                  ☞2
   begin
      return 1 + 2 * desc (this ArrayList)                         ☞3
                          . GetSize return (IM.Integer);
   end;

   var Elts => AM . new Array(1,MaxArraySize);
   var NumElts => IM . new Integer;

   NumElts := 0;
end;

procedure LocalCopy(L:ArrayList, R:ArrayList);                     ☞4
procedure LocalCopy(L:ArrayList, R:ArrayList) is
begin
   var i => im . new integer;

   for i in 1..MaxArraySize do
      TManager.Assign(L.Elts.[i],R.Elts.[i]);
   end for;
end;

!------------------------;
procedure AddBeforeIndex(L: ArrayList, im. Position:integer,
                         T. NewElt:structure) is
begin
   attribute procedure Time return IM.Integer is
   begin
      return 3 + desc (L) . GetSize return (IM.Integer);
   end;

   var i => IM . new Integer;

   if L.NumElts < MaxArraySize and Position >= 1 and
      Position <= (L.NumElts + 1) then
      for i in IM.ReverseSequence(Position,L.NumElts) do
         TManager.Assign(L.Elts.[i+1],L.Elts.[i]);
      end for;
      TManager.Assign(L.Elts.[Position],NewElt);                   ☞5
      L.NumElts := L.NumElts + 1;
   fi;
end;

!------------------------;
procedure Clear(L: ArrayList) is                                  ☞6
begin
   attribute procedure Time return IM.Integer is
   begin
      return 1;
   end;
```

```
      L.NumElts := 0;
   end;

   !------------------------;
   procedure GetIndex(L: ArrayList, im. Position:integer)
      return T.Structure is
   begin
      attribute procedure Time return IM.Integer is
      begin
         return 1;
      end;

      return L.Elts.[Position];
   end;

   !------------------------;
   procedure Length(L: ArrayList)
      return IM.Integer is
   begin
      attribute procedure Time return IM.Integer is
      begin
         return 1;
      end;

      return L.NumElts;
   end;

   !------------------------;
   procedure Members(L: ArrayList)
      yield T.Structure is
   begin
      attribute procedure Time return IM.Integer is
      begin
         return 2 * desc (L) . GetSize return (IM.Integer);
      end;

      var i => IM . new Integer;

      for i in IM.Sequence(1,L.NumElts) do
         yield L.Elts.[i];
         if i > L.NumElts then exitloop; fi;
      end for;
      return;
   end;

   !------------------------;
   procedure Assign(L: ArrayList, R: ArrayList) is                    7A
   begin
      attribute procedure Time return IM.Integer is
      begin
         return 1 +  desc (R) . GetSize return (IM.Integer);
      end;
```

```
      var i => im . new integer;

      L.NumElts := R.NumElts;
      for i in 1..R.NumElts do
         TManager.Assign(L.Elts.[i],R.Elts.[i]);
      end for;
   end;

   !------------------------;
   procedure Equal(L: ArrayList, R: ArrayList)                    ☜7B
      return Booleans.Bit is
   begin
      attribute procedure Time return IM.Integer is
      begin
         return 2 + 3 * desc (L) . GetSize return (IM.Integer);
      end;

      var i => IM . new Integer;

      if not (L.NumElts = R.NumElts) then return False; fi;
      for i in IM.Sequence(1,L.NumElts) do
         if not TManager.Equal(L.Elts.[i],R.Elts.[i]) then
            return False;
         fi;
      end for;
      return True;
   end;
   !------------------------;

   MaxArraySize := 100;                                          ☜8

end;
```

This implementation for lists illustrates the use of local variable and procedure declarations, and the use of initialization statements. It also demonstrates how attributes may be refined, how managers are passed as parameters, how procedure declarations specify that only certain implementation classes are required as parameters and how generalization classes are implemented.

6.3.2.1. Local Declarations and Statements

Notations 1, 4 and 8 pinpoint local declarations and initialization statements for the implementation class. The variable declarations starting at notation 1 represent shared data for the manager that are available to the procedure implementations but unavailable to the application program. These variables are created at notation 1 but only one of them is initialized by the statement at notation 8. Should this representation be selected, the statement at notation 8 would be elaborated when the variable declaration for the list manager was elaborated.

The procedure declarations at notation 4 give the specification and representation of *LocalCopy*, which is a procedure that may be used only inside of the *ArrayListManager*. None of the other procedures in the shown excerpt actually use it, but other procedures in the complete implementation do require the *LocalCopy* procedure, so the declarations were left in as an illustration of local procedures.

6.3.2.2. Refining an Attribute

Notation 2 shows where an attribute is refined. The specification class *List* contained an attribute procedure *Space* for determining the amount space required by an individual list, but that attribute procedure could not use implementation specific information. The *Space* attribute in *ArrayList* has access to the implementation of individual lists, and so may provide a better estimate. Notation 3 shows that the calculation actually depends on the size of the list associated with the individual, and so illustrates how one attribute procedure may call another. Recall that an *ArrayList* simple object must also have a *List* local instance, and since the *List* class contains a declaration for the *GetSize* attribute, the *GetSize* attribute that is to be called will certainly exist.

6.3.2.3. Use of a Manager Parameter

The reason for having the *TManager* identifier in the *ArrayListManager* parameter becomes clear when the line at notation 5 is examined. The manager that is passed in a parameter is used for manipulating the individual elements in the list. In particular, it is necessary to assign one element to another and the passed manager provides the necessary assignment procedure. Therefore it is common that a parameter will have more than one component labeled, since any object that is passed must also have its manager present for operations to be performed on individuals.

6.3.2.4. Requiring an Implementation Class as a Parameter

Notation 6 shows how a procedure implementation requires that the objects it manipulates be implemented with a certain class. Here, the *Clear* procedure will only work on *List* objects that are implemented as *ArrayLists* (or subclasses of *ArrayLists*). This restriction usually eases the process of making representation selections for procedure implementations, since all of the variables and parameters in a procedure implementation may be specified with implementation classes.

6.3.2.5. Implementing Generalization Classes

Because the *ListManager* class inherits the *AssignableManager* class, the *ListManager* class inherits the specifications for the *Assign* and *Equal* procedures as well. The *ListManager* class, acting as a specification class, does not provide implementations for any classes. But *ArrayListManager*, acting as a representation class, should provide implementations for all procedures that are specified in all of its ancestors. Therefore *ArrayListmanager* should provide implementations for the *Assign* and *Equal* procedures. As suggested, these implementation are provided, and can be found at notations 7A and 7B.

In the complete example, the declarations for the specification and implementation of lists are followed by a specification and implementation for sets, which is the other programmer-provided, abstract data type required by the example application. The classes for sets will not be discussed here. They can be found in Appendix E.4.

6.4. A Program: Sort

A small application program was copied from the literature discussing representation selection. The program reads in a collection of numbers, sorts them by successively inserting them into an ordered list (linear search of the list) and then writes out the sorted list [Low 74]. The text of the program is shown below:

```
!----------------------------------------------------;
! INSRT2 example main program                        ;
!----------------------------------------------------;

class MainProgram is
begin

   var IntSetManager => new SetManager(IM.Integer);
   var IntListManager => new ListManager(IM.Integer);        ☜1

   var UnSorted => IntSetManager . new Set
      where SetSize => 50;
   var Sorted => IntListManager . new List
      where ListSize => 50;                                  ☜2
   var Count => IM . new Integer;
   var i => IM . new Integer;
   var Obj1 => IM. new Integer;
   var Obj2 => IM. new Integer;

   ! First construct an Unsorted set;
```

```
IntSetManager.Clear(Unsorted);                                    ☜3A
IM.Read(Count);
for I in IM.Sequence(1,Count) do
   IM.Read(Obj1);
   IntSetManager.Insert(Unsorted,Obj1);
end for;

IntListManager.Clear(Sorted);                                     ☜3B

! Sort the values;

for Obj1 in IntSetManager.Members(Unsorted) do
   Count := 1;
   while Count <= IntListManager.Length(Sorted) do
      Obj2 := IntListManager.GetIndex(Sorted,Count);
      if Obj2 >= Obj1 then
         exitloop;
      else
         Count := Count + 1;
      fi;
   end loop;
   IntListManager.AddBeforeIndex(Sorted,Count,Obj1);
end for;

! Write the sorted list ;

for Obj2 in IntListManager.Members(Sorted) do
   IM.Write(Obj2);
end for;

end;
```

This application program illustrates several unconventional aspects of Paragon programs, such as the presence of manager creations, explicit manager denotation for operations and user-defined representation information. All of these features are missing in the original version of this program which was written in Sail.

6.4.1. Explicit Manager Presence

Because the manager model is explicit in Paragon, the presence of managers must also be explicit. This is illustrated at the points in the program noted 1 and 3.

Notation 1 shows where a manager is explicitly created by the programmer. In other languages, the manager exists without any special actions by the programmer. In the original version of this example, the manager was provided by the translation system in terms of assembly language code. Therefore there was no programmer control over the initialization of the local data in the manager. In Paragon, there may be concerns about the order of initialization of managers, and so the translation system cannot merely create a manager whenever an individual is declared. Instead, a programmer must explicitly provide a manager creation.

Notations 3A and 3B show other examples where the explicitness of the manager is evident. Here, the *Clear* procedure must be called within a particular manager. Because there are two *Clear* procedures, one in the set manager and one in the list manager, the prefixed manager denotes the appropriate procedure to be used. Other languages, such as Clu and Ada, attempt to solve this problem by deriving the manager implicitly by the type of the parameter. Because the use of classes to emulate the manager model is merely a programming convention in Paragon, Paragon instead requires explicit managers to be present in an expression.

6.4.2. User-Defined Representation Information

Because Paragon has a representation-selection mechanism designed into it, an application program can have some representation-selection information present. In particular, the variable at notation 2 contains an attribute association informing the selection system of the expected size of the list. Although other languages permit the programmers to add representation information to variable declarations, for example, use a packed vs unpacked representation, Paragon is different in that the kinds of programmer-provided information are determined by the programmer, not by the translation system. Because the programmer provided the *ListSize* attribute in the *List* class, the programmer may provide the selection system with information by making an attribute association with *ListSize*.

So far, the programmer has provided specifications of abstract data types, implementations of abstract data types and an application program that uses the abstract data types. All that remains for a complete program is a policy procedure for making representation selections. One possible policy procedure is considered next.

6.5. A Policy: Minimum Time and Space

The policy below illustrates features found in many different policies that were written for this thesis. The goal of the policy is to minimize the time-space product of program cost. An exhaustive analysis is performed on all possible implementations in order to find the optimal collection of representations. As usual, interesting features are marked with notations on the right margin. (The discussion continues on pages 193.)

```
!--------------------------------------------------------;
! MinimumTimeSpace
! This is the minimum time space policy.
! It is minimized over a block at a time.
!--------------------------------------------------------;

procedure CalcTS(i:Instance) return im. integer;                 ☜1
procedure CalcTS(i:Instance) return im. integer is
begin
    var TempTime => im . new integer;
    var TempSpace => im . new integer;
    var j => im . new integer;

    TempTime := 0;
    TempSpace := 0;
    ! For each call, if there is a Time attribute, then
      accumulate time*frequency product;
    for j in 1..i.NumP do                                        ☜2A
       if i.ProcCalls.[j]. check time return (im.integer) then☜3A
          TempTime := TempTime +
             (i.ProcCalls.[j] . time return (im.integer))*       ☜3B
             (i.ProcCalls.[j].Frequency);
       fi;
    end for;
    for j in 1..i.NumV do                                        ☜2B
       if i.VarDecls.[j]. check Space return (im.integer) then
          TempSpace := TempSpace +
             i.VarDecls.[j].Space return (im.integer);
       fi;
    end for;
    return TempTime * TempSpace;
end; ! of CalcTS ;

!--------------------------------------------------------;

procedure policy(i:instance);
procedure policy(i:instance) is                                  ☜4
begin
    var PreviousMin => im . new integer;
    var vartemp => im . new integer;
    var ind => im . new integer;
```

```
!------------------------------------------;
procedure DoEval return booleans.bit;
procedure DoEval return booleans.bit is
begin
    var ts => im . new integer;

    ! Try to select procedure implementations and see if a
    ! feasible selection is possible.;
    if i.BindProcs then
        ! Yes, have selection, so get s-t product;
        ts := CalcTS(i);
    else
        ! No feasible proc. impl. selection, so reject choices.;
        return false;
    fi;
    ! Got new s-t value, but is it smaller than previous?;
    if ts < PreviousMin then
        ! Yes, smaller, so save this better value and note
        ! that this implementation should be saved.;
        PreviousMin := ts;
        return True;
    else
        ! Not smaller, punt this set of choices.;
        return False;
    fi;
end; ! of DoEval ;

!------------------------------------------;
! TryAllImpls procedure first lets the class be
! self-implementing and tries all implementation
! combinations of all other variable
! declarations beyond this one. (Current declaration is the
! jth variable declaration in the class or procedure which is
! the doppelganger of i.) After it tries
! self-implementing, TryAllImpls tries every implementation
! for its variable declaration.
! After each implementation selection for itself, all other
! possible implementations for variable declarations beyond
! the jth declaration are considered.
!
! The test in the first statement stops the recursion when
! no more variable declarations are available in the
! block that i denotes. Thus the evaluation function
! is applied (and the current set of implementations are
! noted as being better than what had been seen before).
!
! As an optimization, the TryAllImpls procedure rejects
! implementations that are not locally feasible instead of
! later discovering that they globally infeasible. ;
```

```
procedure TryAllImpls(i:Instance, IM . j: Integer)            ⟵6
   return Booleans.Bit;
procedure TryAllImpls(i:Instance, IM . j: Integer)
   return Booleans.Bit is
begin
   var NextVar => im .new integer;
   var temp => CDRM . new reference;
   var k => im . new integer;
   var FoundBetter => Booleans . new bit;

   ! Assume you can't find anything better.;
   Booleans.Assign(FoundBetter,False);
   ! All variables in i selected?;
   if j > i.NumV then
      ! Yes, so see if a better choice.;
      return DoEval;
   else
      ! No, more variable to selection in i.
      ! We are up to jth variable declaration.;
      NextVar := j + 1;
      ! Leave current var decl alone (self-implementing) and
      ! try all other variable declarations.;
      Booleans.Assign(FoundBetter,TryAllImpls(i,NextVar));
      ! See if worked. If so, save the implementation;
      if FoundBetter then
         i.VarDecls.[j].ImplSet := 0;
      fi;
      ! But keep looking for something better.;
      ! Get the specification class for the jth declaration.;
      CDRM.Assign(temp,i.VarDecls.[j].GetSpec);
      ! Try all children of the specification.;
      for k in 1..temp.↑.NumC do
         ! Is this child locally feasible?;
         if i.VarDecls.[j]
               .LocallyFeasible(temp.↑.Children.[k]) then
            ! Yes, so set current var decl to this child.;
            i.VarDecls.[j].SetImpl(temp.↑.Children.[k]);
            ! And try rest of the var decls in this block.;
            if TryAllImpls(i,NextVar) then
               ! If found a better set of impl, save it.;
               i.VarDecls.[j].ImplSet := k;
               Booleans.Assign(FoundBetter,True);
            fi;
         fi;
      end for;
   fi;
   ! Let previous callers know if a better impl. was found;
   return FoundBetter;
end; ! of TryAllImpls ;
```

```
!----------------------------------------;
PreviousMin := 999999999;                                    ☞7
! Try all implementations for all variables in i,
! starting with variable 1. Ignore whether anything
! was feasible or not.;
if TryAllImpls(i,1) then null; fi;                           ☞8A
! For each var, use the best impl that was found.
! (whole set of impls, not individually the best.);
for ind in 1..i.NumV do                                      ☞8B
    vartemp := i.VarDecls.[ind].ImplSet;
    ! See if a child or the spec was found.;
    if vartemp > 0 then
        ! Yes, use that child number (get the specification
        ! class, then get the vartempth child and assign that
        ! child as the implementation for the indth variable.;
        i.VarDecls.[ind].SetImpl(
                i.VarDecls.[ind].GetSpec.↑.Children.[vartemp]);
    fi;
end for;
! Have made the variable selections, selection the
! procedure implementations. (Assume that it is feasible.);
if i.BindProcs then null; fi;                                ☞8C
! All done with this block, now do the same for the internal
! variables in the variable in this block.
for ind in 1..i.NumV do                                      ☞8D
    Policy(i.VarDecls.[ind]);
end for;
! Now do the same for the internal
! variables in the procedure calls in this block.
for ind in 1..i.NumP do                                      ☞8E
    if not i.ProcCalls.[ind].AlreadySeen then
        Policy(i.ProcCalls.[ind]);
    fi;
end for;

end;
```

The example shows several features that are found in many procedures. Some of these features are local to a couple of statements, while some represent a basic design of the policy. Before examining these local and global features of the policy, a brief overview of the policy's algorithm is provided.

6.5.1. Policy Algorithm

The actual policy procedure declaration starts at notation 4, though the executable part of the policy begins with notation 7. The notations 8A through 8E labels each of the basic pieces of the algorithm.

Notation 8A refers to the statement that calls a procedure which tries every possible implementation for each variable in the block passed to the policy procedure. When the *TryAllImpls* procedure returns, the *ImplSet* variable contains the index of the implementation that provided the minimum time-space product for that block. Thus the policy assumes that only one level of implementations will be provided, since this index is used to pick a child class of the specification class. A value of 0 indicates that no feasible child was found, thus the selected specification should remain untouched.

Notation 8B refers to a loop where all of the selected implementations are actually assigned to the variables in the block. The call of *BindProcs* in the statement following the loop, noted with 8C, then causes the block to be elaborated with implementations. This forces all the appropriate procedure implementations to be selected for the procedure calls in the block.

Once the current block is processed, each object chosen for a variable and each procedure implementation has the policy performed on it for selection of representations for local variables. The loops noted by 8D and 8E perform the policy on the variables and procedure calls respectively.

The way that this algorithm is implemented illustrates some general strategies about policy design. These are considered next.

6.5.2. Global Properties

Like other procedures, policy procedures use various kinds of abstraction to make them easier to write and understand. Some special abstractions that relate to policy procedures are the separation of the evaluation function, the use of local procedures and the block-at-a-time analysis. Each of these is considered in turn.

6.5.2.1. Separate Evaluation Functions

This policy bases its selection of representations on calculations of the space and time product of the block. However, it may be useful to minimize (or maximize) some other evaluation function, for example, just time or just space. Thus one wants the policy procedure to be insensitive to the exact evaluation function.

In the example, the evaluation function is literally removed from the main body of the policy. The *CalcTS* procedure, noted 1, takes a block and calculates a value for that block. This procedure could be changed to return any measure that is desirable and the rest of the system will minimize that value. Thus it is easy to separate the measure used for making selection decisions. Paragon allows the policy to use procedures not declared in it, such as *CalcTS*, and in fact, *CalcTS* was raised to the level of a separate procedure because it is used in several policies. However, policies may also contain local procedures, and local procedures are also a widely used feature.

6.5.2.2. Use of Local Procedures

Policies may contain local procedures and this policy declares two such procedures, *DoEval* and *TryAllImpls*, as noted at 5 and 6 respectively. Each performs a limited function, such as checking for a feasible minimum value and trying all implementations. Many different policies contain local procedures, and thus resemble any moderately sized procedure in any programming language.

6.5.2.3. Block-at-a-Time Analysis

Another common strategy illustrated by this policy is the block-at-a-time analysis. When faced with a possibly changing possibility tree, it is difficult to determine the order in which blocks should be examined. The approach used throughout the example policies is to make selections for the variable declarations in application program first, and then for the variables inside of classes and procedure calls in the application program. This resembles a depth-first search of the possibility tree.

6.5.3. Local Properties

There are several groups of statements that recur in policies, including the example above. These statements are used to make selection within a block, to use attributes and to try all implementations. Each of these groups of statements is considered.

6.5.3.1. Selections within a Block

Whatever the evaluation function used for choosing a selection, the process of making a selection usually requires performing that evaluation over all of the variables and procedure calls in a block. The *for* statements noted at 2A and 2B are frequently found as a way to gather information about variable and procedure calls. Each iterates over their respective arrays in the *Instance* object passed to the containing procedure.

6.5.3.2. Using Attributes

The policy procedure uses attributes to gather information about a program. However, Paragon does not require any given attribute to be present in any given instance. Thus a policy must check to see if an attribute exists before it is called. The frequent, tandem operations of checking and then using an attribute are noted at 3A and 3B.

6.5.3.3. Trying all Implementations

Another common, local phenomenon in policy procedures is the trial of all implementations for all variables. Although both implementations and variable declarations may be stepped through, a coroutine structure is needed for trying each representation for each variable in turn and not a simple *for* loop. One alternative is provided by recursion, and this is the structure used in the *TryAllImpls* procedure. For each possible implementation of a variable declaration, all the following variable declarations have all of their implementations tried. Thus every combination of implementations is covered. A similar algorithm is found in several example policies.

Having all of the pieces for Paragon to process a program, the programmer's application can be analyzed by the translator. The results of running the prototype system on this example are presented in the next section.

6.6. Transformed Program

One of the results of the prototype translation system is a listing of all of the decisions made by the selection system. In this section, some of these listings produced by the prototype are presented.

There are two kinds of listing that are provided: an annotated, pretty-printed[67] version of the source, and a listing of objects and their representations. Each kind of listing will be illustrated and described. The complete output of the translation system from its processing of the example program is provided in Appendix G.

---

[67]Perhaps formatted is a better term, since the annotated programs are *not* pretty.

6.6.1. Annotated Program

The first output of the translator is an annotated, pretty-printed program that can be used for later interpretation of objects.[68] The first excerpt, for part of the *ListManager* specification, is shown below:

```
class listmanager(tmanager : assignablemanager.t : assignable)
   of assignablemanager is
begin
   class list of assignable is
   begin
      attribute var listsize =>
         im.literal(special_make_literal(100));              ☜1
   end;

   procedure addbeforeindex#1653: (1 : list,
                                   im.position : integer,
                                   t.newelt : structure) ;
   procedure clear#1677: (1 : list) ;
   procedure getindex#1712: (1 : list,im.position : integer)
      return t.structure ;
   procedure length#1722: (1 : list) return im.integer ;     ☜2
   procedure members#1751: (1 : list) yield t.structure ;
end;
```

For clarity, most of the declarations have been removed.

There are two details worth noting about the excerpt above. First, each procedure identifier is transformed into a unique identifier. A unique identifier is needed since each procedure specification and implementation is declared with the same identifier. This unique identifier allows later reference to a procedure when procedure implementations are selected. To refer to the procedure specification of *Length*, other parts of the listing will refer to *length # 1722:* (see notation 2).

The second detail worth noting is the presence of a procedure *special_make_literal* (notation 1). This procedure is used to handle literals. Recall that Paragon defines a literal to be a predefined function that returns an appropriate word object. In the current implementation, this result is accomplished by a built-in function *Special_Make_Literal* that takes an integer string and returns an appropriate word object. This procedure is not available to the programmer; it is merely the way that the prototype implements all of the literal functions. But since *Special_Make_Literal* looks like any other function, the system will select a (predefined) implementation for it and lists a call to the function whenever a literal is used.

---

[68] The formatting shown in the thesis is not exactly the same as produced by the prototype translator. The formatting was changed to fit on smaller and fewer pages.

An excerpt of the implementation for *ListManager* is shown below:

```
class arraylistmanager(tmanager:assignablemanager.
                       t:assignable)
   of listmanager is
begin
   var maxarraysize => im.new integer;
   var am => new arraymanager(t.structure);

   class arraylist of list is
   begin
      var elts =>
            am.new array(im.literal#2(special_make_literal#1(1)),
                         maxarraysize);
      var numelts => im.new integer;
      im.assign#5(numelts,
                  im.literal#4(special_make_literal#3(0)));
   end;
```

```
!----------------------------------------------------;
! Source version of addbeforeindex is on page 183.;
!----------------------------------------------------;
procedure addbeforeindex#3173: (1 : arraylist,
                                im.position : integer,
                                t.newelt : structure) is
begin
    var i => im.new integer;
    if booleans.logicaland#10(                                    ☞1
        booleans.logicaland#5(
            im.lessthan#1(1.numelts,maxarraysize),
            im.greaterthanequal#4(position,
                im.literal#3(
                    special_make_literal#2(1)))),
            im.lessthanequal#9(position,
                im.plus#8(1.numelts,
                    im.literal#7(
                        special_make_literal#6(1))))) then
    for i in im.reversesequence#11(position,
                                    1.numelts) do
        tmanager.assign#17(
            1.elts.element#15(
                im.plus#14(i,
                    im.literal#13(
                        special_make_literal#12(1)))),
            1.elts.element#16(i));
    end for;
    tmanager.assign#19(1.elts.element#18(position),
                        newelt);
    im.assign#23(1.numelts,
            im.plus#22(1.numelts,
                        im.literal#21(
                            special_make_literal#20(
                                1))));
    fi;
end;

im.assign#3(maxarraysize,                                          ☞2
        im.literal#2(special_make_literal#1(100)));
end;
```

Two more details become evident from the excerpt above. First, all of syntactic sugar is missing (notation 1). For comparison, the reader may want to examine the implementation given in Section 6.3.2 on page 182. Second, every procedure call in a class and procedure is numbered. For example, the class *ArrayListManager* has three calls at the very end of the fragment above: *special_make_literal # 1*, *literal # 2* and *assign # 3* (notation 2). The numbers serve to identify the calls when an object's representation is listed, since different calls of the same specified procedure will have different numbers appended to them. The numbers also reflect the order of elaboration of the procedure calls in the class or procedure.

The final excerpt of the pretty-printed source is the application program, shown below. Note that the procedure calls in attribute associations are not numbered. This is because no selection is necessary for them and they do not appear in the program after selection is performed. The pretty printer includes them to aid in recalling the original source.

```
class mainprogram is
begin
   var intsetmanager => new setmanager(im.integer);
   var intlistmanager => new listmanager(im.integer);
   var unsorted => intsetmanager.new set
      where setsize => im.literal(special_make_literal(100));
   var sorted => intlistmanager.new list
      where listsize => im.literal(special_make_literal(100));
   var count => im.new integer;
   var i => im.new integer;
   var obj1 => im.new integer;
      var obj2 => im.new integer;

   intsetmanager.clear#1(unsorted);
   im.read#2(count);
   for i in im.sequence#5(im.literal#4(
                            special_make_literal#3(1)),
                          count) do
      im.read#6(obj1);
      intsetmanager.insert#7(unsorted,obj1);
   end for;

   intlistmanager.clear#8(sorted);
   for obj1 in intsetmanager.members#9(unsorted) do
      im.assign#12(count,
                     im.literal#11(special_make_literal#10(1)));
      while im.lessthanequal#14(count,
                                   intlistmanager.length#13(
                                   sorted)) do
         im.assign#16(obj2,
                        intlistmanager.getindex#15(sorted,
                                                     count));
         if im.greaterthanequal#17(obj2,obj1) then
            exitloop;
         else
            im.assign#21(count,
                           im.plus#20(count,
                                        im.literal#19(
                                        special_make_literal#18(
                                        1))));
         fi;
      end loop;
      intlistmanager.addbeforeindex#22(sorted,count,obj1);
   end for;
   for obj2 in intlistmanager.members#23(sorted) do
      im.write#24(obj2);
   end for;
end;
```

6.6.2. Object Listings

In addition to the an annotated source, the translation system gives the results of the policy procedure. For each simple object and procedure call, a listing of the representations of all variables and procedure calls in the simple object or procedure call is produced. The simple object that represents the application program is shown below:

```
instance x12384:. object instance of mainprogram.
   local instance x12385: of mainprogram.
   1 var intsetmanager => arraysetmanager   (x12393:)
   2 var intlistmanager => arraylistmanager   (x12404:)
   3 var unsorted => arrayset   (x12411:)
   4 var sorted => arraylist   (x12477:)
   5 var count => integer   (x12543:)
   6 var i => integer   (x12550:)
   7 var obj1 => integer   (x12557:)
   8 var obj2 => integer   (x12564:)
   1 proc clear => clear#2312: of arraysetmanager   (x12571:)
   2 proc read => read#13: of transputmanager   (x12618:)
   3 proc special_make_literal => special_make_literal#746:
                                  of universal_environment (x12623:)
   4 proc literal => literal#621: of discretemanager (x12630:)
   5 proc sequence => sequence#562: of discretemanager (x12643:)
   6 proc read => read#13: of transputmanager   (x12680:)
   7 proc insert => insert#2176: of arraysetmagager   (x12684:)
   8 proc clear => clear#3466: of arraylistmanager   (x12738:)
   9 proc members => members#2707: of arraysetmanager   (x12785:)
   10 proc special_make_literal => special_make_literal#746:
                                  of universal_environment (x12840:)
   11 proc literal => literal#621: of discretemanager   (x12847:)
   12 proc assign => assign#50: of assignablemanager   (x12860:)
   13 proc length => length#3526: of arraylistmanager   (x12880:)
   14 proc lessthanequal => lessthanequal#324:
                                  of orderedmanager   (x12934:)
   15 proc getindex => getindex#3511:
                                  of arraylistmanager (x12959:)
   16 proc assign => assign#50: of assignablemanager   (x13020:)
   17 proc greaterthanequal => greaterthanequal#351:
                                  of orderedmanager   (x13040:)
   18 proc special_make_literal => special_make_literal#746:
                                  of universal_environment (x13066:)
   19 proc literal => literal#621: of discretemanager   (x13073:)
   20 proc plus => plus#424: of discretemanager   (x13086:)
   21 proc assign => assign#50: of assignablemanager   (x13123:)
   22 proc addbeforeindex => addbeforeindex#3173:
                                  of arraylistmanager   (x13143:)
   23 proc members => members#3747: of arraylistmanager (x13204:)
   24 proc write => write#17: of transputmanager   (x13258:)
```

Each object has associated a unique identifier. For the main program, it is *x12384:*. The simple object for *mainprogram* has only one local instance, since the application program has no parents. As indicated, the main program has eight variables and 24 procedure calls. For each, the listing provides the name of the specification, the name of the implementation, the location of the implementation and the unique identifier of the simple object associated with the implementation. For example, the second variable is *intlistmanager* and is implemented as an *arraylistmanager*. The definite simple object that is associated with the creation component in the variable declaration can be found in the simple object labeled *x12404:*, which is shown below:

```
instance x12404:. object instance of arraylistmanager.
   local instance x12409: of assignablemanager.
   local instance x12410: of listmanager.
   local instance x17880: of arraylistmanager.
   1 var maxarraysize => integer   (x17881:)
   2 var am => arraymanager   (x17895:)
   1 proc special_make_literal => special_make_literal#746:
                                  of universal_environment (x17899:)
   2 proc literal => literal#621: of discretemanager   (x17906:)
   3 proc assign => assign#50: of assignablemanager   (x17919:)
```

Unlike the application program, the *arraylistmanager* has two ancestors, and so a simple object for an *Arraylistmanager* object has three local instances: *assignablemanager*, *listmanager* and *arraylistmanager*. As the first two local instances contain no variable declarations or procedure calls, there is no further information beyond the line listing the local instance. However, the local instance for the *arraylistmanager* class has two variables and three procedure calls, all of which are shown above.

A procedure call has a similar format, except there are no explicit local instances. The listing below gives the selection details for the call of *addbeforeindex* in the application program (the 22nd call). Note that implementation *addbeforeindex #3173:* was selected. If no implementation had been available, the call would have been associated with its specification, here *addbeforeindex # 1653:*.

```
instance x13143:. procedure call of addbeforeindex#3173:
                                  of arraylistmanager.
 1 var i => integer    (x20438:)
 1 proc lessthan => lessthan#252: of orderedmanager    (x20445:)
 2 proc special_make_literal => special_make_literal#746:
                               of universal_environment (x20457:)
 3 proc literal => literal#621: of discretemanager    (x20464:)
 4 proc greaterthanequal => greaterthanequal#351:
                               of orderedmanager    (x20477:)
 5 proc logicaland => logicaland#133: of bitmanager    (x20488:)
 6 proc special_make_literal => special_make_literal#746:
                               of universal_environment (x20500:)
 7 proc literal => literal#621: of discretemanager    (x20507:)
 8 proc plus => plus#424: of discretemanager    (x20520:)
 9 proc lessthanequal => lessthanequal#324:
                               of orderedmanager    (x20543:)
10 proc logicaland => logicaland#133: of bitmanager (x20554:)
11 proc reversesequence => reversesequence#607:
                               of discretemanager    (x20565:)
12 proc special_make_literal => special_make_literal#746:
                               of universal_environment (x20589:)
13 proc literal => literal#621: of discretemanager    (x20596:)
14 proc plus => plus#424: of discretemanager    (x20609:)
15 proc element => element#676: of array    (x20632:)
16 proc element => element#676: of array    (x20648:)
17 proc assign => assign#50: of assignablemanager    (x20664:)
18 proc element => element#676: of array    (x20670:)
19 proc assign => assign#50: of assignablemanager    (x20686:)
20 proc special_make_literal => special_make_literal#746:
                               of universal_environment (x20693:)
21 proc literal => literal#621: of discretemanager    (x20700:)
22 proc plus => plus#424: of discretemanager    (x20713:)
23 proc assign => assign#50: of assignablemanager    (x20736:)
```

In these examples, only predefined procedures were used in the procedure implementations for lists, so the possibility tree is not very deep, and all of the procedure calls of the same procedure implementation look identical. However, Paragon permits one to write a procedure implementation that uses only abstract properties of an object and further allows multiple calls of that procedure with different implementations of parameters. This results in a more interesting possibility tree and is considered next.

6.7. General Procedures

In this example, a program uses the set intersection operation of the abstract data type *Set* in its calculations. Two implementations of sets are provided and are allowed to interact in the intersection procedure. To provide a feasible implementation of the program, a general implementation for the intersection procedure is provided. This procedure implementation uses only abstract operations of its parameters. However, to limit the size of the example, only the barest outline of a program is presented below.

A pretty-printed version of the specification for *sets* is shown below. In all of the following declarations, the manager declaration is suppressed. Only four operations are provided, *Members, IsElement, Insert* and *Intersection*.

```
class set is begin end;

procedure members#1771: (set) yield im.integer ;
procedure iselement#2004: (set,im.integer) return booleans.bit ;
procedure insert#2013: (set,im.integer) ;
procedure intersection#2024: (set,set) return set ;
```

Two implementations for *sets* are provided, called *Set1* and *Set2*. The implementations do not perform any processing; they consist of empty procedure implementations merely as a way to illustrate the selection system.

```
class set1 of set is begin end;

procedure members#2115: (set1) yield im.integer is begin end;
procedure iselement#2130: (set1,im.integer) return booleans.bit
    is begin end;
procedure insert#2137: (set1,im.integer) is begin end;
```

Like the first implementation, the second implementation is missing the *Intersection* procedure.

```
class set2 of set is begin end;

procedure members#2152: (set2) yield im.integer is begin end;
procedure iselement#2165: (set2,im.integer) return booleans.bit
    is begin end;
procedure insert#2174: (set2,im.integer) is begin end;
```

The interesting aspect of this example is the general *Intersection* procedure. Its implementation is shown below:

```
procedure intersection#2102: (l : set,r : set)
   return l.structure is
begin
   var temp => new l;
   var e => im.new integer;

   for e in members#1(r) do
      if iselement#2(l,e) then
         insert#3(temp,e);
      fi;
   end for;
   return temp;
end;
```

The application program contains two sets, and those sets interact in two calls to the *Intersection* procedure, as shown below:[69]

```
class mainprogram is
begin
   var smanager => new setmanager;
   var sv1 => smanager.new set;
   var sv2 => smanager.new set;
   var i => im.new integer;

   if smanager.iselement#2
               (smanager.intersection#1(sv1,sv2),i) then
      null;
   elseif
      smanager.iselement#4
               (smanager.intersection#3(sv2,sv1),i) then
      null;
   fi;
end;
```

A policy is used that forces the first variable, *sv1*, to use representation *set1* and the second variable, *sv2*, to use representation *set2*. After checking for feasibility, the following selections were made:

---

[69]The two calls of *intersection* would normally return the same set. Both calls are included to demonstrate the selection process.

```
instance x2593:. object instance of mainprogram.
   local instance x2594: of mainprogram.
   1 var smanager => setimplmanager (x2595:)
   2 var sv1 => set1   (x2597:)
   3 var sv2 => set2   (x2599:)
   4 var i => integer  (x2601:)
   1 proc intersection =>
               intersection#2102: of setimplmanager   (x2856:)
   2 proc iselement => iselement#2130: of setimplmanager (x2864:)
   3 proc intersection =>
               intersection#2102: of setimplmanager   (x2878:)
   4 proc iselement => iselement#2165: of setimplmanager (x2886:)
```

As expected, the two calls of the *intersection* procedure use the general implementation *intersection #2102:*. However, two different sets of parameters are used, so the two procedure calls be dissimilar. As shown below, this is exactly what happens.

The first call had implementations *Set1* for the left parameter and *Set2* for the right parameter. The resulting selections for the local variables and procedure calls within *intersection #2102* for first call of *intersection* (call *1* in the *mainprogram*, x2856:) are shown below:

```
instance x2856:. procedure call of intersection#2102:
                                  of setimplmanager.
   1 var temp => set1   (x7354:)
   2 var e => integer   (x7357:)
   1 proc members => members#2152: of setimplmanager   (x7364:)
   2 proc iselement => iselement#2130: of setimplmanager (x7375:)
   3 proc insert => insert#2137: of setimplmanager   (x7389:)
```

The variable *temp* should have the same implementation as the left parameter, and indeed it is implemented as *Set1*. As the first call, *members*, uses the right parameter, only the implementation *members #2152:* is feasible, and it is chosen. The calls of *iselement* and *insert* use the left parameter, and so the selected implementations are *iselement #2130:* and *insert #2137:* respectively. Finally, since the returned object from the call of *intersection* is declared to have the same structure as the left parameter, one would expect that the call of the *iselement* procedure on the return object to use the same implementation as for the *iselement* procedure in the call of *intersection*. Examining the second call in the application program shows that implementation *iselement #2130:* is selected, which is the same implementation used in the *intersection* call above.

As the second call of *intersection* (which corresponds to call *3* in the *mainprogram*) has the parameters reversed, one would expect the opposite implementation choices being made for the procedure calls within *intersection #2102*. The second call of *intersection* in the application program is shown, and matches these expectations:

```
instance x2878:. procedure call of intersection#2102
                             of setimplmanager.
1 var temp => set2    (x7432:)
2 var e => integer    (x7435:)
1 proc members => members#2115: of setimplmanager   (x7442:)
2 proc iselement => iselement#2165: of setimplmanager (x7453:)
3 proc insert => insert#2174: of setimplmanager   (x7467:)
```

As this example illustrates, the Paragon design permits the flexibility of using multiple representations for variables while retaining the efficiency of statically determined procedure implementations.

6.8. Recursive Procedures

Another more complicated possibility tree occurs when a program contains recursion. As mentioned in Section 5.5.5.2, the possibility tree would normally be infinite in the presence of recursive procedures. However, Paragon contains a rule that controls the elaboration of procedure calls with implementations, which in turn effectively limits the size of the possibility tree. In this section, the results of processing a program with recursion are illustrated.

6.8.1. Application Program

This recursive application program defines the well-known factorial function. The source for the program, followed by the annotated version, is shown below:

```
class mainprogram is
begin
   procedure Factorial(IM. N: Integer) return IM.Integer;
   procedure Factorial(IM. N: Integer) return IM.Integer is
   begin
      if N <= 0 then
         return 0;
      else
         return N * Factorial(N-1);
      fi;
   end;

   IM.Write(Factorial(3));
end;

!----------------------------------------;
```

```
class mainprogram is
begin
    procedure factorial#1474: (im.n : integer)
    return im.integer ;

    procedure factorial#1537: (im.n : integer)
    return im.integer is
    begin
      if im.lessthanequal#3(n,
            im.literal#2(special_make_literal#1(0))) then
         return im.literal#5(special_make_literal#4(0));
      else
         return im.times#10(n,
                    factorial#9(im.minus#8(n,
                              im.literal#7(
                                  special_make_literal#6(1))))));
      fi;
    end;

    im.write#4(factorial#3(
              im.literal#2(special_make_literal#1(3))));
end;
```

6.8.2. Object Listings

The application program above was found to be feasible when it was elaborated with implementations. Three object listings from the resulting translator output are produced below, one for the main program, one for the call of *factorial* in *mainprogram*, and one for the call of *factorial* in the *factorial* program.

The listing for *mainprogram*, shown below, contains no surprises. The one implementation for *factorial*, that is, *factorial # 1537:*, is chosen.

```
instance x1462:. object instance of mainprogram.
    local instance x1463: of mainprogram.
    1 proc special_make_literal => special_make_literal#1137:
                        of universal_environment (x1684:)
    2 proc literal => literal#646: of discretemanager (x1691:)
    3 proc factorial => factorial#1537: of mainprogram (x1704:)
    4 proc write => write#17: of transputmanager (x1720:)
```

The call of *factorial* in the main program is shown below in the listing for object *x1704:*. Note that this call of *factorial* takes place inside of the *mainprogram*. However, the call in the *factorial* procedure, that is, call number 9 below, takes place in the nested environment of the a factorial procedure inside of the main program. As noted below, the corresponding object for this call is *x4949:*.

```
instance x1704: procedure call of factorial#1537: of mainprogram.
 1 proc special_make_literal => special_make_literal#1137:
                       of universal_environment (x4853:)
 2 proc literal => literal#646: of discretemanager (x4860:)
 3 proc lessthanequal => lessthanequal#324:
                       of orderedmanager (x4873:)
 4 proc special_make_literal => special_make_literal#1137:
                       of universal_environment (x4885:)
 5 proc literal => literal#646: of discretemanager  (x4892:)
 6 proc special_make_literal => special_make_literal#1137:
                       of universal_environment (x4906:)
 7 proc literal => literal#646: of discretemanager  (x4913:)
 8 proc minus => minus#451: of discretemanager  (x4926:)
 9 proc factorial => factorial#1537: of mainprogram  (x4949:)
10 proc times => times#506: of discretemanager  (x4965:)
```

Object x4949: is shown below. Like the listing above, it contains a call of the *factorial* procedure. However, this call takes places inside of a factorial procedure inside of the main program. Hence, this call is *similar* to the call made in object x1704:. Examination of the object associated with the 9th call in object x4949: reveals that the call refers to itself. Thus the same implementation decisions made for the call that originally generated object x4949: should be repeated for the call inside of x4949:. Because the procedure call is similar, no further elaboration of the call with implementations is necessary. Thus there are no more instances of *factorial* in the listing.

```
instance x4949: procedure call of factorial#1537: of mainprogram.
 1 proc special_make_literal => special_make_literal#1137:
                       of universal_environment (x5085:)
 2 proc literal => literal#646: of discretemanager  (x5092:)
 3 proc lessthanequal => lessthanequal#324:
                       of orderedmanager  (x5105:)
 4 proc special_make_literal => special_make_literal#1137:
                       of universal_environment (x5117:)
 5 proc literal => literal#646: of discretemanager  (x5124:)
 6 proc special_make_literal => special_make_literal#1137:
                       of universal_environment (x5138:)
 7 proc literal => literal#646: of discretemanager  (x5145:)
 8 proc minus => minus#451: of discretemanager  (x5158:)
 9 proc factorial => factorial#1537: of mainprogram  (x4949:)
10 proc times => times#506: of discretemanager  (x5197:)
```

The ability to terminate a possibility tree is necessary for a complete analysis of all possible representations in every procedure call. As this example illustrates, termination should come quite quickly as a recursive call is usually "similar" to its previous invocation.

6.9. Some Alternative Policies

The policy in Section 6.5 represents a straightforward implementation of one common criterion for making representation selections. Other criteria and algorithms for selecting representations have been published in the literature. In this section, several of the these other algorithms are presented as a demonstration of how policies can be written in Paragon.[70]

6.9.1. Dynamic Programming

An algorithm developed by Raul Ramirez [Ramirez 80] uses a dynamic-programming algorithm for making representation choices. This section provides a policy that implements his published algorithm.

The policy below actually has three parts. The first part, noted 1, calculates space and time matrices for use by the dynamic-programming algorithm. The published algorithm assumes that tables of spaces and times for the various representations are available for use by the dynamic-programming algorithm. That is not necessarily true in Paragon, so the first part of the policy makes an approximation of the time and space requirements for different representations. No specific evaluation function is provided in the published algorithm, so a space-time product is used.

The second part of the policy, noted 2, provides the initial conditions for the dynamic-programming algorithm. The third part, noted 3, performs the analysis using the recurrence equations in the algorithm. Finally, the fourth part, noted 4, takes the results of the dynamic-programming algorithm and makes the selected choices.

```
procedure policy(i:Instance) is
begin

procedure Ramirez(im. MaxSpace:integer, im. MaxTime:integer,
      im. MaxImpls: integer);
procedure Ramirez(im. MaxSpace:integer, im. MaxTime:integer,
      im. MaxImpls: integer) is
begin
```

---

[70] As a very cursory test to see if the policies were well specified, they were elaborated as main programs and later used to make selections for a program with one variable that had one possible implementation.

```
var CurSpace => im . new Integer;
var CurTime => im . new Integer;
var Infinity => im . new Integer;
var MinCost => im . new Integer;
var MinImpl => im . new Integer;
var NewSpace => im . new Integer;
var Impl => im . new Integer;
var V => im . new Integer;

var AM => new ArrayManager(im.integer);
var AM2 => new ArrayManager( AM.Array(0,MaxTime) );
var AM3 => new ArrayManager( AM2.Array(0,MaxSpace) );
var f => AM3.new Array(1,MaxImpls);
var ImplMatrix => AM3.new Array(1,MaxImpls);

var AM4 => new ArrayManager( AM.Array(0,MaxImpls) );
var S => AM4 . new Array(1,i.NumV);
var T => AM4 . new Array(1,i.NumV);
var Cost => AM4 . new Array(1,i.NumV);

! First, create the matrices for the algorithm to use:
! Space (S), Time (T), and Cost (nothing specified in thesis,
! use S*T as an example) ;

for V in 1..i.NumV do                                         ☞1
   for Impl in 1..i.VarDecls.[V].GetSpec.↑.NumC do
      i.VarDecls.[V].SetImpl(i.VarDecls.[V].GetSpec
                                        .↑.Children.[Impl]);
      if i.BindProcs then fi;
      S.[V].[Impl] := i.VarDecls.[V]. Space return (im.integer);
      T.[V].[Impl] := i.VarDecls.[V]. Time return (im.integer);
      Cost.[V].[Impl] := S.[V].[Impl] * T.[V].[Impl];
      i.VarDecls.[V].SetImpl(i.VarDecls.[V].GetSpec);
   end for;
end for;

! Ramirez's Dynamic Programming Algorithm for
! Data Structure Selection ;

! Initialize the Matrix ;
```

```
for CurSpace in 0..MaxSpace do                                        ☜2
   for CurTime in 0..MaxTime do
      MinCost := Infinity;
      MinImpl := 1;
      for Impl in 1..i.VarDecls.[i.NumV].GetSpec.↑.NumC do
         if S.[i.NumV].[Impl] <= CurSpace and
            T.[i.NumV].[Impl] <= CurTime and
            Cost.[i.NumV].[Impl] < MinCost then
            MinCost := Cost.[i.NumV].[Impl];
            MinImpl := Impl;
         fi;
      end for;
      f.[i.NumV].[CurSpace].[CurTime] := MinCost;
      Imp.Matrix.[i.NumV].[CurSpace].[CurTime] := MinImpl;
   end for;
end for;

! Fill in the Matrix ;

for V in i.NumV - 1 ..1 do                                           ☜3
   for CurSpace in 0..MaxSpace do
      for CurTime in 0..MaxTime do
         MinCost := Infinity;
         MinImpl := 1;
         for Impl in 1..i.VarDecls.[V].GetSpec.↑.NumC do
            if S.[V].[Impl] <= CurSpace and
               T.[V].[Impl] <= CurTime and
               Cost.[V].[Impl] +
               f.[V+1].[CurSpace - S.[V].[Impl]].
                  [CurTime - T.[V].[Impl]]
                  < MinCost then
               MinCost := Cost.[V].[Impl] +
                  f.[V+1].[CurSpace - S.[V].[Impl]].
                  [CurTime - T.[V].[Impl]];
               MinImpl := Impl;
            fi;
         end for;
         f.[V].[CurSpace].[CurTime] := MinCost;
         ImplMatrix.[V].[CurSpace].[CurTime] := MinImpl;
      end for;
   end for;
end for;

! And read the matrix for the appropriate implementations ;
```

```
CurSpace := MaxSpace;                                          ☞4
CurTime := MaxTime;
for V in 1..i.NumV do
   i.VarDecls.[V].SetImpl(i.VarDecls.[V].GetSpec.↑.Children.
            [ImplMatrix.[V].[CurSpace].[CurTime]]);
   NewSpace := CurSpace -
                   S.[V].[ImplMatrix.[V].[CurSpace].[CurTime]];
   CurTime := CurTime -
                   T.[V].[ImplMatrix.[V].[CurSpace].[CurTime]];
   CurSpace := NewSpace;
end for;
end; ! end of Dynamic Programming ;

Ramirez(100,100,10);

end;
```

6.9.2. Branch and Bound

The general technique of branch-and-bound is used throughout artificial intelligence as a way to control the search of a large space [Winston 77]. A branch-and-bound algorithm for making representation choices is presented below. The path being incrementally searched is the list of procedure calls in a given *Instance* object. Note how the evaluation procedure *Eval* is separated from the rest of the policy procedure. Thus it is quite simple to change the optimization criterion as necessary.

```
!--------------------------------------------------------;
! Branch and Bound
!--------------------------------------------------------;

procedure BNB(inst: instance, im . varnum : integer);
procedure BNB(inst: instance, im . varnum : integer) is
begin
   procedure Eval(inst:instance,im . varnum: integer,
      im . implNum: integer, im . procNum: integer)
      return im .integer;
   procedure Eval(inst:instance,im . varnum: integer,
      im . implNum: integer, im . procNum: integer)
      return im .integer is
   begin

      if inst.VarDecls.[varNum].
         LocallyFeasible(SpecDecl.↑.Children.[implNum]) then
         inst.VarDecls.[varNum].
            SetImpl(SpecDecl.↑.Children.[implNum]);
         if inst.BindProcs then null; fi;
         if inst.ProcCalls.[procNum].
            check Cost return (im.integer) then
            return inst.ProcCalls.[procNum].
               Cost return (im.integer);
         else
            return Infinity;
         fi;
      else
         return Infinity;
      fi;
   end;
```

```
    procedure DoSingle; procedure DoSingle is
    begin
       var implNum => im . new integer;
       var MinIndex => im . new integer;
       var aim => new arraymanager(im.integer);
       var Cost => aim . new Array(1,NumDecls);
       var LastConsidered => aim . new Array(1,NumDecls);

       ! Final initial value for all branches ;
       for implNum in 1..NumDecls do
          Cost.[implNum] := Eval(inst,varnum,implNum,1);
          LastConsidered.[implNum] := 1;
       end for;
       while True do
          ! Find current minimum path ;
          MinIndex := 1;
          for implNum in 2..NumDecls do
             if Cost.[implNum] < Cost.[MinIndex] then
                MinIndex := implNum;
             fi;
          end for;
          ! See if done (no more proc to examine) ;
          if LastConsidered.[MinIndex] = inst.NumP then
             exitloop;
          fi;
          ! Not done, so extend path by one ;
          LastConsidered.[MinIndex] :=
             LastConsidered.[MinIndex] + 1;
          Cost.[MinIndex] := Cost.[MinIndex] +
             Eval(inst,varnum,implNum,
                LastConsidered.[MinIndex]);
       end loop;
       CDRM.Assign(MinClass,SpecDecl.↑.Children.[MinIndex]);
    end;

    var NumDecls => im . new integer;
    var SpecDecl => CDRM . new Reference;
    var MinClass => CDRM . new Reference;
    var Infinity => im . new integer;

    Infinity := 999999999;
    CDRM.Assign(SpecDecl,inst.VarDecls.[varnum].GetSpec);
    NumDecls := SpecDecl.↑.NumC;
    if NumDecls > 0 then
       DoSingle;
       inst.VarDecls.[varnum].SetImpl(MinClass);
    fi;
 end;
```

```
|----------------------------;
| Policy procedure starts here;
|----------------------------;
procedure policy(i:instance);
procedure policy(i:instance) is
begin
   var c => im . new integer;

   for c in 1..NumV do
      BNB(i,c);
   end for;
   for c in 1..i.NumV do
      Policy(i.VarDecls.[c]);
   end for;
   for c in 1..NumP do
      if not i.ProcCalls.[c].AlreadySeen then
         Policy(i.ProcCalls.[c]);
      fi;
   end for;
end;
```

6.9.3. Hill-Climbing Heuristic

Another popular technique for controlling the search of alternatives in a large space is hill climbing. A simple hill-climbing (or since the evaluation function is being minimized, hole-falling) algorithm is presented below.

```
|---------------------------------------------------;
| The steepest descent hill climbing               ;
|---------------------------------------------------;
procedure Policy(i:Instance);
procedure Policy(i:Instance) is
begin
   var c => IM . new Integer;
   var j => IM . new Integer;
   var BestClass => CDRM . new Reference;
   var CurClass => CDRM . new Reference;
   var Change => Booleans. new Bit;
   var Dummy => Booleans . new Bit;
   var TempSpace => IM . new Integer;
   var TempTime => IM. new Integer;
   var MinSpaceTime => IM. new Integer;
   var HaveSpaceTime => Booleans. new Bit;
```

```
for c in 1..i.NumV do
    CDRM.Assign(BestClass,i.VarDecls.[c].GetSpec);
    if i.VarDecls.[c].check Space return (IM.Integer) and
       i.VarDecls.[c].check Time(i) return (IM.Integer) then
        MinSpaceTime := 99999999;
        Booleans.Assign(Change,True);
        while Change do
            Booleans.Assign(Change,False);
            CDRM.Assign(CurClass,BestClass);
            for j in 1..CurClass.↑.NumC do
                i.VarDecls.[c].SetImpl(CurClass.↑.Children.[j]);
                Booleans.Assign(Dummy,i.BindProcs);
                TempSpace := i.VarDecls.[c].Space
                                            return (IM.Integer);
                TempTime := i.VarDecls.[c].Time(i)
                                            return (IM.Integer);
                if tempSpace*tempTime < MinSpaceTime then
                    Booleans.Assign(Change,True);
                    CDRM.Assign(BestClass,CurClass.↑.Children.[j]);
                    MinSpaceTime := tempSpace*tempTime;
                fi;
            end for;
        end loop;
        i.VarDecls.[c].SetImpl(BestClass);
    else
        CDRM.Assign(CurClass,i.VarDecls.[c].GetSpec);
        while CurClass.↑.NumC > 0 do
            CDRM.Assign(CurClass,CurClass.↑.Children.[1]);
        end loop;
        i.VarDecls.[c].SetImpl(CurClass);
    fi;
end for;
Booleans.Assign(Dummy,i.BindProcs);
for c in 1..i.NumV do
    Policy(i.VarDecls.[c]);
end for;
for c in 1..NumP do
    if not i.ProcCalls.[c].AlreadySeen then
        Policy(i.ProcCalls.[c]);
    fi;
end for;
end;
```

A particular variant of the hill-climbing algorithm was published by Low [Low 74] for representation selection. An initial hill-climbing procedure assigns representations to all variables. Then each representation is perturbed. After each perturbation, the resulting program is reevaluated to see if a better selection resulted. Low's algorithm in Paragon is expressed below. Note how this particular policy exploits the use of managers mentioned in Section 6.3.1.1 (notation 1).

```
!---------------------------------------------------------;
! Low's policy, again on one block at a time.            ;
!---------------------------------------------------------;

procedure CalcTS(i:Instance) return im. integer;
procedure CalcTS(i:Instance) return im. integer is
begin
    var TempTime => im . new integer;
    var TempSpace => im . new integer;
    var j => im . new integer;

    TempTime := 0;
    TempSpace := 0;
    for j in 1..i.NumP do
        if i.ProcCalls.[j] . check time return (im.integer) then
            TempTime := TempTime +
                (i.ProcCalls.[j] . time return (im.integer))*
                (i.ProcCalls.[j].Frequency);
        fi;
    end for;
    for j in 1..i.numV do
        if i.VarDecls.[j]. check Space return (im.integer) then
            TempSpace := TempSpace +
                i.VarDecls.[j].Space return (im.integer);
        fi;
    end for;
    return TempTime * TempSpace;
end;


procedure CalcVTS(im . v: integer, i:Instance)
        return im. integer;
procedure CalcVTS(im . v: integer, i:Instance)
        return im. integer is
begin
    var call => ProcCall;
    var TempTime => im . new integer;
    var TempSpace => im . new integer;
    var j => im . new integer;
```

```
    TempTime := 0;
    TempSpace := 0;
    let call match i.VarDecls.[v] in i do
       if call . check ManagerTime(i) return (im.integer) then  ⟵1
          TempTime := TempTime +
                         call . ManagerTime(i) return (im.integer);
       fi;
    end let;
    for j in v..i.NumV do
       if v = i.VarDecls.[j].ImplSet and
          i.VarDecls.[j] . check space return (im.integer) then
          TempSpace := TempSpace +
                            i.VarDecls.[j].Space return (im.integer);
       fi;
    end for;
    if i.VarDecls.[v] . check space return (im.integer) then
       TempSpace := TempSpace +
                         i.VarDecls.[v].Space return (im.integer);
    fi;
    return TempTime * TempSpace;
end;

procedure MarkManagers(i:Instance);
procedure MarkManagers(i:Instance) is
begin
   var k => im . new integer;
   var j => im . new integer;

   for j in 1..i.NumV do
      for k in j+1..i.NumV do
      if EnclosingObject(i.VarDecls.[j],i.VarDecls.[k]) then
         i.VarDecls.[k].ImplSet := j;
      fi;
      end for;
   end for;
end;

procedure PerformOnePolicy(i:instance,im . index: integer,
         Booleans. DoingGlobal: Bit);
procedure PerformOnePolicy(i:instance,im . index: integer,
         Booleans. DoingGlobal: Bit) is
begin
   var ManSpec => CDRM . new reference;
   var KidSpec => CDRM. new reference;
   var KidImpl => CDRM. new reference;
   var Best => im . new integer;
   var MinTS => im . new integer;
   var TS => im . new integer;
   var j => im . new integer;
   var k => im . new integer;
   var KidNum => im . new integer;
```

```
procedure SetKids;
procedure SetKids is
begin
   ! First find a kid ;
   for k in index+1..i.NumV do
      if index = i.VarDecls.[k].ImplSet then
         CDRM.Assign(KidSpec,i.VarDecls.[k].GetSpec);
         KidNum := k;
         exitloop;
      fi;
   end for;
   ! Now find an impl ;
   for k in 1..KidSpec.↑.NumC do
      if i.VarDecls.[KidNum].
                    LocallyFeasible(KidSpec.↑.Children.[k]) then
         CDRM.Assign(KidImpl,KidSpec.↑.Children.[k]);
         exitloop;
      fi;
   end for;
   ! And assign the impl to all of the kids ;
   for k in KidNum..i.NumV do
      if index = i.VarDecls.[k].ImplSet then
         i.VarDecls.[k].SetImpl(KidImpl);
      fi;
   end for;
end;

CDRM.Assign(ManSpec,i.VarDecls.[index].GetSpec);
Best := 0;
MinTS := 99999999;
for j in 1..ManSpec.↑.NumC do
   i.VarDecls.[index].SetImpl(ManSpec.↑.Children.[j]);
   SetKids;
   if DoingGlobal then
      TS := CalcTS(i);
   else
      TS := CalcVTS(index,i);
   fi;
   if TS < MinTS then
      MinTS := TS;
      Best := j;
   fi;
end for;
if Best > 0 then
   i.VarDecls.[index].SetImpl(ManSpec.↑.Children.[Best]);
   SetKids;
fi;
end;
```

```
procedure policy(i:instance);
procedure policy(i:instance) is
begin
   var ind => im . new integer;

   MarkManagers(i);
   for ind in 1..i.NumV do
      if i.VarDecls.[ind].ImplSet = 0 then
         PerformOnePolicy(i,ind,False);
      fi;
   end for;
   for ind in 1..i.NumV do
      if i.VarDecls.[ind].ImplSet = 0 then
         PerformOnePolicy(i,ind,True);
      fi;
   end for;
   if i.BindProcs then null; fi;
   for ind in 1..i.NumV do
      Policy(i.VarDecls.[ind]);
   end for;
   for ind in 1..i.NumP do
      if not i.ProcCalls.[ind].AlreadySeen then
         Policy(i.ProcCalls.[ind]);
      fi;
   end for;

end;
```

6.9.4. Simple Constraint

Probably the simplest kind of policy is one that explicitly selects a particular representation. In Paragon, this can only be done by convention between the abstract data type, the variable and the policy. The abstract data type must have an attribute that indicates the implementation, a variable wishing to use explicitly an implementation must use the attribute in its constraint, and the policy procedure must only search for feasible implementations. This approach is error prone and requires a lot of coordination between the abstract data type, policy and variable declaration. However, this approach is developed in this section.

First, a class declaration might be written as shown below:

```
class Complex is
begin
   attribute procedure IsPolar return Booleans.Bit is
   begin return False; end;
```

```
      attribute procedure IsCartesian return Booleans.Bit is
      begin return False; end;
   end;

   class Polar of Complex is
   begin
      attribute procedure IsPolar return Booleans.Bit is
      begin return True; end;
   ...
   end;

   class Cartesian of Complex is
   begin
      attribute procedure IsCartesian return Booleans.Bit is
      begin return True; end;
   ...
   end;
```

The variable using these declarations would choose its implementation by calling the appropriate attribute in its constraint, for example:

```
var MyComplex => new Complex
    such that desc (MyComplex) . IsPolar return (Booleans.Bit);
```

The constraint allows only the the *Polar* implementation of *Complex* to be feasible. Thus a policy would need to only pick a feasible implementation. Such a policy is shown below:

```
!----------------------------------------------------------;
! ExhaustiveFindAnything                                   :
!----------------------------------------------------------;

procedure policy(i:instance);
procedure policy(i:instance) is
begin
   var Completed => Booleans. new Bit;

   procedure TryAllImpls(IM . j: Integer);
   procedure TryAllImpls(IM . j: Integer) is
   begin
      var NextVar => im .new integer;
      var temp => CDRM . new reference;
      var k => im . new integer;
      var ind => im . new integer;

      if j > i.NumV then
         if i.BindProcs then
            for ind in 1..i.NumV do
               Policy(i.VarDecls.[ind]);
            end for;
            for ind in 1..i.NumP do
               if not i.ProcCalls.[ind].AlreadySeen then
                  Policy(i.ProcCalls.[ind]);
               fi;
            end for;
            Booleans.Assign(Completed,CheckFeasibility);
         fi;
      else
         NextVar := j + 1;
         TryAllImpls(NextVar);
         if Completed then return; fi;
         CDRM.Assign(temp,i.VarDecls.[j].GetSpec);
         for k in 1..temp.↑.NumC do
            if i.VarDecls.[j].
               LocallyFeasible(temp.↑.Children.[k]) then
               i.VarDecls.[j].SetImpl(temp.↑.Children.[k]);
               TryAllImpls(NextVar);
               if Completed then return; fi;
            fi;
         end for;
      fi;
   end;

   Booleans.Assign(Completed,False);
   TryAllImpls(1);

end;
```

The programmer should not be required to write convoluted code to be able to select directly an implementation. The current design resulted from my belief that the programmer should not have direct access to the implementations; only attributes should be used. In retrospect, the lack of direct control over the selection of representation may have been a bit too extreme. There are times when a programmer wishes to explicitly select an implementation. One way to provide this ability would be to make the *same as* constraint expressions used in procedure specifications available in any expression (and defining it to return a value that matches *Booleans.Bit*). This would allow one to use any kind of expression in constraints for procedure declarations and permit the use of *same as* expressions to simply state the programmer's intentions, as illustrated below:

```
var MyVar => new Obj
    such that MyVar.structure same as Obj_Impl_1;
```

Another iteration of the Paragon design would probably include this modification.

The programs in this chapter have been processed by a prototype translator for the Paragon language. The next chapter contains a description of the design of the prototype and some measurements performed on it.

Chapter 7
Implementation

The prototype translation system consists of two programs, an LALR(1) parser produced by a parser generation system [Nestor 82] for lexical and syntax analysis and a Lisp program for semantic analysis, feasibility analysis and interpretation.

The parser runs only on Decsystem-20s and produces an intermediate text file (in TCOL format [Newcomer 79]) that is used by the Lisp program. The Lisp program is written in a subset of the Maclisp [MIT 78] and Franzlisp [Foderaro 80] dialects, and runs on both Decsystem-20s and VAX/Unix systems.

This chapter provides a detailed discussion of this prototype translator. I first provide a list of the translator's phases and components. Some static measurements of these phases and components are provided and discussed. Finally, I present some example programs that were processed with the translator. The programs are described and the performance of the translator on these programs evaluated.

7.1. Phase Descriptions

The compiler consists of twelve phases, where phase roughly means "a single pass over the program text". These phases are shown below:

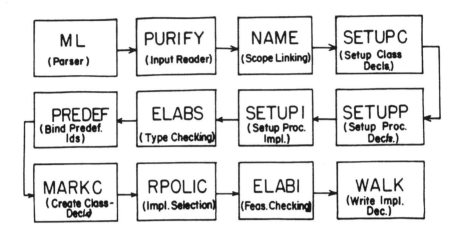

Figure 7-1: Phase Diagram for the Paragon Translator

The phases are executed in order, but may contain pieces or components that are used in other parts of the system. For example, phase ELABI contains procedures for checking the feasibility of a class instantiation or procedure call. These procedures are always executed when the ELABI phase is run, but they are also executed if a policy procedure calls the *CheckFeasibility* procedure during the RPOLIC phase. Some of the interesting components that may appear in more than one phase are discussed in Section 7.2.

An important fact is illustrated by the phase diagram: the design of a Paragon translation system is conventional. After parsing (ML, PURIFY), several bookkeeping phases create links between scopes, classes, and procedure specifications and implementations (NAME, SETUPC, SETUPP, SETUPI). Semantic analysis is then performed (ELABS), the predefined environment is created (PREDEF) and object representations are chosen (RPOLIC). Finally the processed program is made available to later stages of a compiler (WALK).

The only two phases omitted in most systems are MARKC and ELABI. Neither phase is difficult to construct. The former phase exists only to provide information to the policy procedure and hence is an unconventional addition to the translation process. However, the MARKC phase redecorates the class declarations with more links between parent classes and subclasses. Thus the MARKC phase is another bookkeeping phase which is similar to SETUPC. The difference is that the additions to the class declarations are accessible to the policy procedure whereas the decorations added by previous bookkeeping phases are only for internal use.

The ELABI phase is needed because Paragon separates the ideas of specification and implementation all the way to the procedure call level. This phase is not difficult to construct. In most languages, if a procedure call is checked to ensure that it meets specification, and if an implementation meets its specification, then the translation system may conclude that the program is feasible. This is not true for Paragon. Instead an additional pass over the program is required to verify that implementations are present for all procedure calls. But as explained in Sections 5.2.3 and 5.5.5, the algorithm for feasibility checking (elaboration with implementations) is very similar to the algorithm for type checking (elaboration with specifications), so the addition of the ELABI phase requires no breakthrough in compiler technology.

One can therefore conclude that constructing of a Paragon compiler is no more difficult than constructing a compiler for most algebraic languages. One of the significant differences between Paragon and other languages is the presence of the type hierarchy. Thus the use of a type hierarchy should not be eliminated from a language design for fear of implementation difficulties.

Like the overall design of the translator, the designs of individual phases are also quite conventional. The remainder of this section describes each phase of the implemented system.

7.1.1. ML: Parser

The first phase is the parser, called ML[71]. It is a Bliss-36 program automatically created by a parser generator system. The parser accepts text files written in Paragon and produces a TCOL tree in an LG (linear graph) notation, essentially another text file. The TCOL tree also contains a name table for later phases of the translator. The BNF description of Paragon that is used by the parser generator is provided in Appendix B.

---

[71]ML stands for *My Language*. At the time the parser was created, I had no name for Paragon and had to call the parser something.

7.1.2. PURIFY: Input Reader

The second phase of the translator is called PURIFY. This phase reads the TCOL file produced by the parser and creates an internal tree representation. The tree representation used is quite simple: The tree nodes are represented as unique atoms, and the various attributes and pointers attached to a tree node are placed on the property list of the atom. For example, an *if* statement with the following tree fragment:

```
node3: <if statement>
   (test)    (statement)
   /               \
  /                 \
 node4:           node5:
```

would have the internal representation:

```
node3: (test node4: statement node5:)
node4: ....
node5: ....
```

In addition to reading the file, the PURIFY phase also does some simple tree rearranging, usually renaming property identifiers produced by the parser generator and ridding the tree of syntactic sugar. An example of the former transformation is the renaming of the LIST and LISTA properties that are produced by the parser generator into DECLARATION_LIST and STATEMENT_LIST properties, which are used by later phases. Some examples of the latter transformations are changing the symbol ↑ into the identifier *value* and rewriting the expression *a + b* into the more verbose *IM.plus(a,b)*. Sections 3.3.4 and 3.3.5 list all of the syntactic transformations performed by PURIFY.

7.1.3. NAME: Scope Linking

The third phase of the translator, NAME, is responsible for creating pointers between a scope and its enclosing scope, and between each declaration and the scope containing the declaration. These pointers are used during identifier lookup, because if an identifier is not found in one scope, the enclosing scope may eventually be searched as well.

In addition to linking the scopes together, the NAME phase also makes some simple checks for illegal duplicate declarations of identifiers. This is done as an aid to the programmer and is unnecessary for the proper operation of the translator on correct programs.

7.1.4. SETUPC: Setup Class Declarations

The fourth phase of the translator, SETUPC, performs some preprocessing of class declarations for later use in type checking.

First, the ancestors of each class are found and two lists, the leftmost parent order and the leftmost elaboration order, are added to each class declaration. These lists are used primarily for creating simple objects and locating declarations.

With the aid of these lists, the SETUPC phase also tags each class parameter as *inherited* or *defined*. All inherited parameters are also tagged with references to their defining parameters for later semantic checking. (See Appendix A.7 for a discussion of how parameters are inherited.)

This phase also numbers the variables in each class and procedure declaration, although the processing is not directly related to class declarations. When a local instance is created, the objects associated with it are placed in a list; the indices created during this phase are used to retrieve the objects during elaboration with specifications, with implementations and with realizations.

7.1.5. SETUPP: Setup Procedure Declarations

The fifth phase in the translator is called SETUPP. Using the links created by SETUPC, SETUPP associates each procedure implementation with its corresponding specification. Since there is no overloading in Paragon, this can be done by merely examining the names of the procedure specifications in the ancestor classes.

7.1.6. SETUPI: Setup Procedure Implementations

The SETUPI phase creates a list of possible procedure implementations for each procedure specification on a scope-by-scope basis. Initially, a list of all visible procedure specifications is attached to each class and procedure declaration.   Then all visible procedure implementations for each visible procedure specification are also gathered and attached to each class and procedure. During feasibility checking, a list of possible implementations for a procedure call can then be located by merely examining the declaration for the innermost simple object of the environment in which the call is appearing. The inclusion of this phase in the translation system is efficient if one assumes that the use of space to hold the lists of implementations is better than the use of time to search the entire environment each time a procedure call is made to collect possible procedure implementations. Because the translator is running on a Vax with a slow processor but with a large address space, the decision was made to trade space for time.

7.1.7. ELABS: Type Checking and Semantic Analysis

The seventh phase of the translator performs the bulk of the semantic analysis, or more technically, elaboration with specifications. Thus this phase elaborates the universal class declaration and the user's program with specifications. At a practical level, the following tests are included:

- Procedure implementations match their corresponding specifications.

- Classes are properly derived from their parents.

- Object creations are well specified.

- Procedure calls match the appropriate specifications.

- All identifiers denote an appropriate variable, class, procedure or label.

Naturally, the ELABS phase contains procedures for elaborating procedures and classes with specifications. These procedures are used in several components mentioned in other sections. Similarly, elaborating classes and procedures with specifications may require elaboration of attribute variables, so the ELABS phase may use components from the RPOLIC phase.

7.1.8. PREDEF: Locate and Bind Predefined Identifiers

The eighth phase of the translator, PREDEF, is used to locate and bind the predefined classes, variables and procedures in the universal class declaration. Thus the phase finds all predefined declarations such as: the predefined boolean object for use in *if* and *while* statements; the *IM* integer manager; and the *ClassDecl*, *Instance*, *VarDecl*, *ObjDecl* and *ProcCall* classes for use in the MARKC and RPOLIC phases. Similarly, this phase finds all user required declarations: the policy procedure for the selection of object implementations; and the user's main program.

7.1.9. MARKC: Create *ClassDecl* Objects

The ninth phase of the translator, MARKC, creates *ClassDecl* realizations that represent class declarations in the program being processed. References to these *ClassDecl* objects are manipulated by policy procedures to inquire about variable specifications and implementations, and to select implementation classes for object creations.

7.1.10. RPOLIC: Implementation Selection

RPOLIC, the tenth phase of the translator, first elaborates with realizations an *Instance* object for the main program and then executes the policy procedure implementation, passing the newly created *Instance* object as the actual parameter. This phase of the translator contains all of the procedures and run-time support for elaborating Paragon with realizations. Since the elaboration with realizations of indefinite instances is identical to elaboration with specifications, this phase uses some components from the ELABS phase.

7.1.11. ELABI: Feasibility Checking

The eleventh phase, ELABI, checks the program for feasibility. This phase ensures that any implementation choices made by the programmer for variables (via the policy) are compatible with the specifications of those variables and that there is a feasible procedure implementation for every procedure call in the program. Since various components in the ELABI phase are used to check the feasibility of class instantiations and procedure calls, these components may also be executed during the RPOLIC phase during calls of the predefined *CheckFeasibility* and *BindProcs* procedures.

7.1.12. WALK: Write Implementation Decisions

The last phase of the translator, WALK, records all of the choices made for object creations and procedure calls. For every kind of object creation and procedure call, the WALK phase prints a list of variables along with the selected representations, and a list of procedure calls along with the selected implementations. Excerpts of this printout are provided in Section 6.6. In a production system, the transformed program would be passed to a code generation phase.

7.2. Component Descriptions

There are parts of the translator that either do not belong to a particular phase, or are the primary piece of one phase and a minor piece of other phases, or represent a facility that is needed in several phases. These parts of the translator are termed *components* to distinguish them from phases. The prominent components in the translator are described below.

7.2.1. Name Components

Three related components, ES_Name, EI_Name, and ER_Name, are responsible for elaborating name expressions with specifications, implementations and representations respectively. As name expressions are used to express parameters, variables and procedure calls, name expressions are truly the center of the translator for processing Paragon.

These three components are interrelated. For example, when a name expression contains an object creation, and when that object creation is elaborated with specifications, the class mentioned in the name expression will be elaborated with specifications, and any attribute variables in it will be elaborated with realizations. Thus ES_Name could cause ER_Name to be evaluated. Further, these components can be evaluated recursively.

The *Name* translator components contain three subcomponents. One subcomponent controls the processing of class instances, one controls the processing of procedure calls and one controls the processing of local instances. Each set of subcomponents is described below.

7.2.1.1. Create_Class

One set of translator subcomponents, ES_Create_Class, EI_Create_Class and ER_Create_Class, is responsible for the processing of class declarations and name components that denote class instantiations or indefinite instances. Like the three translator components for processing names, each of these three components may call another or recursively call itself. As a simple example, an object creation may contain some parameters that in turn contain an indefinite instance. Thus during the processing of the object creation, a recursive call on a Create_Class subcomponent will be made for the indefinite instance.

7.2.1.2. Create_Call

Another set of related subcomponents is ES_Create_Call, EI_Create_Call and ER_Create_Call. These are analogous to the Create_Class components except that procedure declarations and invocations are processed instead of object creations. Like object creations, one procedure call may require the processing of another procedure call.

7.2.1.3. Create_Local_Instance

The last set of related subcomponents that is discussed here is ES_Create_Local_Instance, EI_Create_Local_Instance and ER_Create_Local_Instance. These subcomponents are responsible for the processing of a block with its declarations and its statements, and are used by both the Create_Object and the Create_Call subcomponents.

7.2.2. MYLET: Function Call Utility

The MYLET[72] component of the translator is used to allow a Lisp function to return multiple values and is completely unrelated to Paragon. In essence, the MYLET function takes a list of identifiers and a function call, evaluates the function, takes the result of the function, which is expected to be a list, and assigns each element of the returned list to the corresponding identifier in the identifier list. MYLET is used widely throughout the translator.

7.2.3. LOOKUP: Symbol Table Processing

The LOOKUP component corresponds to the usual symbol table routines found in most compilers. This component is bit more complicated than symbol table routines in most compilers. In most compilers, a scope is searched to find a declaration that corresponds to a given identifier. Because objects in Paragon have a rather rich structure, the search can be very time consuming. To ameliorate the amount of time spent in searching for an identifier, the LOOKUP component saves various pieces of state information about identifiers in the program tree as it looks them up in an object. This information is used to speed up future searches of identifiers when a class declaration is reelaborated during an object creation or when a procedure declaration is reelaborated during a procedure call.

---

[72] The name MYLET comes from the standard LET macro in Maclisp from which this component was inspired.

7.2.4. COMP: Comparing Objects

The COMP component is responsible for comparing two objects and reporting whether or not they match, and for returning any identifier bindings that result from the matching process. Because object comparison in Paragon is more complicated than the usual name equivalence rule found in most abstract data type languages, the procedures used for determining whether two objects match are correspondingly more complicated. Hence, the translator has a separate component for comparing objects.

7.2.5. GC: Garbage Collector, TIMER: Metering, SW: Switches

Three additional parts of the system do not depend on the details of Paragon but are required in nearly any prototype written in Lisp: GC, the garbage collector; TIMER, the translator metering tool; and SW: the translator debugging switches. Each of the components is briefly described.

Because most of the system is written in Lisp, the style of programming used in the prototype creates a lot of temporary data structures that must be garbage collected when no longer needed. Because the garbage collector belongs to no specific phase, it is considered a distributed component of the translator. The TIMER component records the entrance and exit of various functions in the translator. This component provides the statistics reported in Section 7.3.3. The SW component controls the setting of various debugging switches that the translation system uses.

7.3. Translator Performance

Some measurements of the implemented prototype were performed in an attempt to locate hidden design flaws in the language. These measurements also give some indication of the relative amounts of effort needed to build different pieces a Paragon translator and the relative amounts of processing that is needed for different aspects of Paragon.

Three varieties of measurements are reported: static measurements of the translator, static measurements of the sample programs and dynamic measurements of the translator processing the sample programs. The static measurements reflect the sizes of the phases, components or programs being described. The dynamic measurements reflect the amount of time required to process certain programs by certain pieces of the translator. As the measurement process consumes resources, these numbers should be taken as approximations. A more useful exercise consists of comparing the numbers in the tables to obtain relative sizes and speeds between pieces of the prototype rather than to obtain some absolute performance measurements with which to compare other translators.

7.3.1. Static Measurements of the Translator

Tables 7-1 and 7-2 below give some static measurements of the translator. For each phase and component, a measure of the size of the source code in lines of Lisp source is given, followed by the size of the loaded code in kilobytes of memory.

Phase	# Lines Lisp	# Kilobytes
ML[73]	452	70
PURIFY	613	1[74]
NAME	94	3
SETUPC	235	5
SETUPP	216	7
SETUPI	70	2
ELABS	2050	53
PREDEF	308	9
MARKC	118	3
RPOLIC	2777	70
ELABI	1604	37
WALK	560	19

Table 7-1: Static Sizes of Translator Phases

No effort was made to place the source code into some specific format, such as, elimination of comments or blank lines. Rather, the values for the sizes of source code were simple counts of lines of all of the appropriate files that make up the entry.

The sizes of the loaded programs were calculated by loading them individually into a Franzlisp system. Unless otherwise indicated, the values for the Lisp part of the translator were made using interpretive Lisp programs on a Franzlisp interpreter, running on a Vax

---

[73]Since the parser was generated by a parser generator and is written in Bliss, there is no value for the number of lines of Lisp the ML phase requires. Instead of the number of lines of Lisp, the number of lines of source for the parser generator are given. The memory size is the resulting parser in DecSystem-20 kilowords.

[74]This phase uses compiled Lisp code. It requires 31 kilobytes when not compiled.

11/780 with the Berkeley Unix 4.1 operating system.[75]

Component	# Lines Lisp	# Kilobytes
Lisp System	n/a	599
Utilities[76]	2138[77]	55
COMP	451	11
LOOKUP	344	10
MYLET	28	1
SW	76	0.2[78]
TIMER	51	0.1[79]
Total[80]	11803	885

Table 7-2: Static Sizes of Translator Components

As one might expect, the bulk of the system consists of the sources concerned with elaboration (ELABI, ELABS and RPOLIC) which together comprise about 6355 lines of Lisp, or about 54% of the system source. Similarly, these pieces require about 158 kilobytes or approximately 55% of the total system memory (excluding the underlying Lisp system).

Although the memory size seems rather large, one should recall that most of the Lisp code is interpreted. Compiled Franzlisp is much smaller (and faster) than interpreted Franzlisp. Three pieces of the system were compiled: PURIFY, SW and TIMER. The memory size reductions ran between 80% and 97% for the resulting pieces. Thus a production Paragon translator that was fully compiled would be substantially smaller: between 57 kilobytes (80%)

---

[75]Only three pieces were compiled: PURIFY, SW and TIMER. All measurements for these pieces refer to the compiled versions.

[76]The utilities include a set package, a Lisp debugger, a trace package, a stepper package, a control procedure for running the translator, file handling functions, some special functions and macros for ensuring the program's compatibility with both Maclisp and Franzlisp, access functions for internal data structures, control flow macros, string manipulation functions and error handling functions.

[77]Some of the utilities were provided to me by various people. I have no source size measurements for these utilities. The given number represents the total lines of sources I had access to.

[78]This component uses compiled Lisp code. It requires 1 kilobyte when not compiled.

[79]This component uses compiled Lisp code. It requires 3 kilobytes when not compiled.

[80]All phases and components of the Lisp part of system.

and 9 kilobytes (97%), excluding the underlying Lisp system.[81] Further, there is a great deal of similarity between the three pieces that perform elaboration, so a production design might combine them into a single piece of code, further reducing the final size of the translator. By comparison, the Pascal compiler on the same Unix system requires about 13 kilobytes of memory space and the C compiler requires about 10 kilobytes.[82]

7.3.2. Static Measurements of Some Programs

Several example program fragments were processed by the prototype to measure the dynamic performance of the prototype. This section discusses the program fragments that I used for measuring the performance of elaboration with specifications and implementations. The program fragments used for measuring the performance of elaboration with realizations I defer until Section 7.3.3.3.

Four kinds of program fragments were processed: the predefined environment for Paragon, some specifications of abstract data types, some implementations of abstract data types and some application programs that use abstract data types. Each set of test fragments is described, and then a table listing their static characteristics is provided. The sources for these programs are provided in Appendices E and F.

Although some program fragments may not be translated without others, all of the figures in the tables represent incremental values. For example, an application program may require the predefined environment and some abstract data types to be defined, but the measured values for the predefined environment and the abstract data types are subtracted from the measured values for the entire program. The revised measurements are presented in the tables for the application program fragment.

---

[81] Several attempts were made to compile the entire translation system. Several errors in the compiled code prevented the use of a compiled version of the entire translation system. Some of these resulted from the slightly different semantics of interpreted and compiled Lisp and some were untraceable compiler errors. With enough perseverance, the entire system could have been compiled, but such effort did not seem warranted for the limited number of tests.

[82] One should remember that the Pascal and C compilers contain a parser and a final code generator which the Lisp part of the Paragon system omits. However, the Paragon system contains an additional tree builder in the PURIFY phase and an interpreter that the Pascal and C compilers omit.

7.3.2.1. Predefined Environment

The first program fragment is the predefined environment that is declared in the universal environment, and is denoted *Base* in the tables. The *Base* program fragment includes the declarations of classes for integer objects and boolean objects, the declaration of classes that can be used as type constructors for pointers and arrays, and the class declarations required by the policy procedure. The corresponding procedures for arithmetic, relational operations, logical operations and transput are also declared. The program text for the predefined environment is provided in Section 6.2.

7.3.2.2. Abstract Data Type Specifications

I constructed two general purpose abstract data types for use in application programs: sets and lists. The design of both matched the design in Low's systems as much as possible [Low 74]. Thus the specifications contain a large number of procedures, most of which are not used in the application programs. In addition, the specifications also contain attribute declarations. The interpretation of the attributes is explained with the entire program texts in Appendices E.4 and E.11. Measurements referring to set specifications are denoted *SetSpec* in the tables. *ListSpec* entries in the tables refer to measurements performed on list specifications.

7.3.2.3. Abstract Data Type Implementations

For each abstract data type specification, I programmed several implementations in Paragon. Again, the design of the implementations was taken largely from Low's system [Low 74]. For sets, the following implementations were written:

- An unsorted, singly linked list, *SetULink*

- An sorted, singly linked list, *SetSLink*

- An unsorted array, *SetUArray*

- An sorted array, *SetSArray*

- Shared elements with attribute bits, *SetAttBit*

- BTree, *SetBTree*

The prototype measured the processing of the first five implementations. The program text for all of the implementations can be found in Appendix E.1.

The following implementations were written for lists:

- Singly linked list, *List1Link*

- Doubly linked list, *List2Link*

- Array, *ListArray*

The prototype measured the processing of all of the implementations. The program text for the list implementations can be found in Appendix E.2.

Like their specifications, the implementations of abstract data types also contain attribute declarations which may be used by a policy procedure during the selection process.

7.3.2.4. Application Programs

For application programs, I chose programs that previously appeared in the representation selection literature and rewrote them in Paragon. Three sorting programs (*Insrt2*, *Insrt3*, *Merge*) were copied from Low's thesis [Low 74], a Huffman encoding program (*Huffman*) was copied from a SETL paper [Freudenberger 83] and a transitive closure algorithm (*TransClo*) was taken from Rovner's thesis [Rovner 76]. A simple program to find the maximum of a set (*SetMax*) was also written. The full text of the application programs can be found in Appendix F.

7.3.2.5. Measured Sizes of Programs

Table 7-3 presents some measures of the program fragments in terms of the number of source lines of the text, the number of TCOL nodes produced by the parser, the number of classes declared and the number of procedures declared.

A glance at Table 7-3 above reveals that application programs are significantly shorter than abstract data type specifications and representations. This is due primarily to the absence of local class and procedure declarations in the application programs. The *Huffman* program does declare some local classes and procedures, and its size is significantly larger than that of the other programs.

Program	Source Lines	TCOL Nodes	# Classes	# Procedures
Base	241	944	26	51
SetSpec	220	762	2	35
ListSpec	232	788	2	39
SetULink	294	1290	3	27
SetSLink	313	1372	3	27
SetUArray	227	800	2	27
SetSArray	356	1906	2	27
SetAttBit	334	1560	3	31
List1Link	465	2502	3	34
List2Link	427	2510	3	34
ListArray	290	1602	2	35
Insrt2	47	168	0	0
Insrt3	45	153	0	0
SetMax	35	127	0	0
TransClo	78	295	2	2
Merge	91	406	0	0
Huffman	220	980	6	8
Total	3915	18165	59	377

Table 7-3: Static Sizes of Program Fragments

7.3.3. Dynamic Measurements of Translator

The translation system was exercised in various ways to measure its performance while elaborating program text with specifications, implementations and realizations. Because each of these kinds of elaborations are used in different amounts in different circumstances, three different kinds of measurements were gathered, one for each kind of elaboration.

7.3.3.1. Measuring Elaboration with Specifications

For measuring elaboration with specifications, each program fragment was parsed and semantically checked which corresponds to processing the fragment from the ML phase through the ELABS phase. No representation selection or feasibly checking is appropriate, so the prototype operated on fragments that contained an empty policy and nothing in the main program to instantiate. The performance of the prototype as it operated on these program fragments is reported in two tables: Table 7-4 shows the phase measurements through the ELABS phase; and Table 7-5 shows the measurements for the GC, COMP,

LOOKUP and MYLET components. All the numbers represent seconds of CPU time on a VAX 11/780 interpreting Franzlisp.

These tables give measures of the prototype's performance when doing semantic checking of a program. It should be noted that the measurements in the two tables are not mutually exclusive. For example, some of the time in the ELABS phase was spent doing garbage collection (GC), comparing objects (COMP), looking up identifiers (LOOKUP) and returning multiple values from Lisp functions (MYLET). Thus, the figures should should be viewed as different ways to break down the total time spent in processing the program.

Program	ML	PURIFY	NAME	SETUPC	SETUPP	SETUPI	ELABS	Total
Base	15	145	3	20	2	10	421	616
SetSpec	13	158	0[83]	7	4	8	790	980
ListSpec	13	162	1	9	5	9	697	896
SetULink	19	269	1	12	4	4	1207	1516
SetSLink	20	297	0	12	1	5	1748	2083
SetUArray	14	237	1	15	4	4	1585	1860
SetSArray	24	479	1	19	4	5	2133	2665
SetAttBit	22	353	1	18	6	5	1990	2395
List1Link	31	512	5	27	6	9	1951	2541
List2Link	32	513	1	19	6	8	2226	2805
ListArray	22	331	1	15	7	7	1323	1706
Insrt2	5	28	1	2	1	1	62	100
Insrt3	4	34	0	0	0	1	40	79
SetMax	3	45	1	3	1	1	78	132
TransClo	6	57	1	4	1	1	243	313
Merge	8	100	0	3	0	0	604	715
Huffman	16	223	0	13	6	0	1692	1950
Total	267	3943	18	198	58	78	18790	23352
Total %	1%	17%	0.1%	0.8%	0.2%	0.3%	80%	

Table 7-4: Phase Measurements for Semantic Analysis

From the table above and Table 7-3, we can calculate the overall performance of the semantic analysis at 10 lines of source per minute, or 47 TCol nodes per minute. A more detailed analysis is presented below.

---

83   alue of 0 means that the amount of time required was less than 1 second.

The parsing and bookkeeping phases consume a small fraction of the processing time: less than 3%. Although the elaboration with specifications (ELABS) seems to require over four times the time required by the input reader (PURIFY), one should remember that the PURIFY phase is compiled. Several interpreted versions of PURIFY were run on a subset of the program sources; the interpreted versions ran between 5.4 and 25 times slower than the compiled version.[84] If the ELABS phase were similarly compiled, one should expect a factor of 5 to 25 speedup. Under a 5 fold speedup, the elaboration of *Huffman* (a 220 line program) with specifications would require about five and a half minutes. Although still a rather large value for processing, the speed becomes comparable to the processing required for file reading and minor tree manipulations. Assuming that PURIFY and ELABS still perform equivalent amounts of processing in a production-quality compiler, and given the speed of production-quality tree manipulators [Lamb 80], a production-quality Paragon compiler should be able to type check and semantically process a program quickly.

Another way to analyze the performance of the translator is to consider how much time is spent by various components. Table 7-5 below gives some component measurements (along with a repetition of the total time required for semantic analysis).

---

[84]The different interpreted versions use different combinations of macros and fexprs. The compiled version uses only macros.

Program	GC	COMP	LOOKUP	MYLET	Total Time for Semantics
Base	308	157	110	114	616
SetSpec	279	234	111	96	980
ListSpec	256	266	100	101	896
SetULink	456	988	154	148	1516
SetSLink	632	996	240	293	2083
SetUArray	577	344	252	193	1860
SetSArray	777	727	321	241	2665
SetAttBit	676	1305	290	293	2395
List1Link	767	1803	238	263	2541
List2Link	831	1938	292	300	2805
ListArray	496	541	221	149	1706
Insrt2	214	49	93	39	100
Insrt3	52	0	69	71	79
SetMax	62	0	87	24	132
TransClo	237	113	61	126	313
Merge	452	265	171	192	715
Huffman	991	791	320	326	1950
Total	8063	10517	3130	2969	23352
Total %	35%	45%	13%	13%	

Table 7-5: Component Measurements for Semantic Analysis

The times add to more than 100% because the components are not independent. For example, garbage collection (GC) and Lisp function evaluation (MYLET) occur throughout the COMP and LOOKUP components.

Two interesting facts emerge from the data in Table 7-5: garbage collection consumes much of the processing time and comparing two objects is an important operation in the system. Each of these results is discussed below.

Because the system is written in Lisp, it uses many lists to hold intermediate and temporary structures. For example, every time a procedure call or object instantiation is made, the environment in which the corresponding procedure or class is to be elaborated, is created by making a new list whose CAR is the newly created call or class instance and whose CDR is the call or creation environment. When the call finishes, or the object can no longer be referenced, the storage for this list that describes the new environment may be reclaimed. Normally, this reclamation may be done when the Lisp routine processing the call or instantiation exits with a conventional stack discipline. Lisp has no such stack discipline for the created lists, so they must be garbage collected. The huge number of object creations and procedure calls in a typical program thus creates an enormous number of lists.[85] Another place where the translator creates a lot of lists and then discards them is during MYLET, where the results of a function are packaged in a list, the function returns, the list is taken apart and assigned to individual variables, and then the list is discarded. This occurred about a third of a million times during the experiments. A third occasion when there is a large usage of temporary lists occurs during object comparison, and is discussed in more detail next.

Object comparison takes about half of all of the processing time according to Table 7-5. This seems to be partly the result of garbage collection problems, which are caused by normalizing operations, partly the cost of individual comparison operations, and partly the result of a large number of object comparisons.

Since the comparison functions create many intermediate lists, a lot of garbage collection occurs during execution of the comparison functions. These lists are created because objects, which are represented as lists of simple objects, are subjected to several kinds of normalizing operations. For example, one normalizing operation is the removal of certain simple objects from each list before performing an element-by-element analysis of the lists.[86] Because each normalizing operation may require the creation of a new temporary list, there is an enormous potential for creating a large number of lists, each of which will need to be garbage collected, and the creation of each may cause a garbage collection.

Object matching is also intrinsically expensive. As mentioned in Section 3.4.2.2, two objects may match if they have different number of simple objects. The matching process will ignore some of the simple objects in the actual object during the matching process. The algorithm by which these holes are found could require an exponential number of test comparisons.[87] This searching for holes is one of the reasons that the prototype translator spends approximately 2 tenths of a second per object comparison. Although the example in Section

---

[85] The translation system processed approximately 25 thousand expressions, each of which contained at least one procedure call or object instantiation.

[86] See Appendix A.3 for a complete discussion of how two objects are compared.

[87] The number of tests is exponential in the number of simple objects in the actual object. In particular, if there are a simple objects in the actual object and f simple objects in the formal object, then there are a choose f ways that the objects may be compared.

3.4.2.2 is a bit contrived, the circumstances when a hole appears are quite common, as illustrated below:

```
class universal is
begin
   !----------------------------------------;
   ! Predefined Assignment classes         ;
   !----------------------------------------;
   class AssignableManager is
   begin
      class Assignable is begin end;
      procedure Assign(Assignable,Assignable);
   end;

   !----------------------------------------;
   ! User's Main program                    ;
   !----------------------------------------;
   class MainProgram is
   begin

      !---------------------------------------;
      ! Local "Type" Declaration             ;
      !---------------------------------------;
      class LocalObjectManager of AssignableManager is
         class LocalObject of Assignable is begin end;
      end;

      var LOM => new LocalObjectManager;
      var Obj1 => LOM . new LocalObject;
      var Obj2 => LOM . new LocalObject;

      LOM.Assign(Obj1,Obj2);
   end;
end;
```

The program above is an abbreviated version of the predefined environment which contains the predefined assignment classes and procedure, and the user's program. The user's program declares some kind of local objects that are also assignable. However, the parameter matching for the call of the *Assign* procedure has the same hole problem illustrated with *Kitchens*. Here it is the *MainProgram* simple object that is skipped. Both the *TransClo* and *Huffman* programs have such local declarations. Because nearly every nontrivial program will contain local declarations that are assignable, this problem is recurrent.

Even if object comparison did not require garbage collection and was intrinsically fast, the comparison operation is still a frequently used component and thus accounts for a large fraction of the processing time. Object comparison is performed on every object instantiation and procedure call. In these experiments, for example, about 50 thousand object comparisons were performed. A combination of the garbage collection requirements and the frequency and complexity of the comparison operation accounts for the 45% of the translator's time spent doing object comparison.

These problems are not insoluble. With some slight changes in the language, the number of normalizing operations during object comparison may also be reduced, thus eliminating some of the processing needed for object comparison. Such changes are discussed in Section 8.1. Further, inefficient garbage collection is not needed to reclaim intermediate lists. The comparison algorithm knows exactly when the intermediate list is no longer needed and thus when its storage can be reclaimed. The translation system could also merge the compare and skip-simple-object operations and not create the intermediate list. Therefore a production system will not spend as much time doing object comparison as it would in the prototype.

7.3.3.2. Measuring Elaboration with Implementations

So far, the discussion of translator performance has only considered semantic processing. A rather new kind of processing required by Paragon is *feasibility checking*. This checking is performed by the ELABI phase, so several experiments were performed to calibrate the amount of work required for this phase against the amount of processing required for semantic checking. These experiments and their results are discussed in turn.

The six application programs were translated under two sets of circumstances. Initially, each was checked for feasibility when no selections were performed for the variables in the programs. This represents the minimum amount of time necessary for feasibility checking since the fewest number of procedure implementations will be considered. Under these circumstances, none of the programs were feasible. The application programs were then translated with a single available representation for each of the set and list abstract data types (*SetUArray* and *ListArray*), and with a policy that selected the one available implementation for each variable. Each program was then checked for feasibility, and in fact, all of the programs are feasible with these selections. Thus these experiments provide some measures of the minimum and typical[88] resources required for checking a program's feasibility.

Table 7-6 below gives the raw data (in VAX 11/780 CPU seconds) for the experiments, along with some comparisons between the efforts for feasibility checking and semantic checking.

---

[88] A feasible program is assumed to be typical.

Program	ELABS	ELABI (Infeasible)	% of ELABS	ELABI (Feasible)	% of ELABS	% of Infeasible
Insrt2	62	134	216%	451	727%	337%
Insrt3	40	123	307%	453	1132%	368%
SetMax	78	85	109%	228	292%	268%
TransClo	243	448	184%	958	394%	214%
Merge	604	560	93%	3100	513%	554%
Huffman	1692	893	53%	3798	224%	425%
Total	2719	2243	82%	8988	331%	401%

Table 7-6: Dynamic Performance of Feasibility Checking

The data above reinforce some expectations about execution times for feasibility checking, especially as the proportion of executable statements in a program increases, as the possibility tree grows and as the implementation selections change an infeasible program into a feasible program. A more detailed discussion of these data follows.

Because elaboration with implementations resembles the symbolic execution of a program,[89] one would expect that the higher the proportion of executable statements and object declarations to unexecutable class and procedure declarations, the more time would be spent during elaboration with implementations as compared to elaboration with specifications. Further, one would expect that feasible programs would require more processing than infeasible programs, since a feasible program would have procedure implementations for all procedure calls that would also have to be elaborated with implementations. This is borne out by the data. For example, *Huffman* contains a sizable amount of local class and procedure declarations and thus the processing required for checking the feasibility of an infeasible version of *Huffman* by the ELABI phase is less than for its semantic checking by the ELABS phase. On the other hand, the two insertion sort procedures, *Insrt2* and *Insrt3*, have neither local class nor procedure declarations, so the amount of time for their semantic checking is far less than for feasibility checking.

One would also expect the amount of execution time spent during feasibility checking to increase as the size of the possibility tree increases. When a feasible program is elaborated with implementations, the entire call graph is traced, and thus individual procedures may be elaborated many times during the ELABI phase (once for each call where the selected procedure is used as the implementation), whereas each implementation is elaborated exactly

---

[89] Although the statements in loops are elaborated exactly once and recursion is guaranteed to terminate.

once during the ELABS phase (when checking the declaration of the procedure implementation). Further, the deeper the call graph, the greater the time that is required as compared with ELABS processing. This is again borne out by the data where programs that perform sorting (*Insrt2, Insrt3, Merge*) require several times as much processing for feasibility checking as for elaboration with specifications. This is so striking here (62 vs 451, 40 vs 453, 604 vs 3100) because the list and set operations that are used have internal calls to other procedures, thus these applications have a fairly deep possibility tree to be examined.

The data also indicate that a feasible program generally requires more processing than an infeasible program. Typically, a feasible program has more procedure implementations to consider while an infeasible program may be missing some implementations. These data show an extreme situation; in practice, some infeasible programs may be closer in their processing needs to feasible programs if only a few implementations are missing. Under other circumstances, different implementations may have different call graphs, and thus an infeasible program could require more processing than a feasible program with different selection decisions.

The disquieting fact from these data is that feasibility checking is quite expensive: it varies from approximately the same cost as semantic processing to three times the cost of semantic processing. If performed once, this would not be such a great burden, but the process of checking the feasibility of a program is used to associate attributes with nodes in the possibility tree. Recall that the paradigm for making selections has three steps: pick an implementation; elaborate the program with implementations; and then execute the attributes to gather information about the decisions. Considering many different implementations would require reelaborating the program with implementations many times, at possibly prohibitive cost. The compromise provided by the Paragon system is a facility for checking the feasibility of a block (see *BindProcs* in Section 5.4.2.1), thus limiting the examination to a single node in the possibility tree. In practice, this may not be sufficiently fast for considering many different implementations.

7.3.3.3. Measuring Elaboration with Realizations

Elaboration with realizations takes place when executing the policy procedure and when executing attributes. Because policies and programs can vary widely, there is no general measurement of the time required by any particular policy operating on a particular program. Instead, some measurements were made of the relative speeds of some basic constructs.

The six measurements in Table 7-7 on page 251 were made during the execution of small policy procedures operating on a null application program. To provide a baseline, the execution of a policy with two declarations (for later use) was measured. Specifically, the following policy was executed:

```
procedure policy(i:instance) is
begin
    var j => im . new integer;
    var k => im . new integer;
end;
```

To minimize the effects of calling the policy procedure, the other tests were constructed by placing the construction of interest in a *for* loop. The basic shell with a *for* loop is:

```
procedure policy(i:instance) is
begin
    var j => im . new integer;
    var k => im . new integer;

    for j in 1..1000 do

    end for;
end;
```

In the first nonempty test, the policy procedure declares a local procedure and executes it. The source for this third test is

```
procedure policy(i:instance) is
begin
    procedure TestProc; procedure TestProc is begin return; end;
    var j => im . new integer;
    var k => im . new integer;

    for j in 1..1000 do
        TestProc;
    end for;
end;
```

The fourth test adds some more complexity: a single assignment statement. Recall that a literal is actually a function call, as is the assignment statement, so two procedure calls are being made for each execution of the assignment statement. Unlike the previous example, the procedure *Assign* also has parameters, which makes its call more costly to execute than that in the previous example.[90] The complete text is shown below:

---

[90]The fully expanded name expression for the call would be *IM.Assign(k,IM.Literal(Special_Make_Literal(1)))*.

```
procedure policy(i:instance) is
begin
   var j => im . new integer;
   var k => im . new integer;

   for j in 1..1000 do
      k := 1;
   end for;
end;
```

So far, the policies have dealt with nonattribute procedure calls. Since policies may also use attributes, I performed an experiment to measure the time required for an attribute call. Initially, a baseline policy was executed. Because attributes always return an object, the baseline must also accommodate a returned value so that the way in which the return value is used will not affect the timings. This is accomplished by placing the attribute call in an *if* statement, so that the returned value is used as the test. The baseline can contain the equivalent of the returned value in the same *if* test, thus isolating the differences between the baseline and the sample program to only an attribute call. The actual text of the baseline and the sample programs are shown below:

```
!----------------------------- ;
! This is the baseline ;
!----------------------------- ;

procedure policy(i:instance) is
begin
   var j => im . new integer;
   var k => im . new integer;

   for j in 1..1000 do
      if True then fi;
   end for;
end;

class mainprogram is
begin
   attribute procedure MyAttribute return Booleans.Bit is
   begin return True; end;
end;
```

```
!------------------------------- ;
! The sample containing an attribute call. ;
!------------------------------- ;

procedure policy(i:instance) is
begin
    var j => im . new integer;
    var k => im . new integer;

    for j in 1..1000 do
        if i.MyAttribute return (Booleans.Bit) then fi;
    end for;
end;

class mainprogram is
begin
    attribute procedure MyAttribute return Booleans.Bit is
    begin return True; end;
end;
```

The results of the all of the experiments are tabulated below:

Policy	Policy Execution Time
2 Declarations	33
1000 Iteration For Loop, empty	689
1000 Iteration For Loop, single proc. call	1422
1000 Iteration For Loop, assignment stat.	5117
1000 Iteration For Loop, if statement	1570
1000 Iteration For Loop, attribute call	3376

Table 7-7: Dynamic Performance of Policy Procedure Execution

From these experiments, we can deduce the time required for the continuation of an iterator, the invocation of a procedure, the passing of a parameter and the invocation of an attribute. A discussion of these calculations is presented below, followed by a summary in Table 7-8.

Relatively little time is spent elaborating the empty policy with two declarations: 33 seconds. The elaboration of an iterator adds another 656 seconds of execution time, about half a second per iteration of the *for* loop, which is only continuing an iterator.[91] A single procedure call adds another 733 seconds, or about three-quarters of a second per loop. Thus a parameterless procedure call is about 50% more time consuming than restarting an iterator.

---

[91]Recall that the notation *1..1000* is syntactic sugar for the invocation of a predefined iterator, *IM.Sequence(1,1000)*.

The assignment statement adds another 3695 seconds, or about 3.7 seconds per loop. However, this measurement really corresponds to three procedure calls. In the prototype, literals are implemented in a two procedure call process. The first procedure call emulates the construction of the special literal functions mentioned in Section 3.3.6 by taking the integer literal as a string and returning a *Word* object. The second procedure call is the *Literal* procedure which, as defined by Paragon, takes the *Word* object and returns an *Integer* object. The *Integer* object in turn is the second parameter to the third procedure, namely the *Assign* procedure. Thus there are three procedure calls and a total of four procedure parameter bindings: one for the literal string, one for the *Value* procedure, and two for the *Assign* procedure. If each procedure call without parameters accumulates 733 seconds, then 2199 of the 3695 additional seconds are used for the three procedures' execution overhead and 1496 seconds are used to bind four parameters during the thousand iterations of the loop, or about 0.4 seconds per parameter binding.

The last two policies are used to measure the execution time of an attribute call in the *for* loop. Because the attribute body contains an expression which is identical to the expression in the *if* statement of the baseline, namely *True*, we can subtract the time of the fifth test from the sixth test, giving 1806 seconds for a thousand executions of the attribute call. Thus each attribute call required about 1.8 seconds.

These results are summarized below:

Function	Unit Execution Time
Iteration Continuation	0.66
Parameterless Procedure Call	0.73
Parameter Binding	0.37
Parameterless Attribute Call	1.81

Table 7-8: Unit Execution Times of Policy Procedure

Although the prototype's speed is too slow for interactive use, its speed is sufficiently fast for testing the policy procedures used in these experiments in a batch-mode operation. The primary reason for the slow speed is the implementation of the interpreter. The program tree is merely walked as necessary to perform the required actions. In addition, the added level of Franzlisp interpretation slows execution of Paragon sources. However, Paragon procedures are no more complicated than Pascal or Simula procedures and so a production-quality translator that generates native machine code should do as well as compilers for those languages.

7.4. Conclusions about the Prototype

The implemented prototype served its purpose, namely as an illustration that the type hierarchies can be added to current languages without radical changes to the compiler design. Although the current implementation is slow, the design is conventional, and by comparing the processing requirements consumed by new features of the system, for example, ELABI, with well understood features, for example, ELABS and PURIFY, one can conclude that a production quality version of the new phases should not consume more resources than the more conventional parts of the compiler.

Chapter 8
Retrospective on the Language Design and Implementation

This research was predicated on my belief that type hierarchies provide a natural way to express the refinement process for abstract data types, from specification, to implementation, to selecting a particular implementation. One expression of this belief is the current Paragon design which uses type hierarchies as the basis for its abstract data type features.

On page 20, Chapter 2 provided four sets of specific goals that a language design using type hierarchies should meet. The first two sets of goals dealt with the ways that data abstractions could be specified and used. The third set of goals direct the way that representations for a data abstraction should be selected. The fourth set of goals outlined some requirements that an implementation of a system based on type hierarchies should meet. In this chapter, the Paragon design will be evaluated with respect to these goals. Where imperfections remain, some suggestions for future work are given.

8.1. Abstract Data Type Features

Several goals were presented for the abstract data type features: specifications could be refined; related specifications could be combined in a single module; multiple implementations for an abstract data type could be written. multiple implementations for an abstract data type could be used simultaneously in a program; multiple implementations for an abstract data type could interact in a program; and a single representation could be written for multiple specifications.

These goals were met by the use of classes to define a type hierarchy. Classes allows a programmer to express generalizations. These generalization classes are inherited by specification classes to provide class declarations that serve as specifications for variables. Further refinements of classes, that is, subclasses, can add implementations of the procedure specifications provided in the generalization and specification classes. These subclasses serve as implementations for variables.

Nested classes support the object-manager model of programming. This model uses one class declaration to define a manager of objects and a nested class declaration to define the individuals handled by the manager. The use of nested classes to implement the object-manager model also allows the managers to be inherited by one class while keeping the individuals in separate classes. This shared manager may then have access to both representations of the individuals. Thus the use of nested classes allows a programmer to express multiple representations of a data type that can not only be used simultaneously in a program, but may interact as well.

The packaging of abstract data types in classes also permits details of refinements to be introduced at the proper time. A *Set* could be specified as holding any kind of element while each implementation could specify exactly what additional properties were required of the element for that implementation of *Set* to work.

Many of these effects come naturally because the same mechanism, namely the class declaration, is used for both managers and individuals. For example, class nesting and inheritance permits procedures to be declared in shared managers where they can affect different individuals. Further managers are treated no differently than other instances of classes and so may be created as necessary, passed as parameters and returned from functions.

My major criticism of the class feature in Paragon is that it does not correspond exactly to the object-manager model of programming. Instead, the classes may be used to simulate this model, much in the same way that *goto* and *if* statements may be used to simulate more abstract control statements such as *while*, *case* and *repeat*. Like the *goto* features in assembly languages, the *class* features in Paragon are probably too general to act as the only data structuring mechanism in the language. The problems with this generality becomes evident upon reflection of some of the implications of the design:

- Constraints are required in procedure specifications for refining procedure specifications along with their managers and individuals (Sections 3.5.4 and 4.4.1).

- The expressions in *return* expressions of procedure declarations must use identifiers declared in parameters to properly express the return object of the procedure (Section 4.4.2).

- Comparison of objects is complicated by holes in objects. Holes appear in objects because of intervening declarations of classes and procedures between specification and implementation classes (Sections 3.4.2.2 and 7.3.3.1).

- The language is extremely verbose (every example, also Sections C.4 and C.5).

- Specifications may only be *added* to the hierarchy, never *removed*. Therefore the hierarchy becomes very rigid and difficult to change (Sections 4.4.4 and 4.4.5).

- Implementations are difficult to organize in useful fashion for sharing (Section 4.6.2).

One possible approach towards solving these problems would be to provide more explicit support for the object-manager model. Some salient features of this support include:

- Explicit distinction between managers and individuals;

- Explicit distinction between specifications and implementations;

- Close the scopes that define managers;

- Explicit separation of types and objects;

- Explicit import and export lists for the encapsulation mechanism.

- Implicit combining of managers for implementations;

- Implicit use of managers in expressions;

These features would eliminate the need for nested classes and the all of the notations and semantics that is required for them. Further, these features eliminate differently sized objects so object matching should be much faster. The use of explicit export and import lists can help reduce the cost of feasibility analysis by limiting the possible interactions between representations. The implicit combining of managers and the implicit use of managers in expressions should make the language more concise than Paragon. The separation of types would eliminate the bizarre run-time error where an *indefinite* instance is used as an environment when invoking a procedure. Instead, compile-time analysis could guarantee that a *definite* instance was present when necessary.

A language design that includes those suggestions might be able to avoid many of the problems that befell Paragon. Without such a complete language, however, I would hesitate to state that those specific criteria are enough to ensure a consistent and concise language.

8.2. Describing and Selecting Abstract Data Types

Another set of goals for the design of Paragon is that a programmer should be able to describe and select abstract data types without giving direct access to the implementation. Attributes, policies and possibility trees provide the features that allow the programmers to describe and select abstract data types.

8.2.1. Attributes

Attributes provide a way to describe abstract data types, especially if the specification contains an attribute that may be redeclared by the implementations. The programmer may then use attributes to describe the ways in which implementations differ while protecting the internal details against unauthorized access.

The inclusion of a programmer controlled facility for describing data types is a significant departure from data abstraction languages. Usually, only predefined types have descriptive information available for the different implementations. Thus the attribute facility in Paragon is quite innovative.

Unfortunately, the attribute facility is very verbose. The kinds of information that attributes provide are usually very simple: a formula that defines the amount of space required by a representation; whether performance measurements are being carried out; whether the implementation is a debugging version. Most representation selection systems use a specific format for encoding this data in a readily usable format. In Paragon, general procedures must be written for any piece of information, even simple boolean values. Thus a large amount of program text is consumed providing very little information. An approach for dealing with this problem is presented in Section 8.2.7.

Another problem with attributes is their distributed nature. A programmer cannot readily determine what sorts of representation information are available for an abstract data type without reading all of the implementations of that data type. Unlike most representation selection systems, the representation description is stored with the representation and not collected in some place external to the representations. Further, there is no guarantee that all representations have the same attributes. If one wants to perform a space optimization algorithm in the policy, it would be helpful to guarantee that each representation provides a measure of the space it required. Unfortunately, there is no such method in Paragon for insisting that some set of classes all provide the same set of attributes. The compromise provided by the language is the dynamic selection of attribute procedures. If one wants all representations of an abstract data type to contain a certain attribute, one declares that attribute in the specification. This attribute declaration then serves as a default value. Should any implementation not declare the needed attribute, the attribute declared in the specification can be used by the policy.

An alternative design for attributes would require attribute specifications and implementations just like nonattribute procedures. This has two problems. First, some groups of implementations may have attributes that are not meaningful to all implementations. Therefore it is not appropriate for all implementations to declare that attribute. For example, one may want to include the notion that an implementation performs timing measurements. Only those implementations that have measuring capability should contain attributes that describe the kinds of measurements that are performed, not all implementations.

A second problem is the size of change required when a new attribute is added because of a new implementation. Suppose that a new implementation were added that contains a new facility: the new implementation measures performance. No other implementations measure performance. One would want to add an attribute to that new implementation describing the fact that it measured performance. If specifications and implementations for attributes were required, then the original specification of the abstract data type and every other implementation of the abstract data type would have to be changed to add a specification or implementation, respectively, for this new attribute. Because the addition of a new implementation should not cause such a drastic modification of existing implementations, the approach of using attribute specifications and implementations was rejected.

8.2.2. Policies and Possibility Trees

The design of Paragon included a goal of allowing automatic selection of representations. This is achieved by the policy procedure, which provides the programmer with the ability to specify the criteria for making representation choices. The translation system uses the policy to make the actual representation selections for variables. The primary motivation for the design of the current system was to separate policy and mechanism in the same sense as Hydra [Wulf 74]. I feel that selecting out particular syntactic features of the language for the selection mechanism, such as loop depth, would bias the selection strategy. However, the more features that are made available by the selection mechanism, the greater the convenience for the programmer. One extreme of this situation exists in current compilers: a programmer merely specifies that a program should be optimized for space, leaving to the compiler all of the decisions as to how to make a procedure space efficient. Yet all of the goals for integrating representation selection with data abstraction suggest that the programmer should be deciding how selections should be made, not the compiler. Therefore the translation system should provide the programmer with data about the program and let the programmer institute whatever policy is appropriate. The extreme design is to provide the policy writer, that is, the programmer, with complete access to the parse tree. Such an approach turns the policy writer into a compiler writer, which is considered too inconvenient for the typical programmer. Thus current design of Paragon reflects a compromise to relieve the tension between flexibility and convenience.

The construction of a possibility tree to represent the program and the execution of a policy procedure to make selections are features that attempt to provide the programmer with enough facilities to describe popular selection strategies without requiring the programmer to be a compiler writer. As shown in Sections 6.5 and 6.9, many different selection strategies can be written. Thus the Paragon design subsumes and generalizes many previous representation selection systems.

However, the integration of the selection facilities with the abstract data type features has several problems. At best, the selection facilities represent further compromises between completeness and convenience. These problems can be grouped into three categories: descriptions of the program's variables, descriptions of the program's structure, and storage of intermediate selection decisions.

8.2.3. Anonymous Possibility Tree Nodes

Variables in a program are described by nodes in the possibility tree. But the policy procedure and possibility tree provide only anonymous descriptions of the program's variables and implementations. Because of this anonymity, the policy procedure can either deal in only generalities, or the programmer has to provide many obscure attribute procedures to describe surreptitiously the variable declarations in the program. Because a policy procedure may wish to only deal with certain variables or certain uses of a class, a clearer mechanism is needed. For example, a programmer may know that only the variable *SymbolTable* is important and may wish the policy procedure to consider carefully only that declaration, choosing any feasible implementation for all other variables. A programmer may also wish to write different kinds of policies that work on certain kinds of specifications. One example is a policy that can deal well with selecting set implementations or list implementations. To use such a policy, it is necessary to isolate those variables in the program that are set or list variables, yet all variable declarations look alike to the current policy procedure. A new mechanism should provide direct information about the program's variables' identifiers and specifications, and about the identities of all class declarations.

The reason why the design of this new mechanism is difficult is scope rules. The policy procedure is executed inside of the universal environment, in which all of the policy's identifiers are defined. The class and variable declarations that are manipulated by the policy procedure usually exist in nested scopes that are generally inaccessible to the policy procedure. Thus there is no convenient way to associate the identity of classes or variables in the policy procedure with specific declarations. In the current design, this mapping is provided through the possibility tree and the use of doppelgangers.

In other representation selection systems, this scope problem can be minimized since only one scope, the main program, is analyzed. Thus a special rule can permit the selection system to examine the one scope. In Paragon, the selection process is applied also to local procedures and local data of objects, which gives rise to the possibility tree and nested scopes. Therefore the design of Paragon considers a larger problem than other representation selection systems. I believe that using some abstract representation of the program, such as the possibility tree, is the appropriate data structure for making selection decisions. However, the information represented in the possibility tree is incomplete and anonymous. Therefore more work is needed to provide a more complete data structure and to include specific knowledge about the program's declarations by name rather than by reference.

8.2.4. Parse Tree Availability

The second problem prohibiting convenient use of the selection system is the lack of access to the parse tree of the program. Instead, the writer of a policy sees a possibility tree, which bears resemblance to a call graph. There are many natural questions that can be answered by examining a parse tree and that a policy writer might want to ask:

• In what order are procedures called?

• Are some procedures never called?

- Are there constants in some parameters?

- Is one variable always used in a certain position of a procedure?

- Is a procedure conditionally executed?

- Is a procedure inside of a loop (Possibly an "inner" loop)?

At a more general level of analysis, a policy procedure may wish to perform some kind of control flow reasoning about the program to use some special implementations when appropriate [Hisgen 82], to determine if some constants may be folded which in turn may affect an implementation decision, and to perform assertion propagation in an attempt to supplement attribute-procedure information. Clearly, a piece of the program that is in an inner loop should deserve more attention than a piece of the program that is not. Yet, the policy cannot know which pieces of a program are in such a location. Typical compilers perform these kinds of analyses to determine low level selection details. Higher level decisions, such as whether to use a binary tree or a hash table for an implementation, can also benefit from this information.

Some of these questions can be answered by careful, painstaking analysis of program using the pattern-matching statement. This seems to be a poor substitute for a rather direct question. Similarly, the translation system provides a predefined procedure that returns the number of a times a procedure is called instead of the ability to detect inner loops. In principle, this procedure might invoke a performance verifier as suggested by Shaw [Shaw 79] but in practice no such facility exists. The current system merely asks the programmer for the answer. More realistic approaches in actual systems use a heuristic such as loop depth, a symbolic analysis of the program [Kant 83] or a limited kind of simulation of the system [Low 74]. None of these approaches were added this system.

Other kinds of information cannot be derived from the possibility tree, even with careful and contrived use of pattern matching and attributes. Current compilers gather this information during a flow analysis of the program, during which certain assertions are proposed and propagated through the parse tree and call graph. The current system does not readily admit the collection of such information. Some propagations require intimate knowledge of the operations whereas all operations in Paragon are identically content-free (to the selection algorithm). Many assertions interact strongly with the flow graph of the program through loops and conditions, none of which are available to the policy writer. All of these problems represent future research possibilities for representation selection systems.

8.2.5. Decorating the Possibility Tree

The third major inconvenience in the current selection mechanisms is the presentation of the program structure in the possibility tree. There are two problems with this presentation: no new information may be added to the tree, and the tree may not be altered. The first problem is fairly easy to solve; An alternative design that permits the programmer to add arbitrary decorations to the tree is provided in Section 5.4.2.2.

However, the fact that the structure of the possibility tree is under control of the translation system alone and not the policy is a more difficult problem. Through the use of attributes, a policy may determine that some tree rearranging is appropriate, eliminating some procedure calls, substituting one for another, combining variables, and so on. However, the translation system does not permit the policy to change the tree. Doing so violates the informal specifications for the *Instance* class.[92] One alternative is to provide the programmer with direct access to the parse tree which the policy could then manipulate. When a programmer changes the possibility tree, the corresponding program would be transformed as well. This alternative would eliminate the idea of doppelgangers as well but forces the policy to resemble a compiler phase, a situation that was a priori rejected as being too complex for convenience. Thus the compromise represented by the Paragon design allows the possibility tree to be changed only by the translation system during elaboration with implementations.

Several approaches for solving the shortcomings in the sections above center on different models for making representation selections. Several of these approaches, and their motivations, are described.

8.2.6. Simpler Models

At an empirical level, it is still not clear that multiple representations of abstract data types, let alone multiple and simultaneous representations, have any practical value when dealing with moderately-sized programs. Further, there is little empirical evidence that any selection that is made should be determined at compile time. If true, these observations would suggest a very simple model for making selections of representations.

---

[92] The syntax of Paragon allows the policy to assign any references it desires to the pointers in the tree. However, if such general references were permitted, the underlying translation system would no longer guarantees that the tree will properly match the doppelgangers in the program being analyzed.

It is difficult to show empirically that moderately sized programs do not use large numbers of representations. Some simple observations are possible: None of the example programs in this thesis, which were drawn from the representation-selection literature, really contain a large number of the same data structure that requires radically different implementations. The literature on abstract data types does not seem to require multiple implementations as well. For example, in a widely referenced Clu paper [Liskov 77], there is only one use of each abstract data types: *wordbag*, *wordtree* and *sortedbag*. If no more than one instance of each abstract data type is present in a program, then there is no need for more than one representation to be present in the program at the same time. Further, there is no clear need for more than one representation to even be defined.

There are two places where one does find multiple instances of objects and multiple representations of those instances: in systems with dynamic selection of representations and in systems where the number of abstractions is limited to a small collection of predefined objects.

The applications that use multiple representation of objects make their selection based on some kind of input data, and perform the selection during object creation. For example, as a compiler builds a syntax tree of a program, it may pick different representations of symbols for a symbol table, or different expression nodes for the abstract syntax tree [Sherman 80]. Another example is contained in the Smalltalk system. Here, the entire graphics facility is geared towards the dynamic selection of an appropriate representation of a "displayable" object [Rentsch 83]. In both of these systems, there is no need for a separate selection system, since the program explicitly chooses an appropriate representation based on factors beyond a selection system's realm of knowledge.

The other place where representation selection seems important is when a language or a system provides very few abstractions that have to be used in many ways. This happens in Fortran, where numbers and arrays are the only data abstraction mechanism provided, in data base systems, where tables are the only data abstraction mechanism provided, and in SETL, where sets are the primary data abstraction mechanism. Because these abstractions are used so heavily, there is a significant advantage to having multiple representations for them. For Fortran, a wide body of literature has been developed attacking this specific problem of selecting an appropriate representation for integers, both for the size of the integer and the memory placement of the integer (which are orthogonal aspects of an integer's representation) [Leverett 81]. Similarly, the selection problem for data base systems has been discussed for years [Gotlieb 74, Smith 77] and the implementations of SETL have included a large amount of processing for choosing an appropriate set implementation under many different circumstances [Freudenberger 83]. In these circumstances, the selection system may be simplified by making it more specialized. By needing only to concern itself with integers, or tables, or sets, it may provide explicit facilities for manipulations of those kinds of objects and their operations. With the need to express all possible data abstractions and their uses, the selection mechanism becomes general and difficult to use. Thus a restricted domain could simplify the system.

8.2.7. External Selection Language

Although there may not be a great need for automated selection at compile time, there still exists a need for manual selection of some data types. For example, one can think of a terminal as being an abstract data type and different representations as being different manufacturers' models. A user would like to manipulate an abstract terminal and later manually associate a specific terminal driver with the abstract definition so that the program works on the terminal that the programmer is currently using.

Such an association should be provided by an external selection language. A large amount of work has already been performed on the syntax and semantics that an external selection (or configuration) language should contain, so a discussion will not be presented here. The interested reader may examine some of the previous surveys [Schwanke 82, Tichy 80].

However, the use of an external selection language is not appropriate in all circumstances. When simple module or configuration selection is needed, this approach works well. For more general selection algorithms, the external selection language must contain some notions from the programming language so that it can manipulate the program objects. For Paragon, this includes variable declarations, procedure implementations, and classes. Similarly, the programming language part might have to contain some elements of the external selection language since it must be able to describe the different properties of the implementations and representations. In the past, this approach has been limited to mere naming conventions, where some relation is defined between the names of program entities, such as class names, and the names in the external selection language. Therefore most of these other issues have not been addressed, but are areas for future research.

8.2.8. Program Creation Systems

Another approach to representation selection is through the use of a program generator, either table driven like the PQCC system [Leverett 80, Wulf 80] or expert system driven, such as PSI [Barr 82]. These systems create a program, along with any necessary abstractions, from some description of the task to be completed. Since the program creators have all of the information available about the program that exists, these systems could also make representation choices based on the same information. In many respects, such an approach mimics the manual selection of representations, since in both situations, the program creator is also performing the representation selection. The motivation for separating the tasks of program development and representation selection is no longer present. A program creation system does not become bored or make clerical mistakes during the refinement process, whereas people do. Thus a separation of tasks that is useful for people may not be appropriate when those tasks are performed by machine. Under these circumstances, a representation system would be integrated in the program creation system, and not a separate system as in Paragon.

8.3. Automatic Processing of Paragon Programs

The fourth set of design goals requires that Paragon programs should be compilable. The existence of the prototype translator provides tangible evidence of attaining this goal. The entire language can be semantically checked, representations chosen and the resulting program run. Further, very stringent requirements are place on the translator: each procedure call and object instance may have different implementations; for every procedure call and object instance, the translator must guarantee that a consistent implementation exists; no run-time selection of implementations is permitted. These specific requirements for the translator affected the design of the language and the speed of the resulting translator.

The concept of the three kinds of elaborations is one of the innovations that resulted from the compiler requirements for Paragon. To my knowledge, Paragon is the first language to define elaboration with implementations as a way of ensuring (and expressing) a program's feasibility, that is, as a way to guarantee that a program has all of the necessary implementations for execution.

But with the separation of a program's semantics into three elaborations, and with the requirement that elaboration with specifications and implementations must occur before elaboration with realizations, some programmer convenience is sacrificed. First, heterogeneous data structures are difficult to construct. Second, the global analysis required by feasibility checking makes translation slow and difficult to partition.

8.3.1. Heterogeneous Data Structures

First, the way that a procedure call is elaborated with specifications makes heterogeneous data structures difficult to construct. The difficulty is the direct result of the requirements for automatic processing of programs, in particular, the requirement that the single return type of a function be statically determined. As shown in Section 4.4.3, the elaboration algorithm cannot always determine the exact type of the returned object when more than one kind of object may be returned.

One alternative for solving this problem is to permit the programmer to qualify the results of name components. This is done in Simula through the use of the *QUA* notation (read *qualified*). In Paragon, one might write *f(x) qualified as Matrix* to specify that the return object of *f(x)* should be considered to be a *Matrix*. In general, this assertion must be checked at run time, hence the adoption of this feature violates another goal of guaranteeing no run-time checking or selection.

Once a "qualifying" feature is added, Paragon should also include a way to test the type of an object. As suggested in Section 6.9.4, this could be done by allowing constraint expressions to appear anywhere that other expressions may appear.

8.3.2. Global Feasibility Checking

A second problem with the translation requirements of Paragon is that feasibility checking, that is, elaborating a program with implementations, requires a global analysis of a program. One would like to perform small amounts of separable processing during the analysis of a program, such as the processing of a single procedure or a single class. Instead, all of the calls and object instances must be examined as a whole to determine program feasibility, which causes two problems. First, elaboration with implementations is inefficient. As documented in Table 7-6, feasibility analysis can require three times as much processor time as semantic analysis. Second, the required global analysis renders separate compilation nearly impossible. Usually one can accomplish separate compilation by extracting some small part of each separately compiled piece of a program which can be easily checked with other separately compiled pieces. Because Paragon permits different calls of the same procedure implementation (and different instantiations of the same class) to use different implementation selections for internal variables and procedure calls, the entire implementation of procedures (and classes) must be completed elaborated each time they are used to ensure program feasibility. In short, a separate compilation facility for Paragon would apply only to elaboration with specifications, and a rather sophisticated loader would have to perform elaboration with implementations to ensure feasibility. By contrast, current loaders can usually perform this analysis by merely resolving external references.

One possible solution to this problem would be to force representation selection for each use of a procedure implementation and class to be identical. This would allow the translation system to process a single declaration independently of its use, and hence permit separate compilation. This would also simplify the possibility tree, since only a single block would be considered at a time. There would be no need to perform selection of local procedure calls or class instances and so they could be removed from the tree.

This solution was rejected for two reasons: it eliminated general procedure implementations and it removed the ability to exploit type parameters.

If every procedure implementation had exactly one statically-determined representation choice made for it, then general procedures would be useless. Recall that a general procedure is one that only uses abstract properties of its parameters, such as the *Intersect* procedure below:

```
procedure Intersect(L:Set,R:Set) return Set is
begin
   var i => IM . new Integer;
   ...
   if IsMember(L,i) then
   ...
end;
```

A single implementation choice for the call of *IsMember* would force a single implementation choice for *L* or else probably be infeasible. Both circumstances are unacceptable. Instead, the implementation of *IsMember* should be based on the implementation of *L*, which can change from call to call.

The second reason for rejecting the single implementation of locals in procedures is that I wanted to permit different implementations of local variables when type parameters are used.

In the example for *APLSymbolTable* in Section 4.4.3 (on page 81), the local variables inside of (hypothetical) implementations for the *Insert* procedure may use different implementations that depend on the object passed as a parameter. If exactly one representation were permitted for local variables and procedure calls in each class and procedure implementation, then the *Insert* procedure could not contain a different local variable when the symbol table is created to hold integers than for when the symbol table is created to hold matrices. Thus efficiency of feasibility checking can be obtained at the expense of program inflexibility. Paragon makes a different tradeoff, and allows a flexible set of selection choices at the expense of a large amount of feasibility checking.

8.4. Summary

The significant contributions of this thesis can be grouped into two categories: contributions dealing with language support for abstract data types and contributions dealing with representation selection.

8.4.1. Contributions: Abstract Data Types

Paragon illustrates several innovations using the type hierarchy facility for the specification and implementation of data abstractions. Some of these innovations come directly from the use of the type hierarchy, other comes from the integration of other standard programming language features, such as parameters, with the type hierarchy. Four of these innovations are discussed below.

8.4.1.1. Refining Specifications

The use of multiply inherited classes and the separation of procedure specifications and implementations allows the programmers to write very general specifications and later refine the specifications without adding any implementation details. For example, one may start with the specification that an object may be assigned, then later add specifications that the object is ordered, and finally add specifications that the object is an integer. Thus Paragon provides a general mechanism for writing and refining specifications. The different refinements of specifications are especially useful in parameters, as illustrated by the discrimination-net implementation for sets discussed on page 89.

8.4.1.2. Implementing Abstract Data Types

The class hierarchy and the parameter matching rules provide a new way to refine specifications into implementations of abstract data types. These features allow a programmer to write multiple implementations of abstract data types that may be present simultaneously in a program. Because each refinement for an implementation is named, there is a natural way of distinguishing between different concrete implementations and of defining which details of the concrete implementation are available to a procedure implementation. Because the parameter matching rules are not symmetric, an implementation for an abstract data type may list additional specifications that its parameters must meet. Thus the refinements necessary for the implementation appear with the implementation and are not leaked to the specification of the abstract data type.

8.4.1.3. Combining Representations

The parameter matching rules, the multiple inheritance of classes and the ability to provide multiple procedure implementations for a specification allow a program to use combined representations in a program. Like the implementations of abstract data types, the implementations of procedures may list additional specifications that their parameters must meet, and thus an appropriate procedure implementation can be used when different representations of variables are present. Procedure implementations that specify different concrete representations for their parameters may be written in combined representations. Thus variables that interact may use a procedure that can properly deal with whatever representations those variables use, even if the representations are different.

Further, Paragon allows representations to be combined for unrelated specifications. This is useful when the implementations are related but the specifications are not. One such example is a transaction log, where many different abstract objects must be written into the same log. Thus the log must use a combined representation for all of the abstract objects.

8.4.1.4. Uniform Object Notation

Paragon uses a uniform object notation in variable declarations, parameters and statements. This notation combines the type of an object with the procedures that may operate on that object. Thus this notation eliminates the need for procedure parameters that are usually found in data abstraction languages. Further, the notation distinguishes *indefinite* from *definite* objects. This has the effect of eliminating the need for type parameters and of providing the ability to restrict formal parameters to particular object. One way that this last feature can be used is to require that all arrays passed to a procedure have a lower bound of one.

8.4.2. Contributions: Representation Selection

Paragon advances the state of the art of representation selection in many ways. Some of these innovations come directly from the use of a type hierarchy; others were driven by the goals in Chapter 2. Four of these innovations are discussed below.

8.4.2.1. Describing Abstract Data Types

The attributes are used to describe the classes and procedures in an abstract data type. Because attributes are defined by the programmer, they represent an advance over current compilers that usually provide only predefined attributes. Further, attributes in Paragon may use the entire language, and not merely some scalar values. Thus attributes may describe complex information about a data type. Finally, attributes may be used with any abstract data types and not only predefined types. Thus attributes provide a way to describe the differences between multiple representations of user-defined abstract data types.

8.4.2.2. Organizing Global Program Optimization

A major innovation in Paragon is the ability of the translation system to perform representation selection for all variables and procedure calls in a program. Most representation selection systems perform selection analysis only on the variables in the main program. In Paragon, variables and procedure calls in local procedures and classes also have their representations selected by the same mechanism as the variables and procedure calls in the main program. The Paragon translation system provides a data structure, called the possibility tree, to organize these representation decisions. In addition to providing an organization for the current selection choices, the possibility tree also retains information about previous, rejected selection decisions. This is valuable since old choices are frequently reexamined.

8.4.2.3. Programmer Control of Selection Criteria

Another innovation of the Paragon design is the use of a programmer-provided policy to control the selection of representations. Most compilers or representation selection systems contain predefined algorithms for making representation selection decisions. The criteria embodied by these algorithms may not reflect the criteria that the programmer desires. To change the algorithm requires the programmer to alter the translation system. The design of the translation system for Paragon extracts the algorithm used for making selection decisions from the translator and lets the programmer specify the algorithm using the criteria that the programmer feels are important. The thesis gives several examples of policies that make selection based on a number of criteria using widely differing techniques, such as dynamic programming, hill climbing, step-wise refinement, branch-and-bound searching, exhaustive analysis and direct selection of representations.

8.4.2.4. Feasibility Analysis

Another significant innovation in the Paragon language design is the definition and implementation of feasibility analysis. Feasibility refers to the property that a program has when all selection decisions result in a program that can execute. For example, all variables and procedure calls must have implementations, interacting variables that use different representations must use procedure implementations that can operate on the different concrete representations, and representations for abstract data types that require some special properties of their parameters must ensure that they received the proper kinds of actual parameters. Most languages and systems add restrictions to simplify or eliminate feasibility analysis. For example, one restriction is that any implementation may be used wherever its specification is used. As explained on page 10, such a restriction limits the possible implementations that may be written. Another restriction is that interacting variables must use the same representation. But this ignores other considerations for making selection decisions. This restriction also eliminates the advantages of writing general procedures that use only abstract properties of their parameters. Paragon makes no such restrictions, but instead defines the concept of elaboration with implementations to describe how a program can be checked for feasibility. Further, this thesis describes a translator that implements feasibility checking. Measurements of a prototype show that feasibility checking can require up to three times as much computation as required for semantic analysis.

8.4.3. Future Areas for Related Work

As I was working on this thesis, I thought of several other major directions that could be pursued which would have resulted in a very different thesis. In this section, I briefly discuss some of these related areas where further work might be pursued.

8.4.3.1. Uniform Procedure, Iterator, Object Semantics

Paragon makes a distinction between classes and procedures in several ways: the way that they are declared, the way that they are refined (subclasses vs implementations), the way that they are used (instantiation vs invocation) and the way that their representations are selected (by the policy vs by feasibility analysis). Yet many of the manipulations of classes and procedures are similar: an object is created, the parameters are bound, the local declarations are elaborated and the statements are elaborated. The differences usually concern the lifetime of the created object and the ability to reference the object after its statements have been elaborated. Other languages, such as Beta [Kristensen 83] and SL5 [Hanson 78] try to provide a uniform syntax and semantics for procedures, objects and iterators. Another language design might try to use this uniform approach for defining the storage and operations of an abstract data type and apply a uniform selection technique for picking a representation.

8.4.3.2. Value of Multiple Representations

As I read the literature describing representation selection system, and as I tried to use multiple representations in application programs, I came to have seriously doubts about the need for multiple representations in a program. Clearly, if multiple representations are not needed, then languages do not need to support them and translators do not need to select a representation for variables. Perhaps early researchers who suggested that a dozen or so commonly used data structures such be primitively supported, and that all of the analysis and selection should be moved into the computer and compiler, are correct [Feustal 73]. To understand the need for multiple representations of abstract data types, some empirical research is needed on how abstract data type features are actually used. Unfortunately, there is a lot of question begging here. If one surveys users who do not have languages that support data abstraction or who do not know data abstraction, then the survey will only document the programmers' ignorance or lack of facilities and not the effectiveness of data abstraction.

8.4.3.3. Program Representations for Programmer Manipulation

There are many different ways that programmers make selection decisions. A large variety of these methods can be adapted to Paragon's set of general representation selection features. However, the policy procedure, the attributes and the possibility tree cannot express all the different ways that programmers make decisions. An interesting research area is the analysis of the kinds of information that are necessary for different selection strategies.

8.4.4. Conclusions

The thesis has demonstrated how a type hierarchy can be integrated into a general purpose language design. The thesis demonstrates how a type hierarchy can be used for writing programs using the object-manger model to specify abstractions, refine the specifications, write representations for the abstractions and combine representations as desired. A number of programs were written and translated with a prototype system that processes Paragon. The prototype provides evidence that the language design is well defined and that only conventional compiler technology is necessary for translating languages that include type hierarchies.

There is a lot of intuitive appeal to the model of type hierarchies. Many of the ways that specifications and representations are specified fall naturally into a tree of abstractions, and many refinement paradigms for selecting a representation also search a tree-like structure. All of these are modeled very well by the class hierarchy.

The problems with such an approach are its generality. Although nested and inherited classes nicely express a tree structure, they also express some less useful combinations. Thus a future effort would probably concentrate on the use of an explicit manager model for specifying, representing and selecting abstract data types.

Bibliography

[Balzer 81]   Balzar, Robert.
                Transformational Implementation: An Example.
                IEEE Transactions of Software Engineering SE-7(1):3-14, January, 1981.

[Banatre 81]   Bantare, M., Couvert, A., Herman, D., and Raynal, M.
                An Experience in Implementing Abstract Data Types.
                Software — Practice and Experience 11(3):315-320, March, 1981.

[Barr 82]   Barr, Avron and Feigenbaum, Edward A. (editor).
                The Handbook of Artificial Intelligence.
                William Kaufmann, Inc., Los Altos, California, 1982.

[Barstow 79]   Barstow, David (editor).
                Knowledge-Based Program Construction.
                Elsevier, Amsterdam, 1979.

[Chang 78]   Chang, Ernest, Kaden, Neil E. and Elliott, W. David.
                Abstract Data Types in Euclid.
                Sigplan Notices 13(3):34-42, March, 1978.

[Cheatham 79]   Cheatham Jr., Thomas E., Townley, Judy A. and Holloway, Glenn H.
                A System for Program Refinement.
                In *Proceedings of the 4th International Conference on Software
                    Engineering*, pages 53-62. IEEE Computer Society, September, 1979.

[Curry 82]   Curry, Gael, Baer, Larry, Lipkie, Daniel and Lee, Bruce.
                Traits: An Approach to Multiple-Inheritance Subclassing.
                In Limb, J.O. (editor), *Proceedings, SIGOA Conference on Office
                    Information Systems*, pages 1-9. ACM, SIGOA, June, 1982.
                Also SIGOA Newsletter, Vol. 2, Nos. 1 and 2.

[Dahl 68]   Dahl, O.-J.
                Simula 67 Common Base Language.
                Technical Report, Norwegian Computing Center, Oslo, 1968.

[Dewar 79]   Dewar, Robert B. K., Grand, Arthur, Liu, Ssu-Cheng and Schwartz, Jacob T.
                Programming by Refinement, as Exemplified by the SETL Representation
                    Sublanguage.
                ACM Transactions on Programming Languages and Systems 1(1):27-49,
                    July, 1979.

[Feustal 73]   Feustal, E. A.
                    On the Advantages of Tagged Architecture.
                    IEEE Transactions on Computers C-22(7):644-656, July, 1973.

[Foderaro 80]   Foderaro, John K.
                    The FRANZ LISP Manual
                    Department of Electrical Engineering and Computer Science, University of
                        California at Berkeley, 1980.
                    Distributed with Berkeley/Unix Documentation.

[Freudenberger 83]
                    Freudenberger, Stefan M., Schwartz, Jacob T. and Sharir, Micha.
                    Experience with the SETL Optimiser.
                    ACM Transaction on Programming Languages and Systems 5(1):26-45,
                        January, 1983.

[Ghezzi 77]   Ghezzi, Carlo and Paolini, Paolo.
                    A Language Supporting Abstraction Implementations.
                    In Andre, Jacques and Banatre, Jean-Pierre (editor), *Implementation and
                        Design of Algorithmic Languages: Proceedings of the 5th Annual III
                        Conference*, pages 54-70. IRISA, May, 1977.

[Gillman 83]   Gillman, Robert.
                    INFO-ADA Group Message, Arpanet.
                    May, 1983
                    private communication.

[Goldberg 81]   Goldberg, Adele.
                    Introducing the Smalltalk-80 System.
                    Byte 6(8):14-22, August, 1981.

[Gotlieb 74]   Gotlieb, G. C. and Tompa, Frank. W.
                    Choosing a Storage Schema.
                    Acta Informatica 3:297-319, 1974.

[Hanson 78]   Hanson, David R. and Griswold, Ralph E.
                    The SL5 Procedure Mechanism.
                    Communications of the ACM 21(5):392-400, May, 1978.

[Hisgen 82]   Hisgen, Andy.
                    Towards Optimizations for User-Defined Types: A Program Transformation
                        Approach.
                    Department of Computer Science, Carnegie-Mellon University.
                    May, 1982
                    Ph.D. Thesis Proposal.

[Ichbiah 80]   Ichbiah, Jean, et. al.
                    Reference Manual for the Ada Programming Language.
                    US Government, Washington, D.C., 1980.

[Ingalls 78]   Ingalls, Daniel H. H.
                   The Smalltalk-76 Programming System: Design and Implementation.
                   In *Conference Record of the Fifth Annual ACM Symposium on Principles of
                        Programming Languages*, pages 9-16. ACM, January, 1978.

[Ingalls 81]   Ingalls, Daniel H. H.
                   Design Principles Behind Smalltalk.
                   Byte 6(8):286-298, August, 1981.

[Ingargiola 75]   Ingargiola, Giorgio P.
                   Implementations of Abstract Data Types.
                   In *Proceedings of the Conference on Computer Graphics, Pattern
                        Recognition, & Data Structure*, pages 108-113. IEEE Computer Society,
                        May, 1975.

[Jensen 78]   Jensen, K. and Wirth, N.
                   Pascal User Manual and Report.
                   Springer-Verlag, Mew York, N.Y., 1978.

[Johnson 76]   Johnson, Robert T. and Morris, James B.
                   Abstract Data Types in the MODEL Programming Language.
                   In *Proceedings of Conference on Data: Abstraction, Definition and
                        Structure*, pages 36-46. ACM, March, 1976.
                   Also Sigplan Notices, Vol. 8, No. 2, 1976.

[Kant 83]   Kant, Elaine.
                   On the Efficient Synthesis of Efficient Programs.
                   Artificial Intelligence 20:253-305, 1983.

[Katz 81]   Katz, Shmuek and Zimmerman, Ruth.
                   An Advisory System for Developing Data Representations.
                   In *Proceedings of the Seventh International Joint Conference on Artificial
                        Intelligence*, pages 1030-1036. August, 1981.

[Katzenelson 79]   Katzenelson, Jacob.
                   Clusters and Dialogues for Set Implementations.
                   IEEE Transactions on Software Engineering SE-5(3):256-275, May, 1979.

[Katzenelson 83a] Katzenelson, J.
                   Introduction to Enhanced C (EC).
                   Software — Practice and Experience 13(7), July, 1983.

[Katzenelson 83b] Katzenelson, J.
                   Higher Level Programming and Data Abstractions — A Case Study Using
                        Enhanced C.
                   Software — Practice and Experience 13(7), July, 1983.

[Kristensen 83]   Kristensen, Bent Bruun, Madsen, Ole Lehrmann, Moller-Pedersen, Birger
                        and Nygaard, Kristen.
                   Abstraction Mechanisms in the Beta Programming Language.
                   In *Conference Record of the 10th Annual ACM Symposium on Principles of
                        Programming Languages*, pages 285-298. ACM, January, 1983.

[Lamb 80] Lamb, David Alex, Hisgen, Andy, Rosenberg, Jonathan, Sherman, Mark and
Borkan, Martha.
The Charrette Ada Compiler.
Technical Report CMU-CS-80-148, Carnegie-Mellon University, Computer
Science Department, October, 1980.

[Lamb 83] Lamb, David Alex.
*Sharing Intermediate Representations: The Interface Description
Language.*
Technical Report CMU-CS-83-129, Department of Computer Science,
Carnegie-Mellon University, May, 1983.

[Leverett 80] Leverett, Bruce W., Cattell, Roderic G. G., Hobbs, Steven O., Newcomer,
Joseph M., Reiner, Andrew H., Schatz, Bruce R. and Wulf, William A.
An Overview of the Production-Quality Compiler-Compiler Project.
Computer 13(8):38-49, August, 1980.

[Leverett 81] Leverett, Bruce W.
Register Allocation in Optimizing Compilers.
Technical Report CMU-CS-81-103, Department of Computer Science,
Carnegie-Mellon University, February, 1981.

[Liskov 77] B. Liskov, A. Snyder, R. Atkinson and C. Schaffert.
Abstraction Mechanisms in CLU.
Communications of the ACM 20(8), August, 1977.

[Liskov 81] Liskov, B., Moss, E., Schaffert, C., Scheifler, R. and Snyder, A.
The CLU Reference Manual.
Springer-Verlag, New York, N.Y., 1981.
Lecture Notes in Computer Science No. 114.

[Low 74] Low, James R.
Automatic Coding: Choice of Data Structures.
Technical Report CS-452, Stanford University Computer Science
Department, August, 1974.

[Low 76] Low, James and Rovner, Paul.
Techniques for the Automatic Selection of Data Structures.
In *Conference Record of the 3rd ACM Symposium on Principles of
Programming Languages*, pages 58-67. ACM, January, 1976.

[Low 78] Low, James R.
Automatic Data Structure Selection: An Example and Overview.
Communications of the ACM 21(5):376-385, May, 1978.

[McCune 77] McCune, Brian P.
The PSI Program Model Builder: Synthesis of Very High-Level Programs.
In *Proceedings of the Symposium on Artificial Intelligence and
Programming Languages*, pages 130-139. ACM, August, 1977.
Also Sigplan Notices, Vol. 12, No. 8, August 1977.

[MIT 78]   Unknown MIT Author.
                    Maclisp Manual
                    Department of Electrical Engineering and Computer Science,
                        Massachusetts Institute of Technology, 1978.
                    Transcribed INFO file.

[Mitchell 79]   Mitchell, James G., Maybury, William and Sweet, Richard.
                    Mesa Language Manual.
                    Technical Report CSL-79-3, Xerox Palo Alto Research Center, Systems
                        Development Department, April, 1979.
                    Version 5.0.

[Morgan 81]   Morgan, Chris.
                    Smalltalk: A Language for the 1980s.
                    Byte 6(8):6-10, August, 1981.

[Moss 78]   Moss, John Eliot Blakeslee.
                    Abstract Data Types in Stack Based Languages.
                    Technical Report MIT/LCS/TR-190, Laboratory for Computer Science,
                        Massachusetts Institute of Technology, February, 1978.

[Mylopoulos 80]   Mylopoulos, John, Bernstein, Philip A. and Wong, Harry K. T.
                    A Language Facility for Designing Database-Intensive Applications.
                    ACM Transactions on Database Systems 5(2):185-207, June, 1980.

[Nestor 79]   Nestor, John and Van Deusen, Mary.
                    Red Language Reference Manual
                    Intermetrics, Inc., 701 Concord Ave., Cambridge, MA. 02138, 1979.
                    IR-310-2.

[Nestor 81]   Nestor, J.R. and Beard M.
                    Front End Generator User's Guide
                    Department of Computer Science, Carnegie-Mellon University, 1981.
                    PQCC Internal Documentation.

[Nestor 82]   Nestor, John R. and Beard, Margaret A.
                    Front End Generator System.
                    In Burks, Sharon (editor), *Computer Science Research Review*, pages
                        75-92. Department of Computer Science, Carnegie-Mellon University,
                        Pittsburgh, PA. 15213, 1982.

[Newcomer 79]   Newcomer, Joseph M., Cattell, Roderic G. G., Hilfinger, Paul N., Hobbs,
                    Steven O., Leverett, Bruce W., Reiner, Andrew H., Schatz, Bruce R. and
                    Wulf, William A.
                    PQCC Implementor's Handbook
                    Carnegie-Mellon University, Computer Science Department, 1979.
                    PQCC Internal Documentation.

[Parnas 74]   Parnas, David L.
                    On a "Buzzword": Hierarchical Structure.
                    In *Proceedings of the IFIP Congress 74*, pages 336-339. North-Holland
                        Publishing Co., August, 1974.

[Ramirez 80]   Ramirez, Raul Javier.
                  Efficient Algorithms for Selecting Efficient Data Storage Structures.
                  Technical Report CS-80-18, Faculty of Mathematics, University of Waterloo,
                      March, 1980.

[Reiser 76]   Reiser, John F.
                  Sail.
                  Technical Report AIM-289, Stanford Artificial Intelligence Laboratory,
                      Stanford University, August, 1976.

[Rentsch 83]   Rentsch, Tim.
                  Object Oriented Programming Languages.
                  In Horowitz, Ellis (editor), *Programming Languages: A Grand Tour*, .
                      Computer Science Press, 11 Taft Center, Rockville, MD 20850, 1983.
                  Second Edition, to be published.

[Rovner 76]   Rovner, Paul D.
                  Automatic Representation Selection for Associative Data Structures.
                  PhD thesis, Harvard, 1976.

[Rowe 78]   Rowe, Lawrence A. and Tonge, Fred M.
                  Automating the Selection of Implementation Structures.
                  IEEE Transactions on Software Engineering SE-4(6):494-506, November,
                      1978.

[Schonberg 77]   Schonberg, E. and Liu, S. C.
                  Manual and Automatic Data-Structuring in SETL.
                  In Andre, Jacques and Banatre, Jean-Pierre (editor), *Implementation and
                      Design of Algorithmic Languages: Proceedings of the 5th Annual III
                      Conference*, pages 284-304. IRISA, May, 1977.

[Schwanke 82]   Schwanke, Robert W.
                  *Execution Environments in Programming Languages and Operating
                      Systems.*
                  Technical Report CMU-CS-81-147, Department of Computer Science,
                      Carnegie-Mellon University, May, 1982.

[Schwartz 73]   Schwartz, J. T.
                  *On Programming: An Interim Report on the SETL Project: Installment 1.
                      Generalities; Installment 2. The SETL Language and Examples of its
                      Use.*
                  Research Report, Courant Institute of Mathematical Sciences, Department
                      of Computer Science, New York University, 1973.

[Shaw 79]   Shaw, M.
                  A Formal System for Specifying and Verifying Program Performance.
                  Technical Report CMU-CS-79-129, Carnegie-Mellon University, June, 1979.

[Shaw 81]   Shaw, Mary (editor).
                  ALPHARD: Form and Content.
                  Springer Verlag, New York, New York, 1981.

[Sherman 80]   Sherman, Mark and Borkan, Martha.
                    A Flexible Semantic Analyzer for Ada.
                    In *Symposium on the Ada Programming Language*, pages 62-71. ACM,
                        Boston, December, 1980.

[Smith 77]   Smith, John Miles and Smith, Diane C. P.
                    Database Abstractions: Aggregation and Generalization.
                    ACM Transactions on Database Systems 2(2):105-133, June, 1977.

[Tichy 80]   Tichy, Walter F.
                    Software Development Control Based on System Structure Descripton.
                    Technical Report CMU-CS-80-120, Department of Computer Science,
                        Carnegie-Mellon University, January, 1980.

[VanWijngaarden 69]
                    Van Wijngaarden, A., Mailloux, B., Peck, J. and Koster, C.
                    Report on the Algorithmic Language Algol 68.
                    Numerische Mathematik 14(2):79-218, 1969.

[Weinreb 80]   Weinreb, Daniel and Moon, David.
                    Flavors: Message Passing in the Lisp Machine.
                    A.I. Memo 602, Artificial Intelligence Laboratory, Massachusetts Institute of
                        Technology.
                    November, 1980
                    Also a chapter in the Lisp Machine Manual, [Weinreb 81].

[Weinreb 81]   Weinreb, Daniel and Moon, David.
                    Lisp Machine Manual.
                    Symbolics Inc., California, 1981.
                    Fourth Edition.

[Welsh 79]   Welsh, J. and Bustard, D. W.
                    Pascal-Plus — Another Language for Modular Multiprogramming.
                    Software — Practice and Experience 9:947-957, 1979.

[Winston 77]   Winston, Patrick Henry.
                    Artificial Intelligence.
                    Addison-Wesley, Reading, Massachusetts, 1977.

[Wulf 74]   Wulf, W., Cohen, E., Corwin, W., Jones, A., Levin, R., Pierson, C. and
                        Pollack, F.
                    Hydra: The Kernel of a Multiprocessor Operating System.
                    Communications of the ACM 17, June, 1974.

[Wulf 80]   Wulf, Wm. A.
                    PQCC: A Machine-Relative Compiler Technology.
                    Technical Report CMU-CS-80-144, Carnegie-Mellon University, September,
                        1980.

[Wulf 81]   Wulf, W.A., Shaw, M., Hilfinger, P.N. and Flon, L.
                    Fundamental Structures of Computer Science.
                    Addison-Wesley, 1981.

[Xerox 81]   Xerox Learning Research Group.
                  The Smalltalk-80 System.
                  Byte 6(8):36-48, August, 1981.

Appendix A
Additional Paragon Features

This appendix provides some more details about the Paragon language that were omitted in the main body of the thesis. These miscellaneous topics include the lexical elements of Paragon, matching objects with differing levels of nesting, the initial environments for name expressions, restricting environments in name expressions, environments for parameter elaboration, inheriting class parameters, sharing implementations, procedure constraints, self references and statements. Each of these is discussed in turn.

A.1. Lexical Elements

A.1.1. Character Set

The ascii character set is used. All control characters, that is, characters without graphic representation, are semantically equivalent to blanks.

Characters are grouped together to form *tokens*. A token is an identifier, a numeric literal, a reserved symbol, or a reserved word. White space must separate two consecutive identifiers, reserved words or numeric literals.

A.1.2. Identifiers

An *identifier* is the symbol associated with a procedure declaration, variable declaration, implicit parameter declaration or class declaration when that entity is declared. Reserved words (given later in Section A.1.5) may not be used as identifiers. Two identifiers are identical if they consist of the same sequence of case-independent letters, digits, and underscores.

```
<identifier> :: = <letter> { { _ }? { <letter> | <digit> } } *
<letter>    :: = A | B | ... | Y | Z | a | b | ... | y | z
<digit>     :: = 1 | 2 | ... | 8 | 9 | 0
```

A.1.3. Literals

The only literals permitted in Paragon represent integers. Their semantics are defined in Section 3.3.6.

Two literals are identical ^{f} they consist of the same sequence of digits after all underscores and leading zeros have been removed.

$$\langle integer \rangle ::= \{\ \{\ \langle digit \rangle\ \}+\ \#\ \_\ \}+$$

A.1.4. Special Symbols

Some characters and combinations of characters represent tokens in Paragon. These are listed below. The longest possible sequence of cha.acters is interpreted as a token. Thus the characters < = represents one token and not the two tokens < and = .

;	=>	:=	..	,	(	)	|	&	~
=	<	>	<=	>=	—	+	*	/	.
:	[	]	↑	!				

A.1.5. Reserved words

The following sequences of letters are reserved by the language for special purposes and may not be used by the programmer as identifiers.

and	any	as	attribute	begin	check	class	comment
desc	do	else	elseif	end	exitloop	fi	for
goto	if	in	is	let	loop	match	matches
new	not	null	of	or	procedure	rem	return
same	such	specified	structure	that	then	this	var
when	where	while	with	yield			

A.1.6. Comments

Comments may appear before or after any token in the program. They do not alter the meaning of the program.

$$\langle comment \rangle ::= \{\ comment\ |\ !\ \}\ \langle space \rangle\ \{\ \langle any\ character\ except\ ;\rangle\ \}^*\ ;$$

A.2. Object Creation Expressions

In the thesis, various kinds of expressions are used to create objects in variable declarations without describing which expressions are permitted by the language. Paragon defines several rules that restrict the expressions that may be used as the "type" in variable declarations. This section presents those rules.

Like all expressions, the name expression used as a type is composed of several name components. All but the last name component must be either a parameter or a variable. The last component must have the reserved word *new* and have an identifier that denotes either a class, variable or parameter. No other name component in the expression or in any of its parameters may use the reserved word *new*.

If a variable or parameter identifier is used in the last component, then the environment for the object creation will be the denoted object with the innermost simple object removed, and the underlying class for the object creation will be the class of the innermost simple object denoted by the parameter or variable.

If the class requires parameters for creation, and there are no parameters in the last component of the name expression, then the parameters from the class declaration, variable or parameter denoted in the last name component will be reused. Otherwise the parameters in the name component will be used.

These rules ensure that exactly one new object will be created for each variable declaration and that type parameters may be used to create local variables in a class or procedure.

A.3. Most Preferred Match

The matching rules in Section 3.4.2 apply only to objects that consist of the same number of nested simple objects. Paragon permits objects with different numbers of nested simple objects to match, as mentioned in Section 8.1. This section discusses the additional rules for matching when objects have different numbers of nested objects.

First, a slight change in terminology is needed. Define the relation where two objects match and have the same number of nested simple objects as *pairwise matching*. The rules in Section 3.4.2 define this relation. Then actual object A *matches* a formal object F if A has exactly n more nested simple objects than F, and if after removing some n simple objects from A, then the smaller A pairwise matches F.

However, there may be more than one way that n simple objects may be removed from an actual object for it to match a formal object. Thus Paragon includes two more distinctions in the matching process: *preferred match* and *most preferred match*.

A preferred match occurs when comparing the two different, successful removals of simple objects during the matching process of differently sized objects. The outermost pair of removed simple objects is examined. The removed simple object that was less nested (further out) belongs to the preferred match. If the positions of the outermost removed simple objects are identical, then the same criterion is applied to the next pair of removed simple objects. This process continues until all of the removed simple objects have been considered. Because of the assumption that two different sets of simple objects were removed, there must be some pair of removed simple objects that differ. In the illustration below, the outermost simple object is listed first and the removed simple objects are underlined. The letters refer to the underlying class of the simple object:

Formal:	(	A,		B,		C	)
Actual$_{Match\ 1}$:	(	A,	A,	B,	B,	C	)
Actual$_{Match\ 2}$:	(	A,	A,	B,	B,	C	)
Actual$_{Match\ 3}$:	(	A,	A,	B,	B,	C	)

In example above, *Match 1* is preferred to *Match 2* since the *B* matched in *Match 2* is further out (less nested) than the *B* in *Match 1*. *Match 3* is also preferred to *Match 2* since the *A* matched in *Match 3* is further out than the *A* in *Match 1*. Similarly, *Match 3* is preferred to *Match 2* because the *A* in *Match 3* is less nested than the *A* in *Match 2*.

The most preferred match is a match which is preferred to all others. In the example above, *Match 3* is actually the preferred match of the actual object and formal object. (There is one possible combination of removed simple objects that is not shown, but *Match 3* is preferred to it as well as being preferred to *Match 1* and *Match 2*). When binding parameters during the comparison of two objects, the preferred match is used when more than one match is possible.

A.4. Initial Environments

Section 3.3 postponed a description of the way in which the environment is established for the first component in a name expression. The description is given in this section.

A search for the identifier in the first name component is performed in various scopes until an appropriate declaration is found. That declaration then controls the environment to be used for further elaboration. This search is very similar to that used for looking up identifiers in statically scope languages, such as Algol-60, with additional rules for classes. Specifically, the procedure for determining the declaration of the identifier in the first name component is:

1. The procedure or the fully extended class declaration[93] enclosing the expression is examined for a declaration of the identifier. An identifier implicitly declared in a parameter is consider as being declared in its corresponding procedure or class.

2. If more than one declaration was found, then one of the found declarations must be a procedure specification and the others must be procedure respecifications or implementations. Otherwise at most one declaration must be found and it may not be a procedure implementation. (Recall that a procedure respecification is considered a procedure specification in the absence of a procedure specification. See Section 5.3.5.)

3. If no declaration was found, repeat the first two steps for enclosing blocks, be they procedures or classes. If the universal environment was reached without finding an appropriate declaration, the program is not well specified.

The innermost simple object (and its containing environment) in the environment in which the declaration is found becomes the environment (or more precisely, the declaration environment, see Section A.6) for elaboration of the first name component. Any inner simple objects that were skipped in the search process are ignored.

A.5. Restricting Environments

The returned environment may be restricted for use by the next component in an expression. The syntax of a restriction is the reserved word as followed by a class identifier. Some example classes and the use of as are shown below:

---

[93]The fully extended class declaration is constructed by concatenating all of the class declarations of all ancestors of class along with the class, in leftmost elaboration order.

```
class Parent1 is
begin
   procedure p;
end;

class Parent2 is
begin
   procedure p;
end;

class Son of Parent1, Parent2 is begin end;

var x => new Son;

x as Parent1 . p;        ! Call of p in Parent 1;
x as Parent2 . p;        ! Call of p in Parent 2;
```

In a restriction, the class identifier denotes an ancestor of the underlying class of the last component of the object. When a restriction is present, the search for a declaration of the identifier in the next component is confined to the class declaration of that ancestor. Without a restriction, the procedure of searching the fully extended class declaration for a declaration of the identifier is followed.

To simplify the BNF description in Appendix B, the *as* restriction was deleted. It is never used in any example in the thesis.

A.6. Environments for Parameter Elaboration

In Sections 3.6.4, 5.2.1, 5.2.3 and 5.2.4, a description of procedure invocation or class instantiation was described that included elaboration of parameters.[94] Like all elaborations, elaboration of parameters must occur in some environment. This section defines two kinds of environments, the *statement environment* and the *declaration environment*, and defines how parameters are to be elaborated in these environments.

Every statement is contained in a class or a procedure. Before a statement can be elaborated, the containing class must be instantiated or the containing procedure must be invoked. When either of these events occurs, a new environment is formed and the statements are elaborated in this environment, hence the name *statement environment*.

---

[94] For purposes of discussion, the *return* expression in a procedure and the *yield* expression in an iterator are also parameters.

As a name expression is elaborated, each name component returns an object that is used as the environment for the next name component. This environment is call the *declaration environment*, since this environment is where the declaration for the identifier in the next name component will be found. For the first name component, a special set of searching rules is used to find the declaration environment, as described in Section A.4.

When elaborating a procedure call or class instantiation, the actual parameters in the name component and the formal parameters in the procedure or class declaration are elaborated. The formals are elaborated in the declaration environment and the actuals are elaborated in the statement environment. This is illustrated by the following declarations and procedure calls:

```
class c1(t:any) is
begin
   procedure f1 return t;
end;

class c2 is
begin
   procedure f2(c2);
   v1 => IM . new Integer;
end;

var v1 => new c1(c2);
var v2 => new c2;

v2.f2(v1.f1);
```

Initially *v2* is found, which denotes a *c2* object. Thus *f2* is to be found in the declaration environment *c2*, which it is. Then a procedure call of *f2* is to be elaborated. Thus the parameters in the declaration of *f2* are elaborated in the declaration environment *c2* and the actuals in the statement environment, which is assumed to be the universal class containing the declarations in the program fragment above. The result of elaborating the formal parameter in *f2* in the declaration environment is an indefinite *c2* object. Now the actual parameter must be elaborated in the statement environment. Thus *v1* is found and serves as the declaration environment for the call of *f1*. Repeating the invocation algorithm for the call of *f1*, the return expression for *f1* is elaborated in the declaration environment, and since *t* is bound to an indefinite *c2* object in this environment (because the declaration of *v1* used *c2* as a parameter), the returned object from *f1* is an indefinite *c2* object. Therefore this object is the result from elaborating the actual parameter for the call of *f2* and can be compared with the formal parameter for the call of *f2*, also an indefinite instance of *c2*. The two objects match, and the call of *f2* is well specified.

Note that if the return expression of *f1* had been elaborated in the statement environment, the identifier *t* would have not been found and the name expression would have been ill specified. Had the actual parameter for the call of *f2* been elaborated in the declaration environment, the wrong object would have been selected for v1, namely the integer inside of *c2* and not the variable *v1* inside of the universal class. To avoid these, and other kinds of difficulties, Paragon defines the statement and declaration environments and uses them for the two different kinds of parameter elaborations.

A.7. Inheriting Parameters

Section 3.4.4 provides the basics of declaring and inheriting parameters in classes. That section omitted the details of inheriting parameters from multiple parents and the details of defining new parameters when inheriting already defined parameters. In this section, these details are provided.

All parameters listed in a class declaration are either *inherited* or *defined*. Unlike declarations and statements inherited from ancestor classes, parameters inherited from all ancestors are explicitly represented in a class declaration. Also unlike declarations and statements, inherited parameters come from the ancestors in which the parameters are defined, not from the immediate parents. This is because some parameters of an immediate parent may also be inherited instead of defined, whereas all declarations and statements in an immediate parent are defined in the immediate parent. The distinction between inherited and defined parameters, and the way in which parameters are inherited, are discussed below.

The distinction between inherited and defined parameters is made by position in the parameter list. First, the inherited parameters are given in the parameter list, then the defined parameters. The inherited parameters are listed in leftmost elaboration order. If an ancestor defines more than one parameter, then the class declaration lists the corresponding inherited parameters in the same order. Parameters that are not inherited from an ancestor are said to be *defined* in the class declaration. This is illustrated below:

```
comment Classes to be used as parameter descriptions.
```

```
class A1 is begin end;
class B1 is begin end;
class C1 is begin end;
class D1 is begin end;

comment Classes that have parameters.;

class A(x : A1) is
begin
end;

class B(x : A1, y : B1) of A is
begin
end;

class C(x : A1, z : C1) of A is
begin
end;

class D(x : A1,  y : B1, z : C1, w: D1) of B, C is
begin
end;
```

Here, class A has no parents, and hence no inherited parameters. Thus the the only parameter for A is the defined parameter in A1. Classes B and C each have two parameters. By examining their ancestors in leftmost elaboration order (here, just A), exactly one defined parameter is found, namely the first parameter in class A. Thus the first parameter in classes B and C is inherited (from A). Since B and C have two parameters, the second parameter in each class is a defined parameter.

In a more complicated example, class D has three inherited parameters, one each from A, B, and C, and one defined parameter. Because the leftmost elaboration order for parameters is used, here A, B, C, the first parameter for D is inherited from A, the second from B and the third from C. Note that the parameter from A appears in two different immediate parents, but is only mentioned once in the declaration of class D.

The expression for an inherited parameter need not be identical with the expression used in its defining ancestor class, nor with the expression used in any immediate parent. The objects the expressions denote may be more restrictive than the original parameter. Thus checking between each inherited parameter and the form of the inherited parameter in immediate parents is required. More precisely, if an inherited parameter $P_{c,i}$ is the ith defined *Parameter* for some ancestor class c[95], then the object denoted by the parameter expression must match

---

[95]In general, one can say nothing about where in the parameter list of the class declaration that $P_{c,i}$ will appear.

the object denoted by any parameter expression in an immediate parent that is inherited from
or is defined as $P_{c,i}$. The rule ensures that the objects for parameters in the child are the same
as or more restrictive than the objects used in for an immediate parent. The rule can be
illustrated by altering the previous example as follows:

```
comment Classes to be used as parameter descriptions.;

class A1 is begin end;
class A1B of A1 is begin end;
class A1C of A1 is begin end;
class A1D of A1B, A1C is begin end;

class B1 is begin end;
class B1D of B1 is begin end;

class C1 is begin end;
class C1D of C1 is begin end;

class D1 is begin end;

comment Classes that have parameters.;

class A(x : A1) is
begin
end;

class B(x : A1B, y : B1) of A is
begin
end;

class C(x : A1C, z : C1) of A is
begin
end;

class D(x : A1D,  y : B1D, z : C1D, w: D1) of B, C is
begin
end;
```

The labeling of parameters as defined or inherited is unchanged from the previous example.
But different expressions are used for each parameter, so checking must occur to insure that
the parameters are properly inherited. Specifically, the checking for the first parameter in B
and C checks that A1B and A1C respectively match A1. For class D, there are three inherited
parameters and one defined parameter. The first parameter, A1D, is inherited from class A.
Because both immediate parents B and C also have inherited the first (defined) parameter of
A, checking of A1D must be made against both A1B and A1C. Checks must also be made that
B1D and C1D match B1 and C1 respectively. In this example, all of the objects in the inherited
parameters are compatible with the corresponding parameters in their immediate parents.

There is one last rule for parameters that has not been mentioned. There may be at most one declaration for each identifier implicitly declared in parameters for a class. Among the implications of this rule, no class may inherit parameters from two different ancestors that define the same identifier in the parameter list. This is done to eliminate rules for discriminating between identical identifiers in the parameter list. Because the following declaration has two *I*s declared in its parameters, the class declaration is ill specified:

```
class Illegal(IM . I: Integer, IM . I: Integer) is
begin
end;
```

A.8. Sharing Implementations

As described in Section 4.5.3.3, a single class declaration may be declared that may serve as an implementation class for more than one specification class. However, as Section 4.6.3 noted, there is no way for the selection mechanism to select a single object to be shared for more than one variable, although sets of rules were devised to permit such sharing. In this section, a more detailed discussion of object sharing among variable is provided, including the rules under which such sharing may take place.

Recall that a shared implementation occurs if a single object is able to meet the specifications of more than one variable. As a simple example, assume that there are two kinds of objects: a keyboard, which is an input device, and a display, which is an output device. Corresponding declarations might be:

```
class Keyboard is
begin
   procedure Read;
end;

class Display is
begin
   procedure Write;
end;
```

Although *Keyboard* and *Display* represent two conceptual classes of objects, they frequently may be combined in a single object, say a particular kind of terminal. A corresponding declaration might be:

```
class Teletype of Keyboard, Display is
begin
    procedure Read is begin .... end;
    procedure Write is begin ... end;
end;
```

The class *Teletype* can be used for variables specified as *Keyboards*, *Displays* and *Teletypes*. If a program required a *Keyboard* variable and a *Display* variable, it is reasonable to allow them to share a *Teletype* object. Consider the following program fragment:

```
var k => new Keyboard;
var d => new Display;
...
k.Read;
d.Write;
```

The objects denoted by *k* and *d* might share a single object that was created by instantiating the *Teletype* class. *Teletype* would then be the Implementation for both *k* and *d*.

Paragon permits variables to share a single object for more than one variable. However, indiscriminant sharing of objects is not wise. Consider the following program fragment:

```
var k => new Keyboard;
var t => new Teletype;

k.Read;
t.Read;
```

Sharing a single object that is an instance of *Teletype* is not appropriate here, since the calls to *Read* are conceptually shared by both the keyboard *k* and the teletype *t*. To prevent this kind of interference, Paragon allows only limited kinds of sharing. Specifically, Paragon provides four criteria that must be met for an object to be shared among several variables. Each of these criteria is discussed below. Following the criteria, the method by which a shared object is elaborated is discussed.

A.8.1. Subsuming Implementation Paths

One criterion for deciding if variables interfere with one another when sharing an object depends of the notion of an *implementation path*. This notion is developed in the following series of definitions:

Path   A *path* is a list of class identifiers such that each class in the list is an immediate parent of next class in the list.

Subsume   A path is said to *subsume* another path if the second path is a sublist of the first.

Implementation path

An *implementation path* is a path with the ends of the list being the identifiers of the specification (class used in the variable declaration) and the implementation (class chosen as the implementation).

These definitions are illustrated below:

```
class Company is begin end;
class ServiceCompany of Company is begin end;
class Manufacturer of Company is begin end;
class Conglomerate of ServiceCompany, Manufacturer is
begin
end;

var x => new Company;
var y => new ServiceCompany;
var z => new Manufacturer;
```

One defined path is (*Company, ServiceCompany, Conglomerate*). If the variable *x* is implemented as a *Conglomerate*, then this path is an implementation path for *x*. Another path derived from these class definitions is (*ServiceCompany, Conglomerate*). This path is subsumed by the first path.

Note that there may be more than one implementation path given a specification and an implementation. For example, the path (*Company, Manufacturer, Conglomerate*) is also an implementation path for *x*. Under this interpretation, the path (*ServiceCompany, Conglomerate*) would not be subsumed by the implementation path for *x*.

To prevent interference between the variables that are sharing the object, there must be an implementation path associated with each variable and the implementation for the shared object such that no path subsumes another.

A.8.2. The Environment of the Object

A second criterion requires that the environments for each simple object creation be identical. This is because when an object is shared, the environment containing that object must also be shared.

A.8.3. Parameters in a Shared Implementation

The third criterion tries to ensure that the parameters in the shared object are not improperly shared between any two variables. This is done by partitioning the parameters of the underlying implementation, with a partition being associated with each underlying specification. Thus:

- The inherited parameters in the implementation must not be shared among the specifications, and

- Every parameter in the implementation must appear in the specification of exactly one of the variables.

These rules imply that the parameters only be disjoint outside of the implementation path. To allow a shared parameter outside of the implementation path leaves no way to determine which parameter expression in a variable declaration should be used when a shared object is created.

A.8.4. Variable Interaction

The fourth criterion attempts to prevent use of variables before their declarations have been elaborated.

The order of elaboration of variable declarations can have effects on the results of a program. To minimize undesired interactions, Paragon further limits the use of a shared object to situations where the order of conceptual object creation may be effectively changed. Specifically, the variables declared between the declaration for the first variable and for the last variable sharing an object may not be used in the "type" expression of those variables sharing the object. This effectively allows the moving of all variables that share an object to be placed in the point in the program where the first such variable is declared.

A.8.5. Elaboration of a Shared Implementation

When variables share an object, that object is created and its implementation class elaborated (with implementations or realizations) at the time when the declaration for first variable sharing the object is elaborated. (Sharing is not permitted during elaboration with specifications.) All of the parameters for this implementation, gathered from the corresponding parameters in the variable declarations, are elaborated at this time. When the declarations of the other variables sharing this implementation are reached, their identifiers will be associated with the already created object. No further elaboration of the object takes place.

With these rules and definitions, Paragon has provided a way to share objects. Before these rules can be effectively applied, however, some way must be developed to integrate the rules into the selection mechanism. This was never accomplished.

A.9. Procedure Constraints

Section 3.5.4 provided the most useful procedure constraint that is defined in Paragon. Although not used in any examples, the language does define other kinds of procedure constraints, and they are defined in this section. Further, ways in which constraints may be combined also discussed.

A.9.1. Constraints that Check Matching

In Section 3.5.4, the comparison operation *same as* was defined to test if two objects each matched the other. For example,

```
r.structure same as l.structure
```

checks to ensure that *r* and *l* have the same underlying class. In addition, one may perform a one-sided comparison, that is, see if one object matches the other without insisting on each matching the other. This is done by using the *matches* operation instead of the *same as* operation. For example:

```
r.structure matches l.structure
```

checks to ensure that the underlying class of *r* matches the the underlying class of *l*, but makes no guarantees that the underlying class of *l* matches the underlying class of *r*.

A.9.2. Combining Constraints

Constraints may also be connected using the logical operations &, / and ~, meaning *and, or* and *not* respectively. ~ has the highest precedence (performed first), followed by &, followed by /. The logical operations are associated from left to right. Parentheses may also be used to control the order of comparison and logical operations.

As an example, if the expressions contain no side effects, then

```
r.structure matches l.structure & l.structure matches r.structure
```

is the same as

```
r.structure same as l.structure
```

A.10. Self-References

In Section 3.2.1, three kinds of simple objects were discussed: definite instances, indefinite instances and *any* instances. Paragon provides a fourth kind of simple object, called a self-reference. When used as a name component, a self-reference has the syntax of the reserved word *this* followed by a class or procedure identifier, as illustrated below:

```
class c is
begin
    ...
    this c
    ...
end;
```

A self-reference may appear only in the class or procedure declaration referred to by the identifier, though the declaration need not be the immediately enclosing scope. Further, a self-reference must be the first name component in a name expression.

When elaborated, a self-reference causes the declaration environment to be searched for an instance of the named class or procedure, which in turn becomes the environment returned by the elaboration of the self-reference name component.

Self-references are also used during the checking of class and procedure declarations. Although not mentioned in the main text of the thesis, all declarations are checked to ensure that they are well specified. When a procedure or class declaration is checked, a new simple object for that declaration is made and is called a *self-referent* for the declaration. This self-referent is appended to the environment in which the declaration is being checked (usually another self-referent) and the declarations and statements are elaborated with specifications in this environment. For purposes of comparing objects, self-referents are considered to be the same as definite instances, except that a self-referent of a child class is defined as matching the self-referent of an ancestor class, even though they appear to be two distinct, definite simple objects.

A.11. Statements

Statements provide control flow among the expressions to be elaborated in a Paragon program. After a brief description of statement structure, each kind of statement is described along with its elaborations.

A.11.1. Statement Structure

Each statement may be preceded by any number of labels. A BNF description is shown below:

〈statement〉 :: = { 〈identifier〉 = "〉 }* 〈simple statement〉

A *simple statement* is one that has no labels. There are eleven different kinds of simple statements in Paragon, shown below:

〈simple statement〉 :: =
   〈assignment statement〉 |
   〈subprogram form statement〉 |
   〈return statement〉 |
   〈null statement〉 |
   〈if statement〉 |
   〈while statement〉 |
   〈for statement〉 |
   〈exit statement〉 |
   〈goto statement〉 |
   〈yield statement〉 |
   〈pattern statement〉

The discussion of these statements is grouped into five categories: name expressions, subprogram control statements, conditional statements, loop statements, and goto statements.

A.11.2. Expressions as Statements

〈assignment statement〉 :: = 〈expression〉 : = 〈expression〉

〈subprogram form statement〉 :: = 〈expression〉

〈null statement〉 :: = null

There are three simple statements that are merely expressions: assignment statements, name expressions and null statements. The assignment statement is syntactic sugar for a name expression as defined in Section 3.3.5.

The null statement is always well specified, feasible and defined. For a statements that is an expression, the three kinds of elaboration are performed on the expression whenever the statement is appropriately elaborated. If elaboration of the expression was ill specified, infeasible or erroneous, then the statement is ill specified, infeasible or erroneous respectively, No object may be returned. If an object is returned, the statement is not well specified. No implicit declarations are permitted in the expressions used in the assignment or subprogram form statements. The presence of an implicit declaration renders the statement ill specified.

A.11.3. Subprogram Control Statements

Paragon provides two statements that control the elaboration of procedures, *return* statements and *yield* statements. *Return* statements terminate the invocation of a procedure while *yield* statements suspend a procedure's execution. Each statement is described in more detail below.

A.11.3.1. Return Statement

⟨return statement⟩ :: = return {⟨expression⟩}?

The *return* statement is used to terminate execution of the procedure, and if the procedure is specified to return an object, to provide an object to be returned. The *return* statement may only appear in procedures, not in classes.

If the procedure in which the *return* statement appears specifies no *return* expression, then no expression may be specified in the *return* statement. Since iterators have a *yield* expression and not a *return* expression, *return* statements in iterators may not have an expression. If the procedure in which the *return* statement appears specifies a return object, then every *return* statement in the procedure must have an expression. No implicit declarations are permitted in the expression of a *return* statement. The presence of implicit declarations in the expression renders the *return* statement ill specified.

When a *return* statement is elaborated with specifications, the expression in it is elaborated with specifications and compared with the object that results from elaborating, with specifications, the *return* expression in the procedure declaration. If the elaboration is ill specified or the comparison fails, then the *return* statement is ill specified.

When a *return* statement is elaborated with implementations, the expression in it is elaborated with implementations and compared with the object that results from elaborating, with implementations, the *return* expression in the procedure declaration. If the elaboration is infeasible or the comparison fails, then the *return* statement is infeasible.

When a *return* statement is elaborated with realizations, the expression in it is elaborated with realizations. If elaboration of the expression is erroneous, then the *return* statement is erroneous. The object that results from elaborating the expression is returned as the declaration environment for the next name component and the invocation of the procedure is terminated, that is, no other statements or expressions in the procedure are elaborated. If no expression is present, no object is returned. If the *return* statement appears in an iterator, then the iterator is terminated and elaboration continues with the statement immediately following the *for* loop that invoked the iterator.

A procedure without a *return* expression need not terminate with a *return* statement. Such a procedure may also terminate by reaching the end of the procedure's declaration. However, a *return* statement must be executed for terminating a procedure that specifies a *return* expression. If execution reaches the end of such a procedure without executing a *return* statement, then the invocation of the procedure is erroneous.

A.11.3.2. Yield Statement

⟨yield statement⟩ :: = yield ⟨expression⟩ { when exitloop ⟨statement⟩ }?

The *yield* statement is used to suspend an iterator that is invoked in a *for* statement.

Yield statements may appear only in procedures that yield an object, that is an iterator, though a *yield* statement is not required in an iterator. (An iterator that never executes a *yield* statement will never have the statements in the corresponding *for* loop executed.) Iterators and *for* loops are discussed in Sections 3.7 and A.11.5.1.

When a *yield* statement is elaborated with specifications, the expression is elaborated with specifications and the resulting object compared with the object that results from elaborating, with specifications, the *yield* expression in the iterator declaration. If the elaboration of the expression is ill specified or if the comparison fails, then the *yield* statement is ill specified. The optional statement is then elaborated with specifications. If the optional statement is ill specified, then the *yield* statement is ill specified. No implicit declarations are permitted in the expression of a *yield* statement. The presence of implicit declarations in the expression renders the the *yield* statement ill specified.

When a *yield* statement is elaborated with implementations, the expression is elaborated with implementations and the resulting object compared with the object that results from elaborating, with implementations, the *yield* expression in the iterator declaration. If the elaboration of the expression is infeasible or if the comparison fails, then the *yield* statement is infeasible. The optional statement is then elaborated with implementations. If the optional statement is infeasible, then the *yield* statement is infeasible.

When a *yield* statement is elaborated with realizations, the expression is elaborated with realizations and the resulting object bound to the identifier in the *for* loop that caused the iterator to be invoked. If the elaboration of the expression is erroneous, then the *yield* statement is erroneous. When the *for* loop that invoked the iterator continues the iterator, elaboration of the *yield* statement is completed and control flow resumes in the iterator.

If control passes out of the *for* loop because of the elaboration of a *goto*, *return* or *exitloop* statement, and if the last *yield* statement elaborated for that *for* loop has a statement, then before the loop is exited (but after any expression in the *return* statement is elaborated), then elaboration continues with the statement in the last elaborated *yield* statement. If this statement is erroneous, then the iterator invocation is erroneous. After the optional statement in a *yield* statement has been executed, no other *yield* statement in that iterator may be executed.

A.11.4. Conditional Statement

```
<if statement> :: =
    if <expression> then
        { <statement> ; }*
    { elseif <expression> then
        { <statement> ; }* }*
    { else
        { <statement> ; }* }?
    fi
```

The *if* statement causes conditional execution of statements.

During elaboration with specifications, each expression and statement in the *if* statement is elaborated with specifications in the order in which it appears. The expressions following the reserved words *if* and *elseif* must result in objects that match the predefined boolean object *Booleans.Bit*. If any expression did not match the predefined boolean object, the *if* statement is ill specified. If any of the expressions contained implicit declarations, the *if* statement is ill specified.

The statements in an *if* statement must not return an object, otherwise the *if* statement is not well specified. If any elaboration is not well specified, then the *if* statement is not well specified.

During elaboration with implementations, each expression and statement in the *if* statement is elaborated with implementations in the order in which it appears. If any elaboration is infeasible, then the *if* statement is infeasible.

Elaboration with realizations is discussed in Section 3.8.4.

A.11.5. Loop and Loop Control Statements

Paragon provides three kinds of looping statements: *for* loops, *while* loops and *pattern* loops. *For* and *while* loops are discussed in this section. Since *pattern* loops are inextricably related to the representation selection process, they are discussed completely in Section 5.5.4 and will not be repeated here. A statement that can control the execution of the loop statements, the *exitloop* statement, is also discussed in this section.

A.11.5.1. For Loops

```
<for statement> :: =
    for <identifier> in <expression> { .. <expression> }? do
        { <statement> ; }*
    end for
```

When a *for* loop is elaborated with specifications, the expression following the reserved word *in* is elaborated with specifications (after any transformation because of the syntactic sugaring provided by the .. notation), and the resulting object is compared with the object denoted by the identifier after the *for* reserved word, and then bound to that identifier. If the expression yielding the object was ill specified, then the *for* loop is ill specified. If the expression yielding the object had implicit declarations, then the *for* loop is ill specified. If the object did not result from an iterator invocation, then the *for* loop is ill specified. If the comparison failed, the *for* loop is ill specified. Then the statements in the *for* loop are elaborated with specifications. If any of them were ill specified, then the *for* loop is ill specified.

When a *for* loop is elaborated with implementations, the expression following the reserved word *in* is elaborated with implementations and the resulting object is bound to the identifier following the reserved word *for*. If the elaboration of the expression was infeasible, then the *for* loop is infeasible. Then the statements in the *for* loop are elaborated with implementations. If any of them were infeasible, then the *for* loop is infeasible.

Elaborating a *for* loop with realizations is discussed in Section 3.7.6.

A.11.5.2. While Loops

```
<while statement> :: =
    while <expression> do
        { <statement> ; }*
    end loop
```

A *while* loop provides repeated execution of a group of statements while a certain condition is met.

When a *while* statement is elaborated with specifications, the expression following the reserved word *while* is elaborated with specifications. If the elaboration was ill specified, then the *while* statement is ill specified. If the expression had implicit declarations, then the *while* statement is ill specified. The object that results from the expression elaboration is compared with the predefined boolean object, *Booleans.Bit*. If the comparison failed, then the *while* statement is ill specified. Each statement in the *while* is then elaborated with specifications. If any of these statements were ill specified then the *while* statement is ill specified.

When a *while* statement is elaborated with implementations, the expression following the reserved word *while* is elaborated with implementations. If the elaboration was infeasible, then the *while* statement is infeasible. Each statement in the *while* is then elaborated with implementations. If any of these statements was infeasible then the *while* statement is infeasible.

When a *while* statement is elaborated with realizations, the expression following the reserved word *while* is elaborated with realizations. If the elaboration was erroneous, then the *while* statement is erroneous. If the object returned by elaborating the expression is equal to an object returned by the predefined procedure *True*, then each statement in the *while* loop is elaborated with realizations. If any of these statements were erroneous then the *while* statement is erroneous. This two step process (elaborate the expression, elaborate the statements) repeats as long as the elaboration of the expression results in an object that is equal to an object returned by the predefined procedure *True*, or until a *goto, return* or *exitloop* statement inside of the *while* loop is elaborated with realizations that causes control to leave the *while* loop.

A.11.5.3. Exiting Loops

<exit statement> :: = exitloop { <identifier> }?

The *exitloop* statement forces the elaboration of a loop to be terminated. This statement may appear only inside of a *for* loop, *while* loop or *pattern* loop, with no intervening procedure or class declarations (though intervening statements, such as an *if* statement, are permitted).

When elaborated with specifications, and if no identifier is present, the statement is well specified if it occurs inside of a loop as specified above. If an identifier is present, that identifier must label a loop that is enclosing : ⊕ *exitloop* statement (without any intervening procedure or class declarations) for the *exitloop* statement to be well specified.

Elaboration of an *exitloop* statement with implementations requires no action. If an *exitloop* statement was well specified, then it is also feasible.

Elaboration of an *exitloop* with realizations finishes the elaboration of the statements in the enclosing loop. If the *exitloop* statement contains an identifier, then all enclosing loops up to the loop labeled with the identifier are finished. If iterators in *for* loops are being terminated (see Sections 3.7.6 and A.11.5.1), the loops are terminated from the innermost to the outermost.

A.11.6. Goto Statement

<goto statement> :: = goto <identifier>

The *goto* statement causes a transfer of control to the statement that has the identifier as a label.

When a *goto* statement is elaborated with specifications, the identifier is searched for as a statement label in an enclosing loop, *if* statement, class declaration or procedure declaration. Although intervening *if* statements and loops may be skipped, only the immediately enclosing procedure or class declaration will be examined for the label. If the label cannot be found, then the *goto* statement is ill specified. Note that the search procedure prohibits *goto* statements from specifying a label in a different part of an *if* statement than the part containing the *goto* statement, a label inside of loop that does not contain the *goto* statement, a label outside of the class or procedure declaration that contains the *goto* statement, and a label inside of a class or procedure declaration that does not contain the *goto* statement.

Elaboration of a *goto* statement with implementations requires no action. If a *goto* statement was well specified, then it is also feasible.

Elaboration of a *goto* statement with realizations causes the execution to continue with the statement labeled with the identifier. If a *for* loop is exited by a *goto* statement, any optional statement in the *yield* statement in the corresponding iterator is first executed (see Sections 3.7.6 and A.11.5.1).

Appendix B
Paragon BNF

This appendix gives a slightly edited version of the BNF description used by the parser generator to create the Paragon parser (Phase ML, see Section 7.1.1). After giving the details of the BNF notation, the productions used by the parser generator are listed. The rules have been divided into fives sections: program structure, declarations, statements, expressions and name components.

B.1. Notation

The syntax for Paragon is described in a notation that is an extended BNF with the following conventions [Nestor 81]:

- Nonterminals are enclosed in angle brackets, for example, ⟨identifier⟩ is the nonterminal representing identifiers.

- Terminal symbols are represented as themselves. When a terminal symbol or character conflicts with a nonterminal symbol or character, the terminal symbol will be preceded by a double quotation mark ("). For example, "⟨ denotes the terminal character ⟨ and not the beginning of a nonterminal symbol.

- Production rules are written with a single nonterminal on the left of a :: = symbol followed by sequence of terminal or nonterminal symbols, for example,

    ⟨expression⟩ :: = ⟨primary⟩ ** ⟨expression⟩

- Alternative right hand sides of a production rule with the same nonterminal on the left hand side may be separated by a vertical bar, that is, the | symbol, in a single production. For example:

    ⟨expression⟩ :: = ⟨primary⟩ | ⟨primary⟩ ** ⟨expression⟩

- A sequence of symbols may be bracketed by surrounding it with braces. For example, { ⟨identifier⟩ : ⟨name⟩ } brackets the three symbols ⟨identifier⟩, :, and ⟨name⟩.

- A sequence of symbols is optional in a production if it is surrounded by braces that are immediately followed by a question mark. For example { <identifier> }? denotes an optional identifier.

- A list of zero or more of a sequence of symbols is represented by enclosing the sequence in braces that are immediately followed by an asterisk. For example { <letter> }* indicates zero or more <letter>s.

- A list of one or more of a sequence of symbols is represented by enclosing the sequence in braces that are immediately followed by a plus mark (+). For example { <digit> } + indicates zero or more <digit>s.

- A list of zero or more of a sequence of symbols, separated by another sequence of symbols is represented as two sequences, separated by a hash mark (#) and enclosed by a pair of braces that immediately precede an asterisk (*). For example, the notation

        { <identifier> # , }*

  denotes a list of zero or more <identifier>s separated by commas (,).

- A list of one or more of a sequence of symbols, separated by another sequence of symbols is represented as the above list except that a plus mark (+) is used instead of an asterisk. For example, the notation

        { <parameter> # , } +

  denotes a list of one or more <parameter>s separated by commas (,).

B.2. Program Structure

    <compilation> :: = { <declaration> ; } +

B.3. Declarations

    <declaration> :: =
        <object declaration>
      | <class declaration>
      | <procedure declaration>

    <object declaration> :: =
        { attribute }? var <identifier> = "> <expression>
            { such that <expression> }?
            { where { <attribute association> # , } + }?

    <attribute association> :: = <identifier> = "> <expression>

```
<class declaration> :: =
   class <identifier> { ( { <type name> # , } + ) }?
      { of { <identifier> # , } + }? is
   <block>


<procedure choice> :: = { return <type name> } | { yield <type name> }


<instance formal> :: =  <type name>


<type name> :: = <expression>


<instance constraints> :: =
   such that
   { <or set expression> # , } +


<or set expression> :: = {<and set expression> # "| } +


<and set expression> :: = { <not set expression> # & } +


<not set expression> :: =  { ~ }* <parened set expression>


<parened set expression> :: =
   { <expression>
      { matches | same as } <expression> } |
      { ( <or set expression> ) }


<procedure declaration> :: =
   { attribute }? procedure <identifier> { ( { <instance formal> # , } + )}?
      {<procedure choice>}?
      {of <identifier>}?
      {<instance constraints>}?
      { is <block> }?


<block> :: =
   {specified with}?
   begin
      { <declaration> ; }*
      { <statement> ; }*
   end
```

B.4. Statements

⟨statement⟩ :: = { ⟨identifier⟩ = "⟩ }* ⟨simple statement⟩

⟨simple statement⟩ :: =
   ⟨assignment statement⟩ |
   ⟨subprogram form statement⟩ |
   ⟨return statement⟩ |
   ⟨null statement⟩ |
   ⟨if statement⟩ |
   ⟨while statement⟩ |
   ⟨for statement⟩ |
   ⟨exit statement⟩ |
   ⟨goto statement⟩ |
   ⟨yield statement⟩ |
   ⟨pattern statement⟩

⟨assignment statement⟩ :: = ⟨expression⟩ : = ⟨expression⟩

⟨subprogram form statement⟩ :: = ⟨expression⟩

⟨return statement⟩ :: = return { ⟨expression⟩ }?

⟨yield statement⟩ :: = yield ⟨expression⟩ { when exitloop ⟨statement⟩ }?

⟨null statement⟩ :: = null

⟨exit statement⟩ :: = exitloop { ⟨identifier⟩ }?

⟨goto statement⟩ :: = goto ⟨identifier⟩

⟨if statement⟩ :: =
   if ⟨expression⟩ then
      { ⟨statement⟩ ; }*
   { elseif ⟨expression⟩ then
      { ⟨statement⟩ ; }* }*
   { else
      { ⟨statement⟩ ; }* }?
   fi

⟨for statement⟩ :: =
   for ⟨identifier⟩ in ⟨expression⟩ { .. ⟨expression⟩ }? do
      { ⟨statement⟩ ; }*
   end for

⟨pattern statement⟩ :: =
   let ⟨identifier⟩ match ⟨expression⟩ in ⟨expression⟩ do
      { ⟨statement⟩ ; }*
   end let

```
<while statement> :: =
    while <expression> do
        { <statement> ; }*
    end loop
```

B.5. Expressions

```
<expression> :: = <factor>
```

```
<expression> :: = <expression> <logical operator> <factor>
```

```
<logical operator> :: = and | or
```

```
<factor> :: = <term>
```

```
<factor> :: = <term> <relational operator> <term>
```

```
<relational operator> :: =  = | "< | "> | "< = | "> =
```

```
<term> :: = <primary>
```

```
<term> :: = <unary operator> <primary>
```

```
<term> :: = <term> <additive operator> <primary>
```

```
<unary operator> :: = not | —
```

```
<additive operator> :: = + | —
```

```
<primary> :: = <component>
```

```
<primary> :: = <primary> <multiplicative operator> <component>
```

```
<multiplicative operator> :: = * | / | rem
```

```
<component> :: = <name> | ( <expression> )
```

B.6. Name Components

```
<name> :: = { <name component> # . } +
```

```
%  Description Name Component
<name component> :: = desc ( <expression> )
```

```
%  Numeric Literal Name Component
<name component> :: = <numeric literal>
```

```
%  Definite object name component (this/new)
<name component> :: =
   { { <identifier> : }?
      {this | new} <identifier>
      { ( { <expression> # , } + ) }?
               }

%  Structure (Get class) component
<name component> :: =
   { { <identifier> : }?
      structure
      { ( { <expression> # , } + ) }? }

%  Any component
<name component> :: =
   { { <identifier> : }? any
      { ( { <expression> # , } + ) }?
               }

%  "Check" name components
<name component> :: =
   { { <identifier> : }?
      check <identifier>
         { ( { <expression> # , } + ) }?
      {return ( <expression> ) }? }

%  Array element selection
<name component> :: = [ <expression> ]

%  Pointer Dereference
<name component> :: = ↑

%  Variable, function call, indefinite instance
<name component> :: = <identifier>
<name component> :: = <identifier> : <identifier>
<name component> :: = <identifier> ( { <expression> # , } + )
<name component> :: = <identifier> : <identifier> ( { <expression> # , } + )

%  attribute call
<name component> :: = <identifier> return ( <expression> )
<name component> :: = <identifier> : <identifier> return ( <expression> )
<name component> :: = <identifier> ( { <expression> # , } + )
                                 return ( <expression> )
<name component> :: = <identifier> : <identifier> ( { <expression> # , } + )
                                             return ( <expression> )
```

Appendix C
Conventional Design Issues

Besides the main areas of research, the design of Paragon contained many little details that always appear in a language design. Some of these details were easy to create, since many previous language designs had already worked them out and I could pick the ones I liked. Other features of Paragon were not as common in other languages and so the details were not as easy to define. In some cases, the wrong details were added the language. This section presents some of these uncommon, yet conventional language components, namely iterators, type parameters and literals. This discussion is intended largely as an aid to future language designers, and does not represent research topics, just some friendly advice I learned from this experience.

C.1. Iterators

Iterators were provided as a generalization of the *for* loop construction that is usually present in a language. Unfortunately in Paragon, the index variable used in a *for* loop was designed improperly. First, the *for* loop mechanism violates the one object per identifier rule in Section 2.2.2. Second, an unused object is elaborated and attached to the index identifier. Third, selection analysis is performed on index identifier.

Each of these problems was caused by not realizing that the index variable in the *for* loop is really part of the iterator, and not part of the program that contains the *for* loop. A better way to view the entire iteration process is to consider the *for* loop to be a procedure that takes one parameter, the index variable, and that the iterator calls this procedure every time a yield statement appears in the iterator [Moss 78]. The object associated with the index variable is determined solely by iterator and not by the program containing the *for* loop. In fact, different calls may associate different objects with the index identifier, but this is permitted where the *for* loop becomes a procedure, since it is perfectly reasonable to allow different objects to be passed as parameters to any other procedure. However, this view implies that index variables should not be declared in the program containing the *for* loop, and this is the key mistake in the iterator design.

Because the index variable is declared in an accessible scope of the *for* loop, it will have an object created when that declaration is elaborated. Yet that object will be discarded when the *for* loop is executed the first time. Because the *for* loop makes the previous object unreachable, the declaration creates a wasted object (unless the object was created and used before the *for* loop with the intention of never using the object after the *for* loop, a dubious practice at best). Therefore, no object instantiation should be permitted in the variable declaration for an index variable.

If the variable declaration were present, even without an instantiation name component, it would be represented in the possibility tree and the selection mechanism would attempt to perform object selection on it. But the implementation for the index variable is determined solely by the returned implementation of the iterator, and like all procedure return objects, this implementation is determined by elaborating the call with implementations and not by the policy procedure. Thus no selection should be performed for index variables, and they should not even be declared in the program. Instead, index variables should be implicitly declared in the *for* loop, deriving their specifications and implementations implicitly from the iterator call.

C.2. Type Parameters

The use of type parameters represents a novel aspect of Paragon, since types are passed through the use of indefinite instances. The motivation for this technique was the additional number of names that were present when an extra level of generic instantiation was required to pass type parameters, as in Ada or Clu. In the initial design, a *prototype* was instantiated with *types*, to create more *types*, and then *types* were instantiated with *objects* to create more *objects*. Thus another level of declaration and instantiation was required for each type. This worsened the declaration verbosity problem mentioned in Section C.4 even beyond my patience.

As a result of the decision to use indefinite instances as types, an unusual parameter passing situation could occur and an unusual run-time error was possible. The basis of both of these circumstances is in the inability to determine at compile time if a parameter is a type or an object. A rather contrived example illustrates this:

```
class c is
begin
   procedure pc;
end;

procedure f(p:c) is
begin
   var x => new p;

   p.pc;
end;

var Global => new c;

f(Global);
f(c);
```

The procedure *f* has one parameter, which is an indefinite instance of *c*. The two calls of *f* are well specified, since the definite object *Global* matches the indefinite instance of *c* and the indefinite instance *c* matches itself. Inside of *f*, the parameter *p* is used in two different ways. First, the variable declaration creates a new object with the same structure as the parameter. Thus *p* is used as a type parameter. Second, the procedure call invokes a procedure inside of the parameter, hence using *p* as a definite object: procedures may not be invoked inside of indefinite instances. In general, there is no way at compile time to determine if the passed object will be a definite instance or an indefinite instance. Thus the first call of *f(Global)* is defined but the second call, *f(c)* causes a run-time error when the call of *pc* is attempted inside of an indefinite instance.

The facility shown above permits a programmer to use the same parameter as a type and as an object. However, I have yet to see any value for that specific ability. But, it does cause the described run-time error, so it should probably be corrected in a future language design. The way to deal with this problem is to separate type parameters from nontype (definite object) parameters in expressions. If this could be done without adding another level of explicit instantiation, it would be a better alternative to the current Paragon design. As of this writing, I have not completed a design that I feel would be an adequate substitute for the current design, but I believe that some thought would provide one.

C.3. Literals

Because Paragon contains only objects, and no values, literals represent something of a problem. Usually, one can consider a literal as representing the object with that value. This view leads to problems when parameters are passed by reference, which is the only way that Paragon parameters are passed. The famous early Fortran problem of changing a literal value would result if Paragon adopted the view that literals were names for predefined objects, as is illustrated below:

```
class c(IM. p: Integer) is
begin
   p := 5;
end;
...
var v => new c(4);
```

The creation of the object for the variable v would cause the assignment statement in class c to be executed, changing the value of the object 4 to the value of the object 5.

To eliminate this problem, Paragon adopted the strategy of letting literals denote functions that return new objects with the appropriate value. Thus every time 4 was called, a new object with a value that acted as a four was created and returned. Thus assignment, or any other operation using integers, could be performed on the new object without affecting the value of the literal 4.[96]

This approach has an unusual drawback: it prevents the use of literals in formal parameters. Because Paragon permits definite instances to appear in formal parameters, one may want to use this facility to restrict actuals to include only objects that are composed with a definite instance. A typical example would be specifying a sorting procedure that only worked with arrays having a lower bound of one. One would like to write:

```
procedure Sort(ArrayManager . A: Array(1, IM . N: Integer));
```

which would specify that an array may be passed with a lower bound of one (and the upper bound being bound to the identifier N). In Paragon, however, each occurrence of the literal 1 is a function call that always returns a new object, so when creating an array with a lower bound of 1, a new *Integer* object would result as the lower bound for the *Array* object. This new object is different from the object created for the function call of 1 that is specified in the

---

[96] This also permits the bizarre but well specified statement *1 := 2*.

procedure declaration above. A call on *Sort* using that array would not be well specified since the two definite instances are not identical. To achieve the desired result, the following code fragment would have to be present:

```
var One => IM . new Integer;
var MyArray => AM . new Array(One,100);

procedure Sort(ArrayManager . A: Array(One, IM . N: Integer);

One := 1;
...
Sort(MyArray);
```

This is extremely clumsy and unreliable. After all, there is nothing that prohibits some other assignment statement changing the value of *One* to some other value. Unfortunately, I was unable to devise a better scheme for dealing with this problem. As this use of definite objects in actuals was never used in the example programs, I did not need to place much effort into a better design of literals.

A second problem with literals stems from their status as objects with types and managers. Unlike other variables and procedures, literals have no clearly identified manager to whom they belong. As illustrated throughout the thesis, integers may be used to represent pure numbers or counts of apples or sizes of oranges. Thus a literal must be associated with one of these managers. Paragon defines a literal with no explicit manager to belong to the predefined integers; all other uses of integer literals must have an explicit manager, for example, *AppleManager.4*. Although not convenient, the notation serves well enough for the example programs. In general, the determination of the type of literals can create problems. There was a great deal of discussion during the Ada design about the proper way to handle aggregates, which are another form of literals. Although a seemingly trivial point, future designers of abstract data type languages should give careful consideration to the definition of literals. For the Paragon design, I have two suggestions.

First, add the concept of immutability from Clu. Objects can be specified as immutable or mutable, and parameters can be specified as immutable or mutable. The object matching rules can include another set of tests to ensure that two objects are compatible with respect to mutability. Then integer literals can represent predefined variables that denote immutable objects. I would probably adopt this concept if Paragon were to undergo another design iteration.

A second approach would require a slightly different interpretation for elaborating procedure calls in parameters. The object that is normally returned when a procedure call is elaborated is the object that results from elaborating the *return* expression. However, the procedure invocation actually creates a simple object as well for the elaboration of the body of the procedure (this simple object is present in the possibility tree). In parameters, this simple object might be used instead of the returned object. Then matching is done by comparing the simple objects used for the procedure and not by comparing the returned objects, or perhaps, by comparing both pairs of simple objects. I believe this approach is too complex to be used in general.

C.4. Declaration Verbosity

Another general problem with the Paragon approach is the need to explicitly name everything before it is used. The declaration of a variable with a new type requires five auxiliary declarations: a class to act as a specification for the manager, a class to act as a specification for the individual, a class to act as a representation for the manager, a class to act as a representation for the individual, and a variable declaration that instantiates the manager class. As noted in Section 4.2, other languages contain anonymous manager or individual declarations, and anonymous or implicit manager creations. Much of the verbosity and clumsiness of Paragon could be alleviated by adoption of these techniques.

A similar, but trivial problem, is the lack of multiple object declarations. Each variable declaration created exactly one object. Thus, to declare three integers, one had to write:

```
var i => IM . new Integer;
var j => IM . new Integer;
var k => IM . new Integer;
```

It would have been convenient, and not difficult, to allow multiple object declarations, such as:

```
var i,j,k => IM . new Integer;
```

which could have the same semantics as the first piece of program text. Another iteration of the Paragon design would have included this feature.

C.5. Expression Verbosity

Another drawback in Paragon's use of the manager model is the use of managers throughout expressions to denote the manager in which an operation is declared. The ubiquitous presence of the manager names clutters the program text immensely. Some better syntactic sugar is needed to eliminate the need to explicitly mention the manager. Clu contains such a rule by which the manager (referred to as the *type* in Clu) is determined by the first parameter to the procedure. This was not adopted in Paragon because the manager was not a type, but a separate object. Taking the outermost simple object of the first parameter of a procedure call as the manager may not be correct if the first parameter is composed of more than two simple objects. Further, it is desirable that all such syntactic sugaring be transformable into an identical program. This is not possible since Paragon permits managers to be returned from a procedure call. For example, suppose a programmer wrote $f(a) := b$. A simple rewriting would take the form $manager(f(a)).Assign(f(a),b)$. However, there is no guarantee that the manager returned by the first call of f is the same as returned by the second call of f. Yet a simple analysis following the Clu example would process each parameter and then use the manager of the first, thereby guaranteeing that the manager for the *Assign* procedure had to be identical to the manager of the first parameter, a situation that the programmer could not normally express. In retrospect, this criticism does not seem worth the elimination of this kind of syntactic sugar.

In summary, another approach should concentrate on explicitly providing the manager model of data abstraction, and then include necessary syntactic sugaring and anonymous instantiations to provide conciseness as necessary.

Appendix D
Glossary

Almost Identical   Same as *similar*.

Ancestors   All classes that are inherited transitively (through parents).

Any Instance   An object that results from the instantiation of the predefined, but undenotable class, *any*. All objects match the parameterless *any* instance. If the *any* instance has parameters, then any object that has parameters that match the parameters of the *any* object also matches the *any* object.

Capsule   Red [Nestor 79] term for module.

Class   Smalltalk, Simula and Paragon term for module.

Class Instantiation The process of creating a simple object from a class.

Cluster   Clu term for (data abstraction) module.

Compatible   An object is compatible with another if it matches the other. A component of an object is compatible with another if it matched the other component.

Componont   A component is a single layer or piece in an environment, object, composition, structure or expression.

Compose   To use a parameter, usually a type parameter. Sets are composed with a type to create sets of that type.

Composition   The composition of an object is a list of the unique identifiers, *any* notations and *this* notations that correspond to each of its simple objects. (*any* notation is used when an indefinite instance is ⟨present, *this* notation is used when a self reference is present.)

Creation Environment
    The environment in which a class instantiation takes place. This is the same as the declaration environment for the name component specifying the simple object creation.

Appendix D 322

Declaration Environment

The environment in which the formal parameters are elaborated during an object creation or a procedure invocation. It is so called because the declaration environment provides a simple object for each self reference that is present when the original declaration was elaborated or checking if the declaration (of the class or procedure) was well specified.

Defined Parameters

All parameters in a class declaration that are not inherited.

Definite Instance   A simple object that results from the elaboration of definite simple object creation name component, that is, a name component with the reserved word *new*.

Description Name Component

A description name component provides a way to access the *Instance* object associated with a doppelganger.

Doppelganger   The simple object that results when elaborating object creations or procedure invocations with specifications. A doppelganger is associated with a realization of an *Instance* which is in the possibility tree.

Elaboration with Implementations

One of three kinds of elaboration performed on a program. Elaboration with implementations performs feasibility checking of program. This includes, but is not limited to, finding feasible procedure implementations for every procedure call and checkings that the implementations selected for variables nest properly.

Elaboration with Realizations

One of three kinds of elaboration performed on a program. Elaboration with realizations corresponds roughly to conventional run-time execution of a program.

Elaboration with Specifications

One of three kinds of elaboration performed on a program. Elaboration with specifications corresponds roughly to the semantic analysis of a program.

Envelop   Pascal-Plus [Welsh 79] term for module.

Environment   An environment is an object, i.e., same as *Object*.

Execution   Same as *Elaboration with realizations*.

Expression   Name expressions and syntactic forms that can be transformed into name expressions.

Extended Class Declaration

The list of declarations that results if one concatenates all of the declarations of a class and its ancestors, in leftmost elaboration order.

Form   Alphard term for module.

Function   A procedure that has a *return* expression in its specification.

General Procedure 1. A procedure implementation that only uses abstract properties of an object. An example is a procedure that implements set intersection using only iteration, membership and insertion operations on sets. More precisely, only procedure specifications and other general procedures are visible for all procedure calls in the general procedure declaration

2. A procedure specified in a generalization class, such as *Assign* is in the *AssignableManager*.

Generalized Specification

A specification that is to be further refined into a more restrictive specification before being used to declare objects.

Generalization Class

A class that is inherited by specification classes. Note: this is really a use of a class. A class may be used as a generalization, specification or implementation class.

Identical Simple Object

Two simple objects are identical if they resulted from the same instantiation of a class or the same invocation of a procedure. (Because the same elaboration of the object instantiation or procedure invocation name expression created the identical simple objects, their parameters must be identical as well.)

Identical Objects   Two objects are identical if the corresponding simple objects in each component of the object are identical.

Implementation Class

The class selected as the representation for a variable.

Implementation Path

An implementation path for a variable declaration is a path where one end is the class used as the specification of the variable and the other end is the class used as the implementation of the variable.

Implicit Declaration An implicit declaration of an identifier occurs when a name component is labeled with an identifier followed by a colon. This notation implicitly declares the identifier to denote the object that results from elaboration of the name expression up to and including that name component, or to denote the object that matches the same resulting object during parameter comparison. Implicit declarations are only permitted in parameters.

Indefinite Instance An instance that did not come from a definite (or concrete) object creation. It results from elaborating an indefinite instance name component and corresponds to "any" definite instance of the class in the name component. Operationally, the differences between a concrete or definite instance and an indefinite instance is that only the attribute variables are elaborated in an indefinite instance while all variables are elaborated in a definite instance.

Indefinite Instantiation
The process of creating an indefinite instance.

Inherited Parameters
Parameters that are not defined in a class declaration. Inherited parameters are defined in one of the class's ancestors, though any inherited parameter need not be identical with the parameter so defined in the ancestor. (Inherited parameters need only match the corresponding parameters in immediate parents.)

Instance   1. A simple object that results from elaborating an indefinite instance, object creation, *any* or self-reference name component.

                    2. A predefined class used for realizations in the Possibility Tree.

Invocation Environment
The object in which a procedure invocation takes place.

Interface Module   Mesa phrase for module specification.

Iterator   A procedure that has a *yield* expression in its specification.

Leftmost Elaboration Order
An ordered list of inherited classes in which all transitively inherited parents (that is, ancestors) are listed. It is created by concatenating the leftmost elaboration order of each parent of the class (in order that the parents are given), eliminating duplicate class names when they appear a second time in the list, and appending the class for which the leftmost elaboration order is being defined. The leftmost elaboration order for the example below is *Top, Middle1, Middle2, Bottom.*

```
class Top is begin end;
class Middle1 of Top is begin end;
class Middle2 of Top is begin end;
class Bottom of Middle1, Middle2 is begin end;
```

Leftmost Parent Order

> An ordered list of inherited classes in which all transitively inherited parents (that is, ancestors) are listed. It is created by starting with the class for which the order is being defined and then concatenating the leftmost parent order for each parent in the parent list, eliminating duplications when they appear a second time in the list. The leftmost parent order for the example below is *Bottom, Middle1, Top, Middle2*.

```
class Top is begin end;
class Middle1 of Top is begin end;
class Middle2 of Top is begin end;
class Bottom of Middle1, Middle2 is begin end;
```

Local Instance   A piece of storage that results when making a simple object. There is a bijection between the local instances in a simple object and the class declarations that make up the extended class declaration for the underlying class of the simple object.

Local Instance Set The set of local instances that make up a simple object.

Match   An object matches another if by removing some number of components (including none) of the first, it then pairwise matches the second.

Module   Encapsulation mechanism in a language in which some collection of information is written. Frequently, but not always, modules have identifier visibility rules that permit some subset of the information defined inside of the module to be available to parts of the program outside of the module. Also the Modula and Mesa term for module.

Most Preferred Match

> The match that is used for parameter binding when more than one set of deletions of simple objects between differently sized objects (in nesting levels) results in a successful match.

Name Component   A syntactic unit between two periods (.) in a name expression. This is the basic unit of action in a Paragon program. There are name components for object creation, indefinite instances, *any* instances, self references, procedure invocation, attribute invocation, attribute checking, description and structure extraction. Several kinds of name components are syntactic sugar for other name components, such as integer literals (for example, *3*), array element selection (for example, *[i]*) and pointer dereferencing (*↑*).

Name Expression   A list of name components separated by periods.

Object   An object is an environment. An object is also a set of nested simple objects. Each of the nested objects was instantiated from a class declaration that was nested in the underlying class of the enclosing object.

Object Creation Same as class instantiation when a *new* name component is elaborated.

Package Ada term for module.

Package Body Ada term for module implementation.

Package Specification
 Ada term for module specification.

Pairwise Compatible
 An object is pairwise compatible with another if the two objects have the same number of simple objects and corresponding simple objects are compatible. Compatibility may take place at either the structural (underlying class only) or compositional (creation or invocation expression) level of an object.

Pairwise Match Same as *pairwise compatible.*

Parameter One expression in a list of expressions that follow a procedure or class identifier in a declaration, procedure invocation or class instantiation. Identifiers may be implicitly declared in a parameter by placing them in front of a name component and placing a colon (:) between the identifier and the name component. For example, the expression *IM . i : Integer* may be used as a parameter which implicitly declares *i.*

Path A list of class identifiers such that each identifier denotes a class that is an immediate parent of the class denoted by the following identifier.

Policy Procedure A user-provided Paragon procedure that is interpreted by the translation system for performing representation selections for variables in the user's program.

Possibility Tree A data structure that is manipulated by the policy procedure. The possibility tree represents the user's program.

Preferred Match Given two ways that two objects match, the preferred match is the one which compares the innermost simple objects available and deletes the outermost simple objects available.

Procedure Implementation
 1. A procedure that may be used during elaborations with realizations. This is a procedure that is declared with a block (*begin/end*) and is not a respecification (lacking *specified with.*)

 2. A procedure declaration that is selected for a procedure call during elaborations with implementations.

Realized Instance 1. A instance that results from elaborating an object creation name component with realizations.

2. A definite instance of the predefined *Instance* class that results when the translation system creates the possibility tree.

Realized Simple Object
An instance that results from elaborating an object creation name component with realizations. (Only the first definition for *realized instance*.)

Restricted Class Declaration
The declarations in a single class, excluding the ancestors of the class.

Self Reference 1. A name component that contains the reserved word *this*.

2. A simple object that denotes the containing simple object that results when elaborating a name component that contains the reserved word *this*. These simple objects only result when processing class and procedure declarations.

Shared Specification
A specification that describes more than one kind of object.

Similar Environments
Same as *Similar objects*.

Similar Invocations Same as *Similar procedure calls*.

Similar Objects Two objects are similar if they have the same number of simple objects and their simple objects are similar.

Similar Procedure Calls
Two procedure calls are similar if they use the same procedure implementations, their parameters are similar and their environments are similar.

Similar Simple Objects
Two simple objects are similar if they have the same underlying class, if the objects denoted by their variables are similar and if the parameters are similar.

Simple Object A simple object is created by instantiating a class or invoking a procedure. Simple objects are contained in other simple objects which together make up an environment (or object).

Specific Object Creation
Same as *object creation*.

Specification Class The class denoted by the identifier following the reserved word *new* in an object-creation name component in a variable declaration.

Specified Instance 1. A instance that results from elaborating an instantiation name component with specifications.

2. The instance of an object that results when elaborating the class mentioned in the type of the variable rather then the simple object that results when using the implementation class for the variable.

Specified Simple Object
Same as *specified instance*.

Statement Environment
The environment in which the actual parameters in a name component are elaborated. So called because it is the environment in which the statement containing the parameter is elaborated.

Structure   A list of the underlying classes that were used in the instantiations of an object.

Subsume   One path subsumes another if one path is a sublist of the other.

This Notation A way to denote that the simple object being referenced is the enclosing definite instance of the named class. For example, the notation *this Set* inside of the *Set* class denotes the current definite instance in which the name component *this Set* is being elaborated. The same notation is used when a self reference is represented in the list of simple objects for an object.

Type   The object that results from elaborating, with specifications, the expression following the special symbol = > in a variable declaration.

Type Parameter   A parameter that contains implicitly-declared identifiers that are used in formal parameters or object-creation name components.

Underlying Class The class from which a simple object was instantiated.

Underlying Implementation
The class used as the underlying class for the simple object created or shared in an object-creation name component during elaborations with implementations and realizations.

Underlying Specification
The class specified in the object specification in a specific object creation component, for example, the identifier *Classname* in *new Classname*.

Uninstantiated Environment

>The composition consisting of only self references that denotes the environment of a declaration that is independent of any object instantiations.

Universal Class   The class in which the predefined identifiers, the policy procedure implementation and the user program are declared.

Unrestricted Identifier

>An identifier not in an expression or not preceded by a dot (.) in an expression.

Unspecified Instance

>An instance that did not come from a definite (or concrete) object creation. It results from elaborating an unspecified instance name component and corresponds to "any" definite instance of the class in the name component. Operationally, the differences between a concrete or definite instance and an unspecified instance is that only the attribute variables are elaborated in an unspecified instance while all variables are elaborated in a specific instance.

Unspecified Instantiation

>The process of creating an unspecified instance.

Unused Local Instance Set

>The unused local instance set consists of those local instances that were once used for the simple object associated with a variable but have been removed because classes associated with the local instances are no longer ancestors of, or the same as the implementation class of the variable.

Appendix E
Abstract Data Types Used in the Examples

This appendix gives a brief description of two abstract data types, sets and lists, used in the example programs in Appendix F. First, a brief description of each abstract data type is provided, followed by a short discussion of how attribute procedures perform their measurements. The rest of the appendix contains program text for the specifications and implementations of sets and lists.

E.1. Overview of Sets

The specifications for the sets used as an abstract data type are modeled after the sets specified by Low in his system [Low 74]. The same operations are present, though the names may differ. For example, the membership procedure is called *IsMember* while in Low's system there is explicit syntactic sugaring that corresponds to conventional set notation.

As much as possible, the implementations for sets are also taken from Low's system. One deviation is the use of B-Trees instead of AVL Trees, but this does not invalidate the general goal of providing a reasonable collection of set implementations.

One difference in the semantics between Low's sets and Paragon's sets is that Low allowed the sets to grow to arbitrary sizes while Paragon does not specify if the sets are finite or infinite. Different implementations provide different kinds of sets.

After the specifications for sets, six different implementations are provided. The implementations consist of unsorted and sorted singly-linked lists, unsorted and sorted arrays, a B-Tree implementation and an attribute-bit implementation.

E.2. Overview of Lists

The specifications for the lists used as an abstract data type are modeled after the lists specified by Low in his system [Low 74]. The same operations are present, though the names may differ. For example, the insertion procedure is called *AddBeforeIndex* in Paragon while in Low's system there is explicit syntactic sugaring that corresponds to list insertion.

One difference in the semantics between Low's lists and Paragon's lists is that Low allowed the lists to grow to arbitrary sizes while Paragon does not specify if the lists are finite or infinite. Different implementations provide different kinds of lists.

As much as possible, the implementations for lists are also taken from Low's system. Because the program text for sets illustrates most of the features of Paragon, the list representations need not be extensive for illustrating the language. Therefore, only three implementations of lists are given: singly-linked lists, doubly-linked lists and arrays. These implementations are given after the program text for the list's specification.

E.3. Assumptions about Attribute Procedures

The attribute procedures had to include some measures of time and space requirements so the policy procedures could make selection decisions. Since the thesis is not trying to break new ground in representation-selection algorithms, the values returned by the attribute procedures need not be accurate. Therefore the attributes provide only rough approximations of the space and time requirements. The values returned by the attributes try to capture the asymptotic nature of the implementations. To achieve these approximations, the following guidelines were used for measuring the cost of attributes in implementations:

- Every integer requires 1 unit of space.

- Every bit requires 1 unit of space.

- Every pointer requires 1 unit of space.

- Every array requires *the number of elements* times *the size of the element* units of space.

- Every statement requires 1 unit of time.

- Only the first bracket of a bracketed statement is counted for time units, not both. Thus in a *while* loop, the *while* counts as 1 unit of time and the *end loop* counts as 0 units of time.

- The unit counts for statements in a loop are multiplied by a factor which represents the number of times a loop is executed. In most examples, this is a linear, square or $\log_2$ factor.

These rules are only guidelines. In some procedures, some extra units are arbitrarily added because an assignment statement has many procedure calls in it.

Attributes in specifications were intended to reflect a large but appropriately scaled value. For example, iteration over all elements of a list is proportional to the length of the list, but a large constant factor is included so that the specification appears to perform worse than an implementation.

(Sections E.4 through E.14 have been omitted in this edition. An unabridged version of this thesis is available from Carnegie-Mellon University and contains the complete Paragon text for each implementation.)

Appendix F
Applications Programs

This appendix gives the sources of the application programs described in Section 7.3.2.4. Six programs are provided: a program that finds a set maximum, two insertion sort programs adapted from programs that Low wrote [Low 74], a merge sort program, also written by Low, a transitive closure algorithm adapted from one of Rovner's examples [Rovner 76] and a Huffman encoding program adapted from by a paper by Freudenberger [Freudenberger 83].

F.1. Set Maximum

```
!--------------------------------------------------;
! SetMax example main program                       ;
!--------------------------------------------------;

class MainProgram is
begin

    var IntSetManager => new SetManager(IM.Integer);
    var WorkingSet => IntSetManager . new Set;
    var i => IM . new Integer;
    var j => IM . new Integer;
    var SetSize => IM . new Integer;
    var MaxSeen => IM . new Integer;
    var Total => IM . new Integer;

    IM.Read(SetSize),
    for j in IM.Sequence(1,SetSize) do
        IM.Read(i);
        IntSetManager.Insert(WorkingSet,i);
    end for;

    Total := 0;
    for j in IntSetManager.Members(WorkingSet) do
        Total := Total + j;
    end for;

    IM.Write(Total);

    MaxSeen := -1;
    for j in IntSetManager.Members(WorkingSet) do
        if j > MaxSeen then
            MaxSeen := j;
        fi;
    end for;

    IM.Write(MaxSeen);
end;
```

F.2. Insertion Sort # 1

```
!----------------------------------------------------;
! INSRT2 example main program                        :
!----------------------------------------------------;

class MainProgram is

begin

   var IntSetManager => new SetManager(IM.Integer);
   var IntListManager => new ListManager(IM.Integer);

   var UnSorted => IntSetManager . new Set
      where SetSize => 100;
   var Sorted => IntListManager . new List
      where ListSize => 100;
   var Count => IM . new Integer;
   var i => IM . new Integer;
   var Obj1 => IM. new Integer;
   var Obj2 => IM. new Integer;

   comment First construct an Unsorted set;

   IntSetManager.Clear(Unsorted);
   IM.Read(Count);
   for I in IM.Sequence(1,Count) do
      IM.Read(Obj1);
      IntSetManager.Insert(Unsorted,Obj1);
   end for;

   IntListManager.Clear(Sorted);

   for Obj1 in IntSetManager.Members(Unsorted) do
      Count := 1;
      while Count <= IntListManager.Length(Sorted) do
         Obj2 := IntListManager.GetIndex(Sorted,Count);
         if Obj2 >= Obj1 then
            exitloop;
         else
            Count := Count + 1;
         fi;
      end loop;
      IntListManager.AddBeforeIndex(Sorted,Count,Obj1);
   end for;

   for Obj2 in IntListManager.Members(Sorted) do
      IM.Write(Obj2);
   end for;

end;
```

F.3. Insertion Sort # 2

```
!----------------------------------------------------;
! INSRT3 example main program                        :
!----------------------------------------------------;

class MainProgram is

begin

   var IntSetManager => new SetManager(IM.Integer);
   var IntListManager => new ListManager(IM.Integer);

   var UnSorted => IntSetManager . new Set
      where SetSize => 100;
   var Sorted => IntListManager . new List
      where ListSize => 100;
   var i => IM . new Integer;
   var Obj1 => IM. new Integer;
   var Obj2 => IM. new Integer;
   var Count => IM. new Integer;

   comment First construct an Unsorted set;
```

```
      IntSetManager.Clear(Unsorted);
      IM.Read(Count);
      for I in IM.Sequence(1,Count) do
         IM.Read(Obj1);
         IntSetManager.Insert(Unsorted,Obj1);
      end for;

      IntListManager.Clear(Sorted);

      for Obj1 in IntSetManager.Members(Unsorted) do
         Count := 1;
         for Obj2 in IntListManager.Members(Sorted) do
            if Obj2 >= Obj1 then
               exitloop;
            else
               Count := Count + 1;
            fi;
         end for;
         IntListManager.AddBeforeIndex(Sorted,Count,Obj1);
      end for;

      for Obj2 in IntListManager.Members(Sorted) do
         IM.Write(Obj2);
      end for;

end;
```

F.4. Merge Sort

```
!--------------------------------------------------;
! MERGE example main program                       ;
!--------------------------------------------------;

class MainProgram is

begin

   var IntSetManager => new SetManager(IM.Integer);
   var IntListManager => new ListManager(IM.Integer);
   var ListListManager => new ListManager(IntListManager.List);

   var UnSorted => IntSetManager . new Set
      where SetSize => 100;

   var Sorted => IntListManager . new List
      where ListSize => 100;
   var ListM1 => IntListManager . new List;
   var ListM2 => IntListManager . new List;
   var Merger => IntListManager . new List;

   var OldLists => ListListManager . new List;
   var NewLists => ListListManager . new List;

   var Count => IM . new Integer;
   var infinity => IM . new Integer;
   var Obj1 => IM. new Integer;
   var Obj2 => IM. new Integer;
   var i => IM. new Integer;

   comment First construct an Unsorted set;
   IntSetManager.Clear(Unsorted);
   IM.Read(Count);
   for I in IM.Sequence(1,Count) do
      IM.Read(Obj1);
      IntSetManager.Insert(Unsorted,Obj1);
   end for;

   comment Create list of lists to be merged;
   ListListManager.Clear(OldLists);
   for Obj1 in IntSetManager.Members(Unsorted) do
      ListListManager.AddAfterIndex(OldLists,0,IntListManager.ConstructList(Obj1) );
      comment put new({{ Obj1 }}) into OldLists after 0;
   end for;

   ListListManager.Clear(NewLists);
   Infinity := 999999;
```

```
while ListListManager.Length(OldLists) > 1 do
   while ListListManager.Length(OldLists) > 1 do
      comment The following two are Lops ;
      IntListManager.Assign(LitM1,ListListManager.Grab(OldLists));
      IntListManager.Assign(LitM2,ListListManager.Grab(OldLists));
      IntListManager.Clear(Merger);
      while (IntListManager.Length(LitM1) > 0) or (IntListManager.Length(LitM2) > 0) do
         if IntListManager.Length(LitM1) = 0 then
            Obj1 := Infinity;
         else
            Obj1 := IntListManager.First(LitM1);
         fi;
         if IntListManager.Length(LitM2) = 0 then
            Obj2 := Infinity;
         else
            Obj2 := IntListManager.First(LitM2);
         fi;
         if Obj1 < Obj2 then
            IntListManager.AddAfterIndex(Merger,IntListManager.Length(Merger), Obj1);
            IntListManager.RemoveIndex(LitM1,1);
         else
            IntListManager.AddAfterIndex(Merger,IntListManager.Length(Merger), Obj2);
            IntListManager.RemoveIndex(LitM2,1);
         fi;
      end loop;
      ListListManager.AddAfterIndex(NewLists,0,Merger);
   end loop;
   if ListListManager.Length(OldLists) > 0 then
      ListListManager.AddAfterIndex(NewLists,0,ListListManager.Grab(OldLists));
   fi;
   ListListManager.Assign(OldLists,NewLists);
   ListListManager.Clear(NewLists);
end loop;

IntListManager.Assign(Sorted,ListListManager.Grab(OldLists));

comment Print sorted list;
for Obj2 in IntListManager.Members(Sorted) do
   IM.Write(Obj2);
end for;
end;
```

F.5. Transitive Closure

```
!-------------------------------------------------;
! TransClo example main program                   ;
!-------------------------------------------------;

class MainProgram is
begin

   class PairManager of AssignableManager is
   begin
      class Pair of Assignable is
      begin
         var Domain => IM. new Integer;
         var Range => IM. new Integer;
      end;

      procedure Assign(L:Pair, R:Pair) is
      begin
         L.Domain := R.Domain;
         L.Range := R.Range;
         return;
      end;

      procedure Equal(L:Pair,R:Pair) return Booleans.Bit is
      begin
         return (L.Domain = R.Domain) and (L.Range = R.Range);
      end;
   end;

   var LocalPairManager => new PairManager;
   var PairSetManager => new SetManager(LocalPairManager . Pair);

   var IntSetManager => new SetManager(IM . Integer);
```

```
    var Count => IM . new Integer;
    var i => IM . new Integer;
    var Relation => PairSetManager . new Set;
    var Related => IntSetManager . new Set;
    var NewlyRelated => IntSetManager. new Set;
    var Found => IntSetManager . new Set;
    var Base => IntSetManager . new Set;
    var Temp => LocalPairManager . new Pair;

    comment Read in the relation;
    IM.Read(Count);
    for i in IM.Sequence(1,Count) do
       IM.Read(Temp.Domain);
       IM.Read(Temp.Range);
       PairSetManager.Insert(Relation,Temp);
    end for;

    comment Read in the base for the transitive closure.;
    IM.Read(Count);
    for i in IM.Sequence(1,Count) do
       IM.Read(Temp.Domain);
       IntSetManager.Insert(Base,Temp.Domain);
    end for;

    IntSetManager.Clear(Related);
    IntSetManager.Assign(NewlyRelated,Base);
    while IntSetManager.Size(NewlyRelated) > 0 do
       IntSetManager.Clear(Found);
       for i in IntSetManager.Members(NewlyRelated) do
          for Temp in PairSetManager.Members(Relation) do
             if Temp.Domain = i then
                IntSetManager.Insert(Found,i);
             fi;
          end for;
       end for;
       IntSetManager.Assign(Related,IntSetManager.Union(Related,NewlyRelated));
       IntSetManager.Assign(NewlyRelated,IntSetManager.Subtraction(Found,Related));
    end loop;

    comment Print out the results ;
    for i in IntSetManager.Members(Related) do
       IM.Write(i);
    end for;
end;
```

F.6. Huffman Encoding

```
!---------------------------------------------------;
! Huffman example main program                      ;
!---------------------------------------------------;

class MainProgram is
begin
    comment This program creates a Huffman encoding
            of an integer string ;

    var IntListManager => new ListManager(IM . Integer);

    class CharMapManager of AssignableManager is
    begin
       class CharMap of Assignable is
       begin
          var Domain => IntListManager. new List;
          var Range => IM. new Integer;
       end;

       procedure Assign(L:CharMap, R:CharMap) is
       begin
          IntListManager.Assign(L.Domain,R.Domain);
          L.Range := R.Range;
          return;
       end;
```

```
    procedure Equal(L:CharMap,R:CharMap) return Booleans.Bit is
    begin
       return IntListManager.Equal(L.Domain,R.Domain) and (L.Range = R.Range);
    end;
end;

var LocalCharMapManager => new CharMapManager;
var CharMapSetManager => new SetManager(LocalCharMapManager . CharMap);

class HTreeNodeManager of AssignableManager is
begin
   class HTNode of Assignable is
   begin
      var Domain => IntListManager. new List;
      var Next => IntListManager . new List;
      var Value => IM . new Integer;
   end;

   procedure Assign(L:HTNode, R:HTNode) is
   begin
      IntListManager.Assign(L.Domain,R.Domain);
      IntListManager.Assign(L.Next,R.Next);
      L.Value := R.Value;
      return;
   end;

   procedure Equal(L:HTNode,R:HTNode) return Booleans.Bit is
   begin
      return IntListManager.Equal(L.Domain,R.Domain) and
             IntListManager.Equal(L.Next,R.Next) and
             L.Value = R.Value;
   end;
end;

var HTManager => new HTreeNodeManager;
var HTSetManager => new SetManager(HTManager . HTNode);

class HCodeManager of AssignableManager is
begin
   class HCharCode of Assignable is
   begin
      var Source => IntListManager . new List;
      var CodeValue => IntListManager . new List;
   end;

   procedure Assign(L:HCharCode, R:HCharCode) is
   begin
      IntListManager.Assign(L.Source,R.Source);
      IntListManager.Assign(L.CodeValue,R.CodeValue);
      return;
   end;

   procedure Equal(L:HCharCode,R:HCharCode)
      return Booleans.Bit is
   begin
      return IntListManager.Equal(L.Source,R.Source) and
             IntListManager.Equal(L.CodeValue,R.CodeValue);
   end;
end;

var LocalCodeManager => new HCodeManager;
var CodeSetManager => new SetManager(LocalCodeManager . HCharCode);
var IntListSetManager => new SetManager(IntListManager . List);
```

```
var Temp => LocalCharMapManager . new CharMap;
var Temp1 => LocalCharMapManager . new CharMap;
var Temp2 => LocalCharMapManager . new CharMap;
var Count => IM . new Integer;
var i => IM . new Integer;
var Value => IM . new Integer;
var c => IntListManager . new List;
var s => IntListManager . new List;
var Freq => CharMapSetManager . new Set;
var Chars => IntListSetManager . new Set;
var TempList => IntListManager . new List;
var HTree => HTSetManager . new Set;
var TempHT => HTManager . new HTNode;
var HCode => CodeSetManager . new Set;
var HCD => IntListManager . new List;
var TempCode => LocalCodeManager. new HCharCode;
var B => IntListManager . new List;
var Missing => Booleans. new Bit;
var Found => Booleans. new Bit;

procedure GetMin(CharMapSetManager . F: Set)
   return LocalCharMapManager.CharMap;
procedure GetMin(CharMapSetManager . F: Set)
   return LocalCharMapManager.CharMap is
begin
   var N => IM . new Integer;
   var A => IntListManager . new List;
   var Temp => LocalCharMapManager . new CharMap;
   var FirstTime => Booleans . new Bit;

   IntListManager.Clear(C);
   N := 0;
   Booleans.Assign(FirstTime,True);
   for Temp in CharMapSetManager.Members(F) do
      if FirstTime then
         Booleans.Assign(FirstTime,False);
         N := Temp.Range;
         IntListManager.Assign(C,Temp.Domain);
      elseif Temp.Range < N then
         N := Temp.Range;
         IntListManager.Assign(C,Temp.Domain);
      fi;
   end for;
   Temp.Range := N;
   IntListManager.Assign(Temp.Domain,C);
   CharMapSetManager.Delete(F,Temp);
   return Temp;
end;

comment Read in the string;
IM.Read(Count);
for i in IM.Sequence(1,Count) do
   IM.Read(Value);
   IntListManager.AddBeforeIndex(s,i,Value);
end for;

CharMapSetManager.Clear(Freq);
IntListSetManager.Clear(Chars);
for Value in IntListManager.Members(s) do
   Booleans.Assign(Missing,True);
   IntListManager.Clear(TempList);
   IntListManager.AddAfterIndex(TempList,0,Value);
   for Temp in CharMapSetManager.Members(Freq) do
      if IntListManager.Equal(Temp.Domain,TempList) then
         Booleans.Assign(Missing,False);
         CharMapSetManager.Delete(Freq,Temp);
         Temp.Range := Temp.Range + 1;
         CharMapSetManager.Insert(Freq,Temp);
         exitloop;
      fi;
   end for;
   if Missing then
      IntListSetManager.Insert(Chars,TempList);
      IntListManager.Assign(Temp.Domain,TempList);
      Temp.Range := 1;
      CharMapSetManager.Insert(Freq,Temp);
   fi;
end for;
```

```
HTSetManager.Clear(HTree);
while CharMapSetManager.Size(Freq) > 1 do
   LocalCharMapManager.Assign(Temp1,GetMin(Freq));
   LocalCharMapManager.Assign(Temp2,GetMin(Freq));
   IntListManager.Assign(Temp.Domain,IntListManager.Concatenate(Temp1.Domain,Temp2.Domain));
   Temp.Range := Temp1.Range + Temp2.Range;
   CharMapSetManager.Insert(Freq,Temp);

   IntListManager.Assign(TempHT.Domain,Temp1.Domain);
   IntListManager.Assign(TempHT.Next,Temp.Domain);
   TempHT.Value := 0;
   HTSetManager.Insert(HTree,TempHT);
   IntListManager.Assign(TempHT.Domain,Temp2.Domain);
   TempHT.Value := 1;
   HTSetManager.Insert(HTree,TempHT);
end loop;

CodeSetManager.Clear(HCode);
for TempList in IntListSetManager.Members(Chars) do
   IntListManager.Clear(HCD);
   IntListManager.Assign(B,TempList);
   Booleans.Assign(Found,True);
   while Found do
      Booleans.Assign(Found,False);
      for TempHT in HTSetManager.Members(HTree) do
         if IntListManager.Equal(B,TempHT.Domain) then
            Booleans.Assign(Found,True);
            IntListManager.Assign(B,TempHT.Next);
            IntListManager.AddBeforeIndex(HCD,0,TempHT.Value);
            exitloop;
         fi;
      end for;
   end loop;
   IntListManager.Assign(TempCode.Source,TempList);
   IntListManager.Assign(TempCode.CodeValue,HCD);
   CodeSetManager.Insert(HCode,TempCode);
end for;

comment Print out the results;
for TempCode in CodeSetManager.Members(HCode) do
   IM.Write(IntListManager.GetIndex(TempCode.Source,1));
   for i in IntListManager.Members(TempCode.CodeValue) do
      IM.Write(i);
   end for;
end for;
end;
```

Appendix G
Sample Output of Translator

This appendix gives a minimally edited output from the prototype translator as it operated on the examples in Chapter 6.

```
;;
;; output from compiler 2.0 Mon Jun 13 13:05:55 1983
;;
;; feg version 0
;;
;; input file was fint2f.tcl
;;
;; compilation of fint2f.trn
;;


comment %fint2f.trn;

-----------------------------------------------------------
template output for reading instances.
-----------------------------------------------------------

class universal_environment is
begin
   class transputmanager is
   begin
      class transportable is begin end;

      procedure read#13: (transportable) ;
      procedure write#17: (transportable) ;
   end;

   class assignablemanager is
   begin
      class assignable is begin end;

      procedure assign#50: (l : assignable,r : assignable)
           such that l.structure same as r.structure;
      procedure equal#77: (l : assignable,r : assignable)
         return booleans.bit
           such that l.structure same as r.structure ;
   end;

   class bitmanager of assignablemanager is
   begin
      class bit of assignable is begin end;

      procedure logicaland#133: (b1 : bit,b2 : bit)
         return b1.structure
           such that b1.structure same as b2.structure;
      procedure logicalor#160: (b1 : bit,b2 : bit)
         return b1.structure
           such that b1.structure same as b2.structure;
      procedure logicalnot#171: (b : bit)
         return b.structure ;
   end;

   var booleans => new bitmanager;

   procedure true#213: return booleans.bit ;
   procedure false#221: return booleans.bit ;
```

```
class orderedmanager of assignablemanager is
begin
   class ordered of assignable is begin end;

   procedure lessthan#262: (l : ordered,r : ordered)
      return booleans.bit
         such that l.structure same as r.structure;
   procedure greaterthan#277: (l : ordered,r : ordered)
      return booleans.bit
         such that l.structure same as r.structure;
   procedure lessthanequal#324: (l : ordered,r : ordered)
      return booleans.bit
         such that l.structure same as r.structure;
   procedure greaterthanequal#351: (l : ordered,r : ordered)
      return booleans.bit
         such that l.structure same as r.structure;
end;

class hashablemanager of assignablemanager is
begin
   class hashable of assignable is begin end;

   procedure hash#372: (h : hashable) return im.integer ;
end;

class discretemanager of orderedmanager, transputmanager, hashablemanager is
begin
   class integer of ordered, transportable, hashable is begin end;

   procedure plus#424: (l : integer,r : integer)
      return l.structure
         such that l.structure same as r.structure;
   procedure minus#451: (l : integer,r : integer)
      return l.structure
         such that l.structure same as r.structure;
   procedure unaryminus#461: (l : integer)
      return l.structure ;
   procedure times#606: (l : integer,r : integer)
      return l.structure
         such that l.structure same as r.structure;
   procedure divide#533: (l : integer,r : integer)
      return l.structure
         such that l.structure same as r.structure;
   procedure sequence#562: (lower : integer,upper : integer)
      yield lower.structure
         such that lower.structure same as upper.structure;
   procedure reversesequence#607: (lower : integer,upper : integer)
      yield lower.structure
         such that lower.structure same as upper.structure;

   procedure literal#621: (cm.l : word) return integer ;
   procedure value#632: (i : integer) return cm.word ;
end;

var im => new discretemanager;
class wordmanager
   of assignablemanager, transputmanager is
begin
   class word
         of assignable, transportable is
   begin
   end;
   comment All of the word operations were deleted in this run.;
end;

var cm => new wordmanager;
class arraymanager(elt : any) is
begin
   class array(im.lowerbound : integer,im.upperbound : integer) is
   begin
      procedure element#676: (im.index : integer)
         return elt.structure ;

   end;

end;
```

```
class refmanager(elt : any)
   of assignablemanager is
begin
   class reference
         of assignable is
      begin
        procedure value#713: return elt.structure ;

      end;

   procedure allocate#722: return reference ;
   procedure free#726: (r : reference) ;
   procedure nil#733: return reference ;

end;

procedure special_make_literal#~46: (t : any) return cm.word ;

procedure log2#1271: (im.i : integer) return im.integer ;
procedure log2#1417: (im.i : integer) return im.integer is
begin
   var temp => im.new integer;
   var result => im.new integer;
   var one => im.new integer;
   var two => im.new integer;
   im.assign#3(one,im.literal#2(special_make_literal#1(1)));
   im.assign#6(two,im.literal#5(special_make_literal#4(2)));
   im.assign#9(result,im.literal#8(special_make_literal#7(0)));
   im.assign#10(temp,i);
   while im.greaterthan#11(temp,one) do
      im.assign#13(result,im.plus#12(result,one));
      im.assign#15(temp,im.divide#14(temp,two));
   end loop;
   return result;
end;

procedure square#1430: (im.i : integer) return im.integer ;
procedure square#1451: (im.i : integer) return im.integer is
begin
   return im.times#1(i,i);
end;

class setmanager(t : any)
   of assignablemanager is
begin
   class set
         of assignable is
      begin
         attribute var setsize => im.literal(special_make_literal(10));
      end;

   procedure insert#1475: (s : set,t.e : structure) ;
   procedure delete#1504: (s : set,t.e : structure) ;
   procedure clear#1510: (s : set) ,
   procedure size#1520: (s : set) return im.integer ;
   procedure ismember#1533: (s : set,t.e : structure) return booleans.bit ;
   procedure union#1544: (l : set,r : set) return set ;
   procedure subtraction#1555: (l : set,r : set) return set ;
   procedure members#1565: (s : set) yield t.structure ;

   procedure assign#1620: (l : set,r : set) is
   begin
      var elt => new t;
      clear#1(l);
      for elt in members#2(r) do
         insert#3(l,elt);
      end for;
   end;

end;

class listmanager(tmanager : assignablemanager.t : assignable)
   of assignablemanager is
begin
   class list
         of assignable is
      begin
      attribute var listsize => im.literal(special_make_literal(100));
      end;
```

```
    procedure addbeforeindex#1653: (l : list,im.position : integer,t.newelt : structure) ;
    procedure addafterindex#1666: (l : list,im.position : integer,t.newelt : structure) ;
    procedure removeindex#1674: (l : list,im.position : integer) ;
    procedure clear#1677: (l : list) ;
    procedure getindex#1712: (l : list,im.position : integer)
        return t.structure ;
    procedure length#1722: (l : list) return im.integer ;
    procedure first#1732: (l : list) return t.structure ;
    procedure grab#1742: (l : list) return t.structure ;
    procedure members#1751: (l : list) yield t.structure ;
    procedure constructlist#1761: (t.elt : structure) return list ;

end;

class arraysetmanager(tmanager : assignablemanager.t : assignable)
    of setmanager is
begin
    var arrayofobjectmanager => new arraymanager(t.structure);
    var maxarraysize => im.new integer;
    class arrayset
            of set is
    begin
        var elts => arrayofobjectmanager.new array(im.literal#2(special_make_literal#1(1)),maxarraysize);
        var lastused => im.new integer;
        im.assign#5(lastused,im.literal#4(special_make_literal#3(0)));
end;

    procedure localcopy#2040: (l : arrayset,r : arrayset) ;
    procedure localcopy#2101: (l : arrayset,r : arrayset) is
    begin
        var i => im.new integer;
        for i in im.sequence#3(im.literal#2(special_make_literal#1(1)),r.lastused) do
            tmanager.assign#6(l.elts.element#4(i),r.elts.element#5(i));
        end for;
    end;

    procedure insert#2176: (s : arrayset,t.e : structure) is
    begin
        var i => im.new integer;
        for i in im.sequence#3(im.literal#2(special_make_literal#1(1)),s.lastused) do
            if tmanager.equal#5(s.elts.element#4(i),e) then
                return ;
            fi;
        end for;
        im.assign#9(s.lastused,im.plus#8(s.lastused,im.literal#7(special_make_literal#6(1))));
        tmanager.assign#11(s.elts.element#10(s.lastused),e);
    end;

    procedure delete#2277: (s : arrayset,t.e : structure) is
    begin
        var i => im.new integer;
        for i in im.sequence#3(im.literal#2(special_make_literal#1(1)),s.lastused) do
            if tmanager.equal#5(s.elts.element#4(i),e) then
                tmanager.assign#6(s.elts.element#6(i),s.elts.element#7(s.lastused));
                im.assign#12(s.lastused,
                             im.minus#11(s.lastused,im.literal#10(special_make_literal#9(1))));
                return ;
            fi;
        end for;
    end;

    procedure clear#2312: (s : arrayset) is
    begin
        im.assign#3(s.lastused,im.literal#2(special_make_literal#1(0)));
    end;

    procedure size#2327: (s : arrayset)
        return im.integer is
    begin
        return s.lastused;
    end;
```

```
procedure ismember#2405: (s : arrayset,t.e : structure)
    return booleans.bit is
begin
    var i => im.new integer;
    for i in im.sequence#3(im.literal#2(special_make_literal#1(1)),s.lastused) do
        if tmanager.equal#5(s.elts.element#4(i),e) then
            return true#6;
        fi;
    end for;
    return false#7;
end;

procedure union#2536: (l : arrayset,r : arrayset)
    return arrayset is
begin
    var o => new arrayset;
    var i => im.new integer;
    localcopy#1(o,l);
    im.assign#2(o.lastused,l.lastused);
    for i in im.sequence#5(im.literal#4(special_make_literal#3(1)),r.lastused) do
        if booleans.logicalnot#8(ismember#7(o,r.elts.element#6(i))) then
            im.assign#12(o.lastused,im.plus#11(o.lastused,
                                               im.literal#10(special_make_literal#9(1))));
            tmanager.assign#15(o.elts.element#13(o.lastused),
                               r.elts.element#14(i));
        fi;
    end for;
    return o;
end;

procedure subtraction#2647: (l : arrayset,r : arrayset)
    return arrayset is
begin
    var o => new arrayset;
    var i => im.new integer;
    for i in im.sequence#3(im.literal#2(special_make_literal#1(1)),l.lastused) do
        if booleans.logicalnot#6(ismember#5(r,l.elts.element#4(i))) then
            im.assign#10(o.lastused,im.plus#9(o.lastused,im.literal#8(special_make_literal#7(1))));
            tmanager.assign#13(o.elts.element#11(o.lastused),l.elts.element#12(i));
        fi;
    end for;
    return o;
end;

procedure members#2707: (s : arrayset)
    yield t.structure is
begin
    var i => im.new integer;
    for i in im.sequence#3(im.literal#2(special_make_literal#1(1)),s.lastused) do
        yield s.elts.element#4(i);
    end for;
    return ;
end;

im.assign#3(maxarraysize,im.literal#2(special_make_literal#1(100)));
end;

class arraylistmanager(tmanager : assignablemanager.t : assignable)
    of listmanager is
begin
    var maxarraysize => im.new integer;
    var am => new arraymanager(t.structure);

    class arraylist
        of list is
    begin
        var elts => am.new array(im.literal#2(special_make_literal#1(1)),maxarraysize);
        var numelts => im.new integer;
        im.assign#5(numelts,im.literal#4(special_make_literal#3(0)));
    end;

    procedure localcopy#2771: (l : arraylist,r : arraylist) ;
    procedure localcopy#3031: (l : arraylist,r : arraylist) is
    begin
        var i => im.new integer;
        for i in im.sequence#3(im.literal#2(special_make_literal#1(1)),maxarraysize) do
            tmanager.assign#6(l.elts.element#4(i),r.elts.element#5(i));
        end for;
    end;
```

```
procedure addbeforeindex#3173: (1 : arraylist,im.position : integer,t.newelt : structure) is
begin
   var i => im.new integer;
   if booleans.logicaland#10(
         booleans.logicaland#5(
            im.lessthan#1(l.numelts,maxarraysize),
            im.greaterthanequal#4(position,im.literal#3(special_make_literal#2(1)))),
         im.lessthanequal#9(position,
                            im.plus#8(l.numelts,im.literal#7(special_make_literal#6(1))))) then
      for i in im.reversesequence#11(position,l.numelts) do
         tmanager.assign#17(
            l.elts.element#15(in.plus#14(i,im.literal#13(special_make_literal#12(1)))),
            l.elts.element#16(i));
      end for;
      tmanager.assign#19(l.elts.element#18(position),newelt);
      im.assign#23(l.numelts,im.plus#22(l.numelts,im.literal#21(special_make_literal#20(1))));
   fi;
end;

procedure addafterindex#3341: (1 : arraylist,im.position : integer,t.newelt : structure) is
begin
   var i => im.new integer;
   if booleans.logicaland#7(
         booleans.logicaland#5(
            im.lessthan#1(l.numelts,maxarraysize),
            im.greaterthanequal#4(position,im.literal#3(special_make_literal#2(0)))),
         im.lessthanequal#6(position,l.numelts)) then
      for i in im.reversesequence#11(
            im.plus#10(position,im.literal#9(special_make_literal#8(1))),l.numelts) do
         tmanager.assign#17(l.elts.element#15(im.plus#14(i,im.literal#13(special_make_literal#12(1)))),
                            l.elts.element#16(i));
      end for;
      tmanager.assign#22(l.elts.element#21(
                            im.plus#20(position,im.literal#19(special_make_literal#18(1)))),
                         newelt);
      im.assign#26(l.numelts,im.plus#25(l.numelts,im.literal#24(special_make_literal#23(1))));
   fi;
end;

procedure removeindex#3463: (1 : arraylist,im.position : integer) is
begin
   var i => im.new integer;
   if booleans.logicaland#5(
         im.greaterthanequal#3(position,im.literal#2(special_make_literal#1(1))),
         im.lessthanequal#4(position,l.numelts)) then
      for i in im.sequence#9(
            im.plus#8(position,im.literal#7(special_make_literal#6(1))),l.numelts) do
         tmanager.assign#15(
            l.elts.element#10(i),
            l.elts.element#14(im.plus#13(i,im.literal#12(special_make_literal#11(1)))));
      end for;
      im.assign#19(l.numelts,im.minus#18(l.numelts,im.literal#17(special_make_literal#16(1))));
   fi;
end;

procedure clear#3466: (1 : arraylist) is
begin
   im.assign#3(l.numelts,im.literal#2(special_make_literal#1(0)));
end;

procedure getindex#3511: (1 : arraylist,im.position : integer)
   return t.structure is
begin
   return l.elts.element#1(position);
end;

procedure length#3526: (1 : arraylist)
   return im.integer is
begin
   return l.numelts;
end;

procedure first#3546: (1 : arraylist)
   return t.structure is
begin
   return l.elts.element#3(im.literal#2(special_make_literal#1(1)));
end;
```

```
procedure grab#3674: (l : arraylist)
   return t.structure is
begin
   var temp => new t;
   var i => im.new integer;
   if im.greaterthan#3(l.numelts,im.literal#2(special_make_literal#1(0))) then
      tmanager.assign#7(temp,l.elts.element#6(im.literal#5(special_make_literal#4(1))));
      for i in im.sequence#13(
         im.literal#9(special_make_literal#8(1)),
         im.minus#12(l.numelts,im.literal#11(special_make_literal#10(1)))) do
         tmanager.assign#19(
            l.elts.element#14(i),
            l.elts.element#18(im.plus#17(i,im.literal#16(special_make_literal#15(1)))));
      end for;
      im.assign#23(l.numelts,im.minus#22(l.numelts,im.literal#21(special_make_literal#20(1))));
      return temp;
   fi;
end;

procedure members#3747: (l : arraylist)
   yield t.structure is
begin
   var i => im.new integer;
   for i in im.sequence#3(im.literal#2(special_make_literal#1(1)),l.numelts) do
      yield l.elts.element#4(i);
      if im.greaterthan#5(i,l.numelts) then
         exitloop;
      fi;
   end for;
   return ;
end;

procedure constructlist#4012: (t.elt : structure)
   return arraylist is
begin
   var tl => new arraylist;
   im.assign#3(tl.numelts,im.literal#2(special_make_literal#1(1)));
   tmanager.assign#7(tl.elts.element#6(im.literal#5(special_make_literal#4(1))),elt);
   return tl;
end;

procedure assign#4063: (l : arraylist,r : arraylist) is
begin
   var i => im.new integer;
   im.assign#1(l.numelts,r.numelts);
   for i in im.sequence#4(im.literal#3(special_make_literal#2(1)),r.numelts) do
      tmanager.assign#7(l.elts.element#5(i),r.elts.element#6(i));
   end for;
end;

procedure equal#4166: (l : arraylist,r : arraylist)
   return booleans.bit is
begin
   var i => im.new integer;
   if booleans.logicalnot#2(im.equal#1(l.numelts,r.numelts)) then
      return false#3;
   fi;
   for i in im.sequence#6(im.literal#5(special_make_literal#4(1)),l.numelts) do
      if booleans.logicalnot#10(tmanager.equal#9(l.elts.element#7(i),r.elts.element#8(i))) then
         return false#11;
      fi;
   end for;
   return true#12;
end;

im.assign#3(maxarraysize,im.literal#2(special_make_literal#1(100)));
end;

class mainprogram is
begin
   var intsetmanager => new setmanager(im.integer);
   var intlistmanager => new listmanager(im.integer);
   var unsorted => intsetmanager.new set
      where setsize => im.literal(special_make_literal(100));
   var sorted => intlistmanager.new list
      where listsize => im.literal(special_make_literal(100));
   var count => im.new integer;
   var i => im.new integer;
   var obj1 => im.new integer;
   var obj2 => im.new integer;
```

```
         intsetmanager.clear#1(unsorted);
         im.read#2(count);
         for i in im.sequence#5(im.literal#4(special_make_literal#3(1)),count) do
            im.read#6(obj1);
            intsetmanager.insert#7(unsorted,obj1);
         end for;

         intlistmanager.clear#8(sorted);

         for obj1 in intsetmanager.members#9(unsorted) do
            im.assign#12(count,im.literal#11(special_make_literal#10(1)));
            while im.lessthanequal#14(count,intlistmanager.length#13(sorted)) do
               im.assign#16(obj2,intlistmanager.getindex#15(sorted,count));
               if im.greaterthanequal#17(obj2,obj1) then
                  exitloop;
               else
                  im.assign#21(count,im.plus#20'count,im.literal#19(special_make_literal#18(1))));
               fi;
            end loop;
            intlistmanager.addbeforeindex#22(sorted,count,obj1);
         end for;

         for obj2 in intlistmanager.members#23(sorted) do
            im.write#24(obj2);
         end for;
      end;

   end;

   ----------------------------------------------------------
   the user's program
   ----------------------------------------------------------

   instance x12384:. object instance of mainprogram.
      local instance x12385: of mainprogram.
      1 var intsetmanager => arraysetmanager (x12393:)
      2 var intlistmanager => arraylistmanager (x12404:)
      3 var unsorted => arrayset (x12411:)
      4 var sorted => arraylist (x12477:)
      5 var count => integer (x12543:)
      6 var i => integer (x12550:)
      7 var obj1 => integer (x12557:)
      8 var obj2 => integer (x12564:)
      1 proc clear => clear#2312: of arraysetmanager (x12571:)
      2 proc read => read#13: of transputmanager (x12618:)
      3 proc special_make_literal => special_make_literal#746: of universal_environment (x12623:)
      4 proc literal => literal#621: of discretemanager (x12630:)
      5 proc sequence => sequence#562: of discretemanager (x12643:)
      6 proc read => read#13: of transputmanager (x12680:)
      7 proc insert => insert#2176: of arraysetmanager (x12684:)
      8 proc clear => clear#3466: of arraylistmanager (x12738:)
      9 proc members => members#2707: of arraysetmanager (x12785:)
      10 proc special_make_literal => special_make_literal#746: of universal_environment (x12840:)
      11 proc literal => literal#621: of discretemanager (x12847:)
      12 proc assign => assign#50: of assignablemanager (x12860:)
      13 proc length => length#3526: of arraylistmanager (x12880:)
      14 proc lessthanequal => lessthanequal#324: of orderedmanager (x12934:)
      15 proc getindex => getindex#3511: of arraylistmanager (x12959:)
      16 proc assign => assign#50: of assignablemanager (x13020:)
      17 proc greaterthanequal => greaterthanequal#351: of orderedmanager (x13040:)
      18 proc special_make_literal => special_make_literal#746: of universal_environment (x13066:)
      19 proc literal => literal#621: of discretemanager (x13073:)
      20 proc plus => plus#424: of discretemanager (x13086:)
      21 proc assign => assign#50: of assignablemanager (x13123:)
      22 proc addbeforeindex => addbeforeindex#3173: of arraylistmanager (x13143:)
      23 proc members => members#3747: of arraylistmanager (x13204:)
      24 proc write => write#17: of transputmanager (x13258:)

   instance x12393:. object instance of arraysetmanager.
      local instance x12395: of assignablemanager.
      local instance x12396: of setmanager.
      local instance x17568: of arraysetmanager.
      1 var arrayofobjectmanager => arraymanager (x17576:)
      2 var maxarraysize => integer (x17579:)
      1 proc special_make_literal => special_make_literal#746: of universal_environment (x17587:)
      2 proc literal => literal#621: of discretemanager (x17594:)
      3 proc assign => assign#50: of assignablemanager (x17607:)

   instance x17576:. object instance of arraymanager.
      local instance x17578: of arraymanager.
```

```
instance x17579:. object instance of integer.
   local instance x17583: of assignable.
   local instance x17581: of ordered.
   local instance x17582: of transportable.
   local instance x17583: of assignable.
   local instance x17584: of hashable.
   local instance x17585: of integer.

instance x17587:. procedure call of special_make_literal#746: of universal_environment.

instance x17594:. procedure call of literal#621: of discretemanager.

instance x17607:. procedure call of assign#50: of assignablemanager.

instance x12404:. object instance of arraylistmanager.
   local instance x12409: of assignablemanager.
   local instance x12410: of listmanager.
   local instance x17880: of arraylistmanager.
   1 var maxarraysize => integer (x17881:)
   2 var am => arraymanager (x17895:)
   1 proc special_make_literal => special_make_literal#746: of universal_environment (x17899:)
   2 proc literal => literal#621: of discretemanager (x17906:)
   3 proc assign => assign#50: of assignablemanager (x17919:)

instance x17881:. object instance of integer.
   local instance x17885: of assignable.
   local instance x17883: of ordered.
   local instance x17884: of transportable.
   local instance x17885: of assignable.
   local instance x17886: of hashable.
   local instance x17887: of integer.

instance x17895:. object instance of arraymanager.
   local instance x17897: of arraymanager.

instance x17899:. procedure call of special_make_literal#746: of universal_environment.

instance x17906:. procedure call of literal#621: of discretemanager.

instance x17919:. procedure call of assign#50: of assignablemanager.

instance x12411:. object instance of arrayset.
   local instance x12412: of assignable.
   local instance x12413: of set.
   local instance x18188: of arrayset.
   1 var elts => array (x18210:)
   2 var lastused => integer (x18226:)
   1 proc special_make_literal => special_make_literal#746: of universal_environment (x18190:)
   2 proc literal => literal#621: of discretemanager (x18197:)
   3 proc special_make_literal => special_make_literal#746: of universal_environment (x18234:)
   4 proc literal => literal#621: of discretemanager (x18241:)
   5 proc assign => assign#50: of assignablemanager (x18254:)


instance x18210:. object instance of array.
   local instance x18225: of array.

instance x18226:. object instance of integer.
   local instance x18230: of assignable.
   local instance x18228: of ordered.
   local instance x18229: of transportable.
   local instance x18230: of assignable.
   local instance x18231: of hashable.
   local instance x18232: of integer.

instance x18190:. procedure call of special_make_literal#746: of universal_environment.

instance x18197:. procedure call of literal#621: of discretemanager.

instance x18234:. procedure call of special_make_literal#746: of universal_environment.

instance x18241:. procedure call of literal#621: of discretemanager.

instance x18254:. procedure call of assign#50: of assignablemanager.
```

```
instance x12477:. object instance of arraylist.
   local instance x12478: of assignable.
   local instance x12479: of list.
   local instance x18523: of arraylist.
   1 var elts => array (x18545:)
   2 var numelts => integer (x18561:)
   1 proc special_make_literal => special_make_literal#746: of universal_environment (x18525:)
   2 proc literal => literal#621: of discretemanager (x18532:)
   3 proc special_make_literal => special_make_literal#746: of universal_environment (x18569:)
   4 proc literal => literal#621: of discretemanager (x18576:)
   5 proc assign => assign#50: of assignablemanager (x18589:)


instance x18545:. object instance of array.
   local instance x18560: of array.

instance x18561:. object·instance of integer.
   local instance x18565: of assignable.
   local instance x18563: of ordered.
   local instance x18564: of transportable.
   local instance x18565: of assignable.
   local instance x18566: of hashable.
   local instance x18567: of integer.

instance x18525:. procedure call of special_make_literal#746: of universal_environment.

instance x18532:. procedure call of literal#621: of discretemanager.

instance x18569:. procedure call of special_make_literal#746: of universal_environment.

instance x18576:. procedure call of literal#621: of discretemanager.

instance x18589:. procedure call of assign#50: of assignablemanager.

instance x12543:. object instance of integer.
   local instance x12547: of assignable.
   local instance x12545: of ordered.
   local instance x12546: of transportable.
   local instance x12547: of assignable.
   local instance x12548: of hashable.
   local instance x12549: of integer.

instance x12550:. object instance of integer.
   local instance x12554: of assignable.
   local instance x12552: of ordered.
   local instance x12553: of transportable.
   local instance x12554: of assignable.
   local instance x12555: of hashable.
   local instance x12556: of integer.

instance x12557:. object instance of integer.
   local instance x12561: of assignable.
   local instance x12559: of ordered.
   local instance x12560: of transportable.
   local instance x12561: of assignable.
   local instance x12562: of hashable.
   local instance x12563: of integer.

instance x12564:. object instance of integer.
   local instance x12568: of assignable.
   local instance x12566: of ordered.
   local instance x12567: of transportable.
   local instance x12568: of assignable.
   local instance x12569: of hashable.
   local instance x12570: of integer.

instance x12571:. procedure call of clear#2312: of arraysetmanager.
   1 proc special_make_literal => special_make_literal#746: of universal_environment (x19469:)
   2 proc literal => literal#621: of discretemanager (x19476:)
   3 proc assign => assign#50: of assignablemanager (x19489:)

instance x19469:. procedure call of special_make_literal#746: of universal_environment.

instance x19476:. procedure call of literal#621: of discretemanager.

instance x19489:. procedure call of assign#50: of assignablemanager.

instance x12618:. procedure call of read#13: of transputmanager.

instance x12623:. procedure call of special_make_literal#746: of universal_environment.
```

```
instance x12630:. procedure call of literal#621: of discretemanager.

instance x12643:. procedure call of sequence#562: of discretemanager.

instance x12680:. procedure call of read#13: of transputmanager.

instance x12684:. procedure call of insert#2176: of arraysetmanager.
    1 var i => integer (x19612:)
    1 proc special_make_literal => special_make_literal#746: of universal_environment (x19620:)
    2 proc literal => literal#621: of discretemanager (x19627:)
    3 proc sequence => sequence#562: of discretemanager (x19640:)
    4 proc element => element#676: of array (x19663:)
    5 proc equal => equal#77: of assignablemanager (x19679:)
    6 proc special_make_literal => special_make_literal#746: of universal_environment (x19689:)
    7 proc literal => literal#621: of discretemanager (x19696:)
    8 proc plus => plus#424: of discretemanager (x19709:)
    9 proc assign => assign#50: of assignablemanager (x19732:)
    10 proc element => element#676: of array (x19738:)
    11 proc assign => assign#50: of assignablemanager (x19754:)

instance x19612:. object instance of integer.
    local instance x19616: of assignable.
    local instance x19614: of ordered.
    local instance x19615: of transportable.
    local instance x19616: of assignable.
    local instance x19617: of hashable.
    local instance x19618: of integer.

instance x19620:. procedure call of special_make_literal#746: of universal_environment.

instance x19627:. procedure call of literal#621: of discretemanager.

instance x19640:. procedure call of sequence#562: of discretemanager.

instance x19663:. procedure call of element#676: of array.

instance x19679:. procedure call of equal#77: of assignablemanager.

instance x19689:. procedure call of special_make_literal#746: of universal_environment.

instance x19696:. procedure call of literal#621: of discretemanager.

instance x19709:. procedure call of plus#424: of discretemanager.

instance x19732:. procedure call of assign#50: of assignablemanager.

instance x19738:. procedure call of element#676: of array.

instance x19754:. procedure call of assign#50: of assignablemanager.

instance x12738:. procedure call of clear#3466: of arraylistmanager.
    1 proc special_make_literal => special_make_literal#746: of universal_environment (x19927:)
    2 proc literal => literal#621: of discretemanager (x19934:)
    3 proc assign => assign#50: of assignablemanager (x19947:)

instance x19927:. procedure call of special_make_literal#746: of universal_environment.

instance x19934:. procedure call of literal#621: of discretemanager.

instance x19947:. procedure call of assign#50: of assignablemanager.

instance x12785:. procedure call of members#2707: of arraysetmanager.
    1 var i => integer (x20021:)
    1 proc special_make_literal => special_make_literal#746: of universal_environment (x20029:)
    2 proc literal => literal#621: of discretemanager (x20036:)
    3 proc sequence => sequence#562: of discretemanager (x20049:)
    4 proc element => element#676: of array (x20072:)

instance x20021:. object instance of integer.
    local instance x20025: of assignable.
    local instance x20023: of ordered.
    local instance x20024: of transportable.
    local instance x20025: of assignable.
    local instance x20026: of hashable.
    local instance x20027: of integer.

instance x20029:. procedure call of special_make_literal#746: of universal_environment.

instance x20036:. procedure call of literal#621: of discretemanager.

instance x20049:. procedure call of sequence#562: of discretemanager.
```

```
instance x20072:. procedure call of element#676: of array.

instance x12840:. procedure call of special_make_literal#746: of universal_environment.

instance x12847:. procedure call of literal#621: of discretemanager.

instance x12860:. procedure call of assign#50: of assignablemanager.

instance x12880:. procedure call of length#3526: of arraylistmanager.

instance x12934:. procedure call of lessthanequal#324: of orderedmanager.

instance x12959:. procedure call of getindex#3511: of arraylistmanager.
  1 proc element => element#676: of array (x20285:)

instance x20285:. procedure call of element#676: of array.

instance x13020:. procedure call of assign#50: of assignablemanager.

instance x13040:. procedure call of greaterthanequal#351: of orderedmanager.

instance x13066:. procedure call of special_make_literal#746: of universal_environment.

instance x13073:. procedure call of literal#621: of discretemanager.

instance x13086:. procedure call of plus#424: of discretemanager.

instance x13123:. procedure call of assign#50: of assignablemanager.

instance x13143:. procedure call of addbefo.eindex#3173: of arraylistmanager.
  1 var i => integer (x20438:)
  1 proc lessthan => lessthan#252: of orderedmanager (x20445:)
  2 proc special_make_literal => special_make_literal#746: of universal_environment (x20457:)
  3 proc literal => literal#621: of discretemanager (x20464:)
  4 proc greaterthanequal => greaterthanequal#351: of orderedmanager (x20477:)
  5 proc logicaland => logicaland#133: of bitmanager (x20488:)
  6 proc special_make_literal => special_make_literal#746: of universal_environment (x20500:)
  7 proc literal => literal#621: of discretemanager (x20507:)
  8 proc plus => plus#424: of discretemanager (x20520:)
  9 proc lessthanequal => lessthanequal#324: of orderedmanager (x20543:)
  10 proc logicaland => logicaland#133: of bitmanager (x20554:)
  11 proc reversesequence => reversesequence#607: of discretemanager (x20565:)
  12 proc special_make_literal => special_make_literal#746: of universal_environment (x20589:)
  13 proc literal => literal#621: of discretemanager (x20596:)
  14 proc plus => plus#424: of discretemanager (x20609:)
  15 proc element => element#676: of array (x20632:)
  16 proc element => element#676: of array (x20648:)
  17 proc assign => assign#50: of assignablemanager (x20664:)
  18 proc element => element#676: of array (x20670:)
  19 proc assign => assign#50: of assignablemanager (x20686:)
  20 proc special_make_literal => special_make_literal#746: of universal_environment (x20693:)
  21 proc literal => literal#621: of discretemanager (x20700:)
  22 proc plus => plus#424: of discretemanager (x20713:)
  23 proc assign => assign#50: of assignablemanager (x20736:)

instance x20438:. object instance of integer.
  local instance x20442: of assignable.
  local instance x20440: of ordered.
  local instance x20441: of transportable.
  local instance x20442: of assignable.
  local instance x20443: of hashable.
  local instance x20444: of integer.

instance x20445:. procedure call of lessthan#252: of orderedmanager.

instance x20457:. procedure call of special_make_literal#746: of universal_environment.

instance x20464:. procedure call of literal#621: of discretemanager.

instance x20477:. procedure call of greaterthanequal#351: of orderedmanager.

instance x20488:. procedure call of logicaland#133: of bitmanager.

instance x20500:. procedure call of special_make_literal#746: of universal_environment.

instance x20507:. procedure call of literal#621: of discretemanager.

instance x20520:. procedure call of plus#424: of discretemanager.

instance x20543:. procedure call of lessthanequal#324: of orderedmanager.
```

instance x20554:. procedure call of logicaland#133: of bitmanager.

instance x20565:. procedure call of reversesequence#607: of discretemanager.

instance x20589:. procedure call of special_make_literal#746: of universal_environment.

instance x20596:. procedure call of literal#621: of discretemanager.

instance x20609:. procedure call of plus#424: of discretemanager.

instance x20632:. procedure call of element#676: of array.

instance x20648:. procedure call of element#676: of array.

instance x20664:. procedure call of assign#50: of assignablemanager.

instance x20670:. procedure call of element#676: of array.

instance x20686:. procedure call of assign#50: of assignablemanager.

instance x20693:. procedure call of special_make_literal#746: of universal_environment.

instance x20700:. procedure call of literal#621: of discretemanager.

instance x20713:. procedure call of plus#424: of discretemanager.

instance x20736:. procedure call of assign#50: of assignablemanager.

instance x13204:. procedure call of members#3747: of arraylistmanager.
    1 var i => integer (x21040:)
    1 proc special_make_literal => special_make_literal#746: of universal_environment (x21048:)
    2 proc literal => literal#621: of discretemanager (x21055:)
    3 proc sequence => sequence#562: of discretemanager (x21068:)
    4 proc element => element#676: of array (x21091:)
    6 proc greaterthan => greaterthan#277: of orderedmanager (x21107:)

instance x21040:. object instance of integer.
    local instance x21044: of assignable.
    local instance x21042: of ordered.
    local instance x21043: of transportable.
    local instance x21044: of assignable.
    local instance x21045: of hashable.
    local instance x21046: of integer.

instance x21048:. procedure call of special_make_literal#746: of universal_environment.

instance x21055:. procedure call of literal#621: of discretemanager.

instance x21068:. procedure call of sequence#562: of discretemanager.

instance x21091:. procedure call of element#676: of array.

instance x21107:. procedure call of greaterthan#277: of orderedmanager.

instance x13258:. procedure call of write#17: of transputmanager.

Index

Bepa 1

Abstraction 6
Actual object 49
Ada 22, 23, 26, 29, 45, 74, 86, 88, 92, 120, 189, 314, 317
Algol-68 24, 39
Allocate 175
Almost identical 321
Alphard 10, 22, 29, 75, 89
AlreadySeen 146
Ancestor 40
Ancestors 321
And 169
Any instance 39, 321
Arithmetic operations 46
Array 173
Array element selection 45
ArrayManager 173
Arrays 173
Assign 168
Assignable 168
AssignableManager 168
Attribute association 128
Attribute identifier 128
Attribute procedure invocation 151
Attribute value 128
Attributes 14, 120

Balzer 21
Banatre 24
Barr 21, 266
Barstow 127
Beta 273
BindProcs 141
Bit 169
BitManager 169

Capsule 321